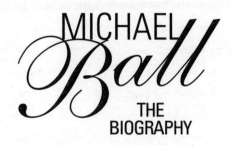

MICHAEL
Ball

THE
BIOGRAPHY

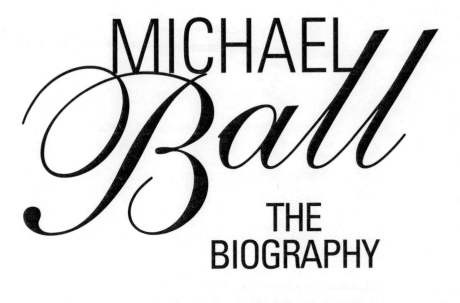

MICHAEL *Ball*

THE BIOGRAPHY

WILLIE ROBERTSON

JOHN BLAKE

Published by John Blake Publishing Ltd,
3 Bramber Court, 2 Bramber Road,
London W14 9PB, England

www.johnblakepublishing.co.uk

www.facebook.com/Johnblakepub facebook
twitter.com/johnblakepub twitter

First published in hardback in 2012

ISBN: 978 1 85782 674 6

British Library Cataloguing-in-Publication Data:

A catalogue record for this book is available from the British Library.

Design by www.envydesign.co.uk

Printed and bound in Great Britain by CPI Group (UK) Ltd

1 3 5 7 9 10 8 6 4 2

Papers used by John Blake Publishing are natural, recyclable
products made from wood grown in sustainable forests.
The manufacturing processes conform to the
environmental regulations of the country of origin.

Every attempt has been made to contact the relevant
copyright-holders, but some were unobtainable. We would
be grateful if the appropriate people could contact us.

Contents

INTRODUCTION

A Boy From Nowhere

Michael Ball was asked if he had mapped out a path when he started his career in the entertainment business back in the mid-1980s. He replied: 'Oh, God, no. I just knew I loved the environment, I loved new challenges. I don't think you can ever plan a career because any time you make a plan and a decision, something will come along to change it.'

But this most talented actor and singer, this most polished of British stage performers, this charming baritonal tenor, the man with the soft demeanour and mop of curly hair, did know one thing for certain. From that moment on 14 July, 1984, at the Aberystwyth Arts Centre, when the double doors swung open upstage and he stood alone as John the Baptist, a 22-year-old in the musical *Godspell*, and he stilled the theatre singing the line quoted from the Bible 'Prepare ye, the way of the Lord', the feeling was one of enchantment. And it was an emotion he wanted to experience again and again.

'With the audience, there is a moment when you know you have got them,' Michael told BBC Radio 4 in March 2008. 'Quite often, you don't know why you have them, the stars are lining for some reason, the sound is absolutely right, the atmosphere is absolutely right, you are part of the rollercoaster as much as the audience; those occasions are really rare – but when they happen it is super sexuality, it is fantastic.'

Almost before he had time to absorb his debut, Michael was performing on the stage in Manchester in *The Pirates of Penzance* and in London's West End in *Les Misérables*. *The Phantom Of The Opera*, *Aspects Of Love*, *Chitty Chitty Bang Bang*, *Hairspray* and *Sweeney Todd* followed to name but a few. And then there was Broadway, the pinnacle for any theatre performer. The reviews weren't great, but the audiences seemed to appreciate him.

He was the British entrant for the *Eurovision Song Contest* after taking himself almost to the top of the UK singles chart. He was the host of television and radio shows. He was controversially appearing with opera companies on either side of the Atlantic. He was upsetting the stuffed shirts of the classical music world by being the first 'light entertainer' to have his own *Prom*. And he was – and still is – the adored singer with a legion of fans, who relished every one of his 17 solo albums up to 2012, most of which went gold or platinum. They packed his concerts across the world.

The awards came, too. The first in 1989 as the *Variety Club*'s Most Promising Artiste and then his coveted Laurence Olivier Award in 2008 for his stunning performance as Edna

Turnblad in *Hairspray*. Andrew Lloyd Webber, that doyen of the stage musical in the 20th and 21st centuries, said: 'Michael has a God-given voice. He is that very rare thing – a natural singer who can just get on stage and deliver.'

Not only did Michael grace the productions of Baron Lloyd Webber in Britain and the United States of America, but he also proved a success in the rival camp of musical-writing legend Stephen Sondheim. 'I love the business I'm in. It's my joy – and my passion,' said Michael. 'I always used to sing along to records and the radio, and everyone used to tell me to shut up. It's amazing to think people now actually pay to listen to me.'

The risks and pitfalls of the industry he learned quickly. 'You can say, "Right, I'm going to do this show for this amount of time." But it could close, so you are out of work,' he told the *Liverpool Echo* in 2011. 'Sometimes two jobs come along at the same time – which one are you going to do? So you are constantly at crossroads that can take you down different directions. But I don't take any of it for granted. And the longer it goes on, the more it surprises me. I thought I'd have been caught out years ago.'

Getting that balance right is the trick for Michael. He added: 'There is a danger in being a Jack-of-all-trades because you might be regarded as spreading yourself too thin. But I really enjoy tackling the different musical styles. I would love to have been a rocker, but then I would also love to have been Frank Sinatra or Dean Martin. And, of course, I adore musical theatre, so being given the opportunity to do a bit of everything is ideal.'

His interest in music was particularly honed when he was

just eight years old and living in South Africa. 'There was no TV but in our rented house we inherited a record collection, which included albums by Sinatra, Billie Holiday and Ella Fitzgerald,' he explained. 'They were my musical gurus. My mother played the piano, and we would gather round, singing numbers by Irving Berlin or George Gershwin.'

Now thousands of fans adore his solo concerts each year as well as his theatrical performances. 'It's because I'm an actor and not just a singer that I get into the character of the singer as opposed to just singing the notes,' he told *Portsmouth News* in 2007. 'But I really had no idea I could make my living from singing. Basically, as long as there is an audience I am happy. There is not much else that gives you that kind of a buzz. I approach every song I do as I would approach a song from the theatre: it's lyric based, it's story based, it's character based.'

But does he consider himself an actor or a singer? 'I started off as an actor, very much considering and thinking of myself as an actor, but I've done so much singing now, and concentrated so much on that, that I think maybe I've slipped over into the other side.'

Michael amazingly has never had a singing lesson. He said: 'The way I like to sing, the songs I like to sing, are about emotion and about performing and about the heart. If you worry too much about the sound, hitting the note, you loose the intensity of what you are trying to sing.'

His image as Mr Nice Guy – 5ft 11in tall with twinkling blue eyes and a permanent white-toothed smile – does not bother him. 'I think I'm approachable,' he told *The Times* in 2001. 'And while I'll tend towards melancholy in my off-stage life, it's not in my nature to be miserable on stage. I'll always switch it on. Does that make me nice? Well, guilty as charged. I quite deliberately tried to provide something for everyone. People want to feel they have been entertained – and you do that by giving them as much as you can.'

But Michael puts an understandable gloss on what has been a long, character-building struggle, through some ridiculous highs and lows. From the sanctuary of a loving family through to the school years he hated with a passion. From the zenith of a man in his mid-20s originating a role on a West End stage in London, through to the depths of being too frightened to even leave his home, too frightened to get on a London Underground train, desperately and hopelessly trying to reverse a downward spiral by seeking solace in drink and drugs.

Yet in one woman, at a time when those in theatreland did not associate him with romantic trysts involving the fairer sex, Michael discovered a saviour; someone who put his life back on the rails. Their meeting was captured on television, an assignation inspired by him singing his hit single, 'Love Changes Everything'. Well, Love did precisely that – changed everything for him when Cathy McGowan, a television and fashion icon from the Swinging Sixties, arrived to interview him. And in the years ahead, more than 20 of them together, he could boast: 'Cathy takes care of me, and helps organise my life, that's her priority.'

Michael's story – from the little-boy-lost, the teenager going nowhere, to the contented artist recognised as Britain's premier stage musical performer – is the stuff upon which people create the wonderful pieces of theatre on which he thrives.

What makes him different from other artists? 'I've always

said I'll consider anything that comes through my letterbox,' he contested. 'I'm prepared to take risks in the fields of entertainment – such as host a radio show, record a new album, perform in *Sweeney Todd*, host my own TV chat show. Unlike a lot of actors, I'm as comfortable being myself in public as I am being a character.'

There have been traumas along the way. At least twice he came close to dying, but he has battled through all the set-backs, simply seeking contentment in his professional work and his home life, the latter of which he has guarded stoutly. 'When I come home, I want to shut the door,' he said. 'I think if you open the door, it's difficult to close it afterwards.'

There are no biographies about Michael Ball, not before this one – official or otherwise. He does give interviews but he focuses in the main on the production he is about to appear in or the album he is about to release. He told *Woman's Weekly* as far back as 1994: 'I'm normally quite forthright and able to talk about things but I feel very protective about my private life. All I do is provide entertainment, a bit of light relief in troublesome times. That's what I give and I don't think it means everybody then has an automatic right to pry into things that I'm not giving away to the public.

'I don't have any need to be a celebrity. I'm not interested. I am interested in being proud of the work I do, and I am. I like what I do. I don't need to be recognised. I never want to be fodder. I'm not interested in being in newspapers or magazines. If I'm realistic, I know I communicate better through music than I would through speaking.'

And he is philosophical about the future. In 2004, he said:

'Even if I'd never worked again, I could say I've starred on Broadway – they can't take that away from me.'

Michael Ball's story is an amazing tale of determination. And this book provides a peek behind the scenes into his life; the life of one of Britain's most accomplished musical stage entertainers of all time.

CHAPTER 1

I Dreamed
A Dream

Had Michael Ashley Ball been born 22 miles to the east, he would have arrived most fittingly into this world at Stratford-upon-Avon, perhaps the most famous of theatre towns. Instead, the second son of teacher Ruth and car industry executive Tony entered stage left, rather unspectacularly in England's West Midlands at Bromsgrove in Worcestershire.

Michael's mother Ruth Parry Davies was born at Mountain Ash, a small town in Rhondda Cynon Taf. His father, Anthony George Ball, was a product in November 1934 of the market town of Bridgwater in Somerset, where he was brought up by parents, Harry and Mary Irene, and where he attended the local grammar school.

Tony, at the age of 17, despite having aspirations to be an actor, was persuaded by Harry, who was in the motor industry, to take an apprenticeship in engineering – and in 1951 he was indentured with the Austin Motor Company's plant at Longbridge in Warwickshire.

The couple married in 1957, living within driving distance of Tony's work. When their first son Kevin arrived two years later, Tony was already a business success being the man responsible for the launch in that year of the iconic small car, the Mini, which was voted the second most influential car of the 20th-century with more than 1.5 million rolling off the production line.

By the time Michael came along on 27 June 1962, Tony had become Austin's UK car sales manager. That meteoric rise from apprentice on the shop floor to company executive within eight years would be mirrored, and even bettered, by Michael's rapid transition from drama school student to London West End star.

As far as his heritage goes, Michael had a dilemma. Was he Welsh or English? 'I'm Wenglish,' he insisted during a Question and Answer session with his own fan club. 'My mum is Welsh. I don't know what the laws are but in the Jewish religion you take on whatever nationality or religion that the mother is. I've always had a huge affinity for Wales. Technically I'm not, I'm English, and I am very proud to be British.

'I don't think I am going to differentiate between the two unless it comes to rugby and war. If we go to war or we fight an international on the rugby pitches, I'm a Welshman. But I support the English football team. I'm a very healthy mixture of the two. There's something a bit more exciting about being a Celt. It's lovely having a history like that, and there's something very moving about being part of a tribe. I'm British but I have Welsh ancestry and I'm very proud of it, so I'm a Wenglishman.'

Michael was delighted in 2010 when BBC One Wales helped him trace his roots. When it was revealed the Ball family – the English line – had a history of first cousins marrying, he joked: 'We're all inbred. Thank God the Welsh came along.'

Yet it transpired that even his father's side had a Welsh connection. In 1850, Michael's great-great-great grandfather William Ball and wife Jane moved to Cardiff from Glastonbury having lost two sons, Henry and George. But this venture did not have a 'happy ever after' ending because Jane died in childbirth shortly afterwards and William returned to England alone.

Michael's maternal great-grandfather, Arthur Parry, was abandoned by his parents shortly after his birth in the 1870s, leaving him at the age of 13 to travel from his home in Maesteg to the then prosperous mining town of Mountain Ash in the Welsh Valleys.

It was there that Arthur married and had a daughter, Agnes Parry, Michael's grandmother and a lady for whom he still holds a particular affection. He spent many a happy time during his school holidays playing in and around the Cadwallader Street home in Mountain Ash where his mother Ruth was raised – her father was a coal miner – and where his uncle Tom and aunt Denise still live.

'My gran was a typical matriarchal leader of the family and the community,' he said on the show. 'People looked up to her and would always go to her for advice and help. Everyone called her Lil. An extraordinary woman, fiercely proud and protective and she loved us grand-kids to distraction. She made us feel that we could do anything, she was as proud as anything when I went into the music business.'

One of Michael's most prized possessions to this day is Agnes' gold wedding ring, which he wore on his little finger until eventually putting it on a chain round his neck. 'Gran promised it to me when I was about seven, and my mother gave it to me at her funeral,' he said. 'Gran meant the world to me. I spent a lot of time with her. When I was at boarding school, where the food was terrible, she would send me boxes of Welsh cakes.'

Michael was heartbroken when Agnes died in 1984 just five days before she was due to watch him perform in *The Pirates Of Penzance* at the Manchester Opera House. 'It was just devastating,' he told the film crew. 'She hadn't been ill or anything – but the reviews had come out for *Pirates* and she had been to almost everyone's house in the town showing them. She just dropped down dead, far too young, of a heart attack.'

Tracing his family background, with the help of that television programme, helped him 'realise why I still wear the ring and why she is still such an integral part of my life. The ring is an unbreakable bond, it's a symbol of that and that's what I have with her and that's what I have with Wales, an unbreakable bond.'

He was distraught when he thought one day that he had lost the ring while on a beach during a holiday in Portugal. 'It was covered in suntan oil, I decided to take it off and put it down on the towel next to me,' he said. 'Later, I stood up to go, picked up the towel and then remembered the ring. I really freaked out. My friends and I did this search around and, after four hours, we finally found it. I feel as if it's my lucky charm, and I still feel my grandmother is watching over me.'

His memories of Agnes are many, not least of visiting Castell Coch, a 19th-century Gothic revival castle that was built on what remained of a 13th-century fortification. The imposing building is situated on a hillside high above the tiny village of Tongwynlais, which has a population of only 2,000, to the north of Cardiff in the River Taff Valley. Michael said: 'My gran would say, "That's where Father Christmas lives." There's an industrial site opposite with pungent smells and they said the wicked wizard lives there. I believed it.'

He also recalls how Agnes told him that 'the greatest singer in her opinion was Mahalia Jackson', the African-American gospel singer whose extraordinary career lasted from the 1930s through to her death at the age of 60 in 1972. He told BBC Radio 4's *Desert Island Discs*: 'I remember being finally convinced that she was the greatest female vocalist who had ever lived when I was watching a film called *Imitation Of Life* (1959) with Lana Turner, a melodramatic movie. The final scene is extraordinary where they are having a huge funeral and there is Mahalia Jackson singing this song "Trouble Of The World". To watch the woman singing and the belief and sincerity is hard to beat.'

Michael's personal history is 'an indelible part' of his life and he is delighted he knows 'where things started'. Those things, most importantly, included his great appreciation for music and singing. To this day, as a proud member of the

Mountain Ash Male Voice Choir, Michael finds himself welcomed back to rehearsals for a rendition of 'Calon Lân', the rousing Welsh hymn.

He boasts how he used to sing with the choir alongside his uncle Tom, whom he describes as 'a beautiful lyric tenor', and with his mum – 'a good pianist but not really a great singer whatever she may believe' – on keyboard.

Michael said: 'Music generally is a big part of my family life, just as it is a part of Welsh tradition. I love the idea that if you get three Welshmen together, you've got a male voice choir. I understand the power of music. I understand the therapeutic nature of music, the sense of community that music engenders, so I totally understand why it still goes on; choirs come together as a focal point for a community.'

Though Michael was born at Bromsgrove in the West Midlands – and the family lived 12 miles to the south in the tiny parish of Tibberton, which in 2011 had a population of less than 500 – his first real memories are of Dartmoor in Devon, to where the family moved when he was three years old.

He describes his time, until he was eight years old, in the tiny village of Crapstone as 'idyllic'. The rather unfortunately named but wonderfully rural Crapstone, a mile from Yelverton and nine miles from Plymouth, is probably only really known for hosting a Ministry of Defence site until the 1980s, a hangover from the Second World War when the area was strategic because of its close proximity to RAF Harrowbeer. The word 'crap' is a West Country version of 'crop' so the area, which was first populated in 1546, means literally 'crop of stones', a reflection of the clusters of huge boulders that appear in abundance across this particular landscape.

The young Michael, all chubby faced and curly locks, thrived in Devon, with such places to enjoy as Yelverton Rock. He said: 'It was a great playground for a kid. I really love the West Country, it's gorgeous with a great way of life and with friendly people.'

The scenic beauty of the region and its changing hues through the various season captured the imagination of Michael. He described one of his best childhood memories as 'waking up to a white Christmas in 1969'. He explained to *Best* magazine: 'All the ponies had got into our garden and we had to chase them out before we could open presents. Mum was worried about the plants being trampled, but that didn't matter nearly as much as the fact that the garden was absolutely covered in snow.'

Such memories have made Christmas such a special time for Michael. In an interview with *Hello!* magazine, Michael revealed: 'We always had amazing Christmases. Mum did everything – the cooking, tidying up, washing up. And she wouldn't have it any other way. We had a family tradition where we could open one present after church on Christmas Eve, and then no one could open the rest until we were all around the tree in the morning.'

The majority of young children seem to love dressing up and singing. and Michael was no exception. Whether, at three years old, he was inspired by his mother's piano playing or even having the remotest idea that his father had harboured a desire in his early years to be an actor, Michael seemed to just love singing and being the centre of attention.

His mother Ruth said: 'From a tiny tot, he was always putting on a character and entertaining us. I mean he has never had any inhibition. He has never been shy – a touch of precociousness when he was tiny but I always knew he was going to go on stage.'

Michael told *Woman's Weekly* magazine in 2004: 'At three-and-a-half, I was in a local panto where I upstaged everybody horribly. In the middle of a rendition of "My Favourite Things", from *The Sound Of Music*, I walked to the front of the stage and started to play a pretend saxophone.'

He has also recounted this story involving the song 'Do-Re-Mi' and 'miming with a trumpet', but that matters not, the youngster simply relished performing, with his parents encouraging all three of their children – sister Katherine was born in 1970 – to take up amateur dramatics.

Michael claims his first ever performance was 'playing an urchin in an amateur panto version of *Aladdin*, aged three. I thought, "I love this."'

He also 'absolutely loved' his first school, Plymouth College Prep, where he attended from the age of five in 1967. The school – at St Dunstan's Abbey, The Millfields, in Plymouth – has always prided itself on its 'small class sizes and the excellent teaching from enthusiastic staff', an aspect that was certainly appreciated by young Master Ball. Another famous Michael, a certain chap named Michael Foot, who went on to become leader of the Labour Party from 1980 to 1983, had also attended the same prep school.

Cherished childhood memories seem all the more powerful when you can recall the minor details, and Michael can certainly do that. He told the *Daily Mail* in 2011: 'The teachers were Miss

Neeno, who was scary, and Miss Lillicrap, who was kind. Miss Neeno and I had a falling out over music. She was trying to explain why you had to have five lines to write the notes on. I wasn't having that. "Why can't you just put the dots anywhere?" I asked. I was inquisitive but, yes, I was cheeky, too.'

But he wasn't cheeky and brave all the time. In 1970, this mite of an eight-year-old was frightened nearly to death of the popular BBC series *Doctor Who*, especially when Patrick Troughton, who had played the Time Lord from 1966, morphed into Jon Pertwee. 'You know that thing that kids used to watch it from behind the sofa,' said Michael. 'I was so scared of the music I had to watch it from outside, through the window, at the back of the sofa. I was honestly petrified.'

Yet music, even when it scared him, had a huge influence on the young Michael. He remembered: 'There were three musicals that were my staples as a kid – *Mary Poppins*, *The Sound Of Music* and *Chitty Chitty Bang Bang*.'

And it was his love of the latter that led him more than three decades later to snap up the lead role as Caractacus Potts in the stage play in London's West End, with him explaining: 'The chance to lead the cast in my favourite childhood fantasy film was too good to turn down.'

The young Michael was subconsciously coupling his love of music, nurtured from that Welsh background, and a love of theatre, which was enriched by trips with his father to Stratford-upon-Avon, to lay the foundations from which he could build his successful musical career. There were influences all around him and the young lad was carefully noting each down mentally and storing them away to build the bedrock of his ambitions.

He revealed to the *London Evening Standard*: 'When I think what the Sherman Brothers did – *Mary Poppins*, *The Aristocats*, *The Jungle Book* – I can honestly say those songwriters wrote my childhood.'

And equally the theatre and the movies he watched played their parts. When asked for his favourite lines from a song, he once quoted: 'There's got to be a morning after, if we can hold on through the night'. And he explained: 'It comes from "The Morning After". It was the theme to *The Poseidon Adventure*, sung by Maureen McGovern. I first heard it when I was nine years old and I thought it was the greatest song ever.'

The influences just kept coming for Michael, whose only regret from his early years seems to be 'not learning to play the piano as a child – I can't read music'. But then he was probably too busy at a young age collecting and reading his beloved comics, another interest he would take through to adulthood. He said when in his 40s: 'I loved them as a kid, and it has stayed with me. Comics and graphic novels, mainly the DC and Marvel ones. *Batman*, *The Justice League of America*. That makes me a bit of a nerd, doesn't it?'

In 1970, Tony's work saw the family move from their quiet Dartmoor haven to a busier life at Farnham in Surrey. Michael, a lad from the country, was then sent to the private Barfield School, on the Guildford Road in Runfold. He said: 'I didn't like this one because I didn't know any of the other boys and it was very sporty, which I'm not.'

He was just about getting used to his new Surrey surroundings when, after just seven or eight months, the Balls were up and on their travels once again. Tony's rise up the executive ladder within the car industry had elevated him to the position of UK car sales manager with Austin Motor Company, from 1962–66, and sales and marketing executive with the British Motor Corporation from 1966–67 before he was appointed to head up the British arm of the South African-owned Barlow Rand Group. Such was his success that he was appointed managing director of the huge dealership Barlow Rand Ford. The only problem was that the role was based in South Africa.

So Michael, eight years old going on nine, woke up in the mornings not staring at the rural beauty of Devon or the leafy streets of Surrey but instead at SA.

Yet the fact that the location was now Cape Town mattered not to the development of Michael's interests. He told *Women's Weekly* in 2004: 'South Africa was stunning but the country was in the grip of apartheid. There was no television, it was banned. Cinema films were censored, so we spent three years listening to the World Service and singing around the piano. We had to provide our own entertainment. Mum played and we all sang along. It was a rented house and I discovered a record collection of songs from the shows – cast recordings of 1950s musicals, Sinatra's Capitol Years, Dinah Washington, Ella Fitzgerald – and we would sing along to them every evening. That's where I got the bug. I immediately identified with the notion of telling a story and building a character through song.'

But school in South Africa, just as it had done with Barfield, and just as it would do at Plymouth College senior section in the years ahead, proved problematic for Michael. In an interview with the *Daily Mail*, Michael said: 'I was sent to Bishops, the preparatory school for a college that was the equivalent of Eton. Because I joined late and didn't speak Afrikaans, some of the teachers picked on me. But while I wasn't particularly happy at school, I loved the outdoor life and the weather.'

However, life took another rather sharp turn for Michael. He explained: 'My elder brother, Kevin, was a boarder at Plymouth College back in the UK. When I was 11, my parents gave me the choice of joining my brother back in Devon or waiting until my father had finished in South Africa and returning to England with them to go to day school. Well, what did I know? I was a child. Kevin is four years older than me and I worshipped him, so I opted for the former.'

While Ruth and Tony stayed with Katherine in South Africa – until his father transferred with the role as head of Barlow Rand European Operations – Michael went to the senior school within Plymouth College, this time as a boarder, perhaps hoping to recapture some of those wonderful early West Country experiences. Reality turned out to be very different. 'I was terribly homesick but determined not to let anyone know, least of all my brother, who almost entirely ignored me anyway. But I did start to make some good friends of my own.'

Plymouth College, an independent school for boys in Devon, with places for day pupils and boarders, was founded in 1877 and offers the motto *Dat Deus Incrementum* – far from original as a number of schools boast the same Latin dictum, not least Westminster School in London. It means 'God gives growth'. Michael described the school and his time there, most eloquently to the respected *Financial Times* newspaper, as 'shit'.

More philosophically, he explained to *Women's Weekly*: 'It's an experience you survive and it does toughen you up. But it's a ghastly thing. I'm told I was keen to go, but then I wanted to do the same as my big brother – and the truth is you shouldn't ask an 11-year-old what he wants because he doesn't know.' He continued: 'Looking back, I would much rather have been at home and if I had children of my own, I would never send them away to school. I didn't know there was any real alternative, but it was a horrible experience. I think boarding schools are rotten. It changed life at home, too.'

But Michael explained that he was not critical of his parents for their efforts in trying to provide 'the best education possible'. He said: 'My parents have a very working-class background and it's that classic thing of thinking that a private education is the best thing that you can do for your kids. But it was just rubbish.

'The college was terribly sporty and academic which I was so not. I loved shows, loved dressing up and I was quite precocious. There was a certain amount of outlet for that but at the end of the day you want to be at home. You try to fit in and be all things to all men – you try to be popular, you try to be funny, you try to be clever – but you don't have any time to unburden yourself. Never show yourself, so you just store it all up. It means that you become really unused to unburdening.'

Michael loathed exercise to such an extent that he pretended he had a heart condition to get out of cross-country running. How ironic that as he grew older he became so into 'keeping fit' that he would list it as one of his recreations in his entry for Debrett's *People Of Today*.

Once the harrowing memories were long enough away, Michael was able to look back not so much in anger but with a touch of humour at his school days, not least because of his convincing acting performance of a child with heart problems.

He said in an interview with the *Daily Telegraph Australia*: 'I was so desperate to get out of running that I made myself hyperventilate in front of the sports master, just managing to gasp out that I wasn't allowed to run because of my heart. It worked. I never had to do cross-country at all that term. Later, I invented a musical appreciation society, which I said I had to attend so that I could avoid other sports.

'I suspect I hated sports so much because I wasn't the best at it – I don't like doing anything I'm not the best at. I was always the fat boy in class.'

The lack of warmth within his school environment pushed Michael down the well-trodden path, some might even say 'rights of passage', of getting himself into trouble and rebelling against life in general. It was as a 12-year-old that he started smoking, a habit that would stay with him for three decades and lead to constant battles to try to quit. He revealed to *Tope Santé*: 'I was one of the first boys in my class to nip behind the bicycle sheds for a cigarette and the habit stuck, unfortunately. I was frequently caught and caned.'

At 13, it wasn't such a bad age for Michael as he managed to sneak his first kiss. 'It was at school with a girl called Helen,' he told *Saga* magazine. 'She was the daughter of the housemaster at Plymouth College, and the only girl around, so she was very popular.'

But by the time he was 14, life started to bite. He told the *Daily Mail*: 'I hit puberty, I'd become a bit disenchanted. I've always been quite quick with a ready answer, which got me into no end of trouble. I can't count the number of times I was caned. I'd been at the school two weeks when it happened the first time. It was a physics class and we were sitting in rows. A boy behind me called me a rude name, so I turned round and chinned him.

'He hit his head on the bench. There was a slight scratch which he then squeezed for all he was worth to get as much blood running down his face as possible. I was flogged – three strokes on my bottom which stung like hell – but I was damned if I was going to cry.'

Michael's school troubles continued. 'When I was 15, there were some boys who used to shoplift – I never did that – but they used to bring the stuff back and I'd sell it. I gave them a cut and did quite well out of it,' he recounted in a press interview with *Songs of Praise Magazine*. 'After a couple of months, I got caught and was caned. I had been threatened with expulsion, so I got off quite lightly. But up until then, we really thought what we were doing was harmless fun. It wasn't until the implications of the whole thing were explained to us that we understood why we shouldn't have been doing it in the first place.'

By the time Michael was 16, he wanted to be anywhere except Plymouth College. 'As I moved into my teens, I did less and less work. When I was a bit older, I would sneak out to X films or to pubs that would turn a blind eye. I was lost in my own little world. I hated the rules. Why couldn't I wear my shoes in the house? Why did I have to go to bed when I wasn't sleepy? It's why I rebelled.'

And with the value of hindsight and the maturity of adulthood, Michael explained to the *Scotsman*: 'I wasn't happy. I was unfocused and carrying all the rubbish around with me, as you do at that age. I had no real idea what to do. I had self-image issues because I was a big fat boy. I failed all my mock O-Levels, and they told me not to come back after I'd sat the real ones. But then I promptly passed all nine and they had to give me the form prize for passing most O-Levels.'

But such was the animosity between Plymouth College and Michael that the school did not inform him or even invite him to the speech day, though he said in later years, with more than a hint of sarcasm: 'I'm in the prospectus now.'

As a 16-year-old, Michael knew not where life was taking him but, despite the fact he was worried 'no one would want to see me on the stage', he knew he would love to perform. And his teenage years had not been completely moribund; not least because he attended the performances of three important pieces of theatre.

Shortly after his parents returned to Britain in 1971 and settled back at Farnham in Surrey, his father took him to the theatre, one of a number of trips that the pair would make. Tony always harked back to his original ambition of wanting to be an actor, which his parents refused to let him do telling him to get a trade instead. Michael said: 'When we moved to the UK, I attended my first theatre, I believe it was *West Side Story*. And I fell in love with it. That's when I decided to try to become a professional singer.'

Secondly, Michael attended his first West End show – *Jesus Christ Superstar* at the Palace Theatre in Cambridge Circus, London. He said to the *Express*: 'I was about 12 and I thought, "Wow, this is what I want to do." I was completely blown away by *JCS*, it was such a magnificent production. The music was amazing and it turned out to be the event that changed my life. I was completely enthralled by the show – it was such a momentous experience that I decided there and then that I wanted to be involved in musical theatre. I'd always loved music and theatre and, from that moment on, I decided I couldn't even think about doing anything else.'

And thirdly came Michael's first genuine experience of William Shakespeare. He went with his father to a Royal Shakespeare Company production at Stratford-upon-Avon, which impressed Michael greatly. He said: 'As a 13-year-old, I sat through *King Lear* and it all came alive for me.'

This appreciation of the Bard was so important to Michael's development because prior to this he had major doubts. He explained to *Radio Gloucester*: 'Shakespeare got ruined for me at school, as inevitably happens. Unless you've got a really great English Lit teacher, Shakespeare can become totally daunting and you just don't want to know about it. But I went to see it – where it should be seen, at the theatre, played by wonderful performers – and never had a fear of it, I loved it.'

Those three experiences pressed all the right buttons and Michael pushed himself forward to take part in the school productions at his dreaded Plymouth College.

He explained to the *Daily Mail*: 'There had been an English teacher called Mr Greaves in the fourth year. The Upper Sixth were doing a version of *King Lear* that year. As luck would have it, Dad had just taken me to the fabulous Trevor Nunn production at Stratford starring Donald Sinden, Judi Dench and Michael Williams. Back at school, Mr Greaves cast me as the Fool, even though I was two years younger – a fantastic experience. I then had a great time in school productions.'

And such was his enthusiasm that he joined a local dramatics group, the Surrey County Youth Theatre, when he was 15 going on 16.

When Michael, despite being armed with his O-Levels, was not invited back to Plymouth College to sit his A-levels, he headed off to the local sixth-form college in Farnham, Surrey. He had established in his own mind that theatre was the only thing that really interested him, though on the surface he still was very much the tearaway teenager.

He told *Women's Weekly*: 'Once I got involved in youth theatre, I quickly realised that nothing else excited me to this degree. But my natural rebelliousness had become well established. Initially, at sixth-form college I studied English, sociology and economics. I did well in English, I'd never heard of sociology, and at the end of my first year the teacher handed back my economics multiple-choice paper saying, "This is an extraordinary result, Michael. In studies, it has been shown that chimpanzees faced with multiple-choice would get 12 per cent of the answers right. You scored nine". So I abandoned economics.

'I couldn't think what else to do at the end of my two years there, so I went to college in Guildford to start reading law. I was aimless, lost.'

Michael tried everything, even selling holidays on the streets. 'I was wearing lederhosen in Guildford, Woking and Leatherhead, trying to give out leaflets for coach holidays to Switzerland,' he told the *Sunday Express*.

But he also had a little dabble into the world of entertainment, a young man with a varied taste in music, everything from The

Carpenters to Joni Mitchell and Pink Floyd. 'One of the girls and I from college discovered this underpass in Guildford between Debenhams and the high street, and we would busk every Saturday. We would make a tidy little bit that would help us party for the weekend. It was fun and I think people liked us doing it, so I always felt as if there was a place for me, and if someone would recognise what I do I would be all right. I was learning that I could make a noise that people would listen to.'

But he didn't seem to care too much about his appearance back then, a far cry from the dapper gent we all know these days. The fansite *JustBall.net* quotes him saying: 'Because I was a fat kid, I used to be Mr Oxfam. On one occasion, I was walking down Farnham High Street and I really thought I was the business. I had on these baggy dungarees and bright red hennaed hair. In fact, I looked so ludicrous that my mother crossed the road to disown me.'

An inspiration for Michael at the age of 17 was John Travolta in the hit movie *Grease*. 'Every Thursday afternoon for about 14 weeks, a load of us would bunk off to go and watch it. I thought he was the coolest guy on Earth,' he revealed to *The Lady*.

But that adulation was hardly giving Michael's life any particular direction. His father Tony said: 'He had got his O-levels and his A-levels and so I said to him, "Why don't you go to university and take a drama degree, if acting is what you want to do. If you don't make success on the stage you could always end up teaching drama."'

The rebellious youngster replied: 'Dad, what a negative attitude that is.'

Yet there is a more significant reason as to why life had

become so depressing for the adolescent Michael, a horrendous event took place, so painful mentally and physically that he very rarely speaks about it.

When asked in November 1999, whether he regretted never having his own children, he claimed that he had only recently realised what a 'monumental change it would make to my life if I were to have kids'. He explained to *My Weekly*: 'I used to think I could handle it, but I don't now. This business is quite selfish and often unfair on children.'

However, this explanation followed an interview – published first in a *Mail on Sunday* magazine a month earlier – in which he spoke openly for the first time of his 'secret sadness' that he could 'never know the joys of being a father'.

He explained in graphic detail how he narrowly escaped death but suffered appalling injuries as an 18-year-old when he took his brother Kevin's place in a charity parachute jump. 'The jump went wrong,' said Michael. 'The parachute failed to open properly and I plummeted to the ground. I was going to Earth at four times the speed I was meant to and got dragged along the floor.'

He was inflicted with horrific injuries. Doctors told him his back was seriously damaged, but he had also ruptured a groin and had suffered internal bleeding. 'They said I was mangled and cut up inside and I had to have lots of delicate operations,' he explained. 'I was in and out of hospital and getting very depressed.'

Those injuries, he revealed, meant he underwent surgery and treatment over a period of four years and, according to the article in 1999, a reluctance to share with girls the grim truth that he was impotent and that he felt like a 'freak'.

Michael was quoted as saying: 'It was very difficult to come to terms with. I was so embarrassed by what had happened to me down below that I didn't tell anyone for six months. All I ever thought was, "Will I ever be normal?" I didn't feel adequate to be with the rest of the lads running with all the girls. I didn't have a sexual relationship for more than four years.'

This incident, and its impact on his immediate future, provides a far greater understanding of why Michael was having trouble staying positive and his life, as happens with so many teenagers, seemed to be drifting in that too-often-seen rudderless manner. But he did have the Surrey County Youth Theatre group to give him a degree of focus – and he made appearances in performances of *The Boyfriend* in 1980 and in *Under Milk Wood* the following year.

He admitted in an interview with *Songs of Praise Magazine*: 'By the age of 18, I had absolutely no direction in my life. I really needed something that I could focus on so that I could find my path and stay out of trouble. I was a drop-out and quite badly behaved; I used to indulge in stuff, booze and soft drugs and all that sort of stuff. And I was really without direction and I really badly needed something. What saved me was the Surrey County Youth Theatre. I loved nothing more than either standing in the middle of the stage singing or swinging a sword around in the manner of Errol Flynn.'

He continued, 'A great lady called Kay Dudeney, a tough bird, ran it and she obviously saw something in me. One day, she asked if I'd ever thought of going to drama school. It seems ridiculous but it had never occurred to me. She told me that she thought I had a future as an actor.'

Well, that was enough to inspire Michael and to nurture his love of theatre into a defined ambition. He told *Women's Weekly* that Kay 'used her influence' to get him a late audition at the Guildford School of Drama. 'They agreed to see me and they offered me a place. Kay helped me to get a grant for my tuition fees. I didn't tell Mum and Dad until it was a *fait accompli*, because I was slightly worried about their reaction, but they were absolutely delighted.

'Kay, who is sadly dead now, was instrumental in getting me started. I wasn't the most diligent of students but, looking back, I realise it changed my life forever. It suddenly kind of clicked and I went almost overnight into this environment that I knew I wanted to be in. At last, I was a square peg in a square hole.'

CHAPTER 2

Losing My Mind

So Michael packed up his troubles in his old kit bag in September 1981 and travelled the 10 miles from the family home in Farnham, Surrey, for a new start at Guildford School of Acting – on the University of Surrey's Stag Hill Campus where such luminaries as Bill Nighy, Brenda Blethyn and Celia Imrie had trodden the same boards, or rather corridors, before him.

Guided by his mentor Kay Dudeney, Michael enrolled on the acting course in preference to the musical theatre and singing courses. One problem he had from the outset at GSA was his jaundiced view of the school environment, especially when it came to doing any sort of exercise. True, he had the problem of the surgery following his parachute catastrophe, but an in-built Plymouth College phobia of sport prompted him to stay well clear of the strenuous stuff.

He said in later years: 'In the mornings, early mornings, they did their dance classes, so I invented a heart condition to get out of it. And I'm regretting it now. I love the dancing.'

But when it came to qualifying in 1984 after negotiating successfully the three-year course, Michael had a musical trick up his acting sleeve. He told *Woman's Weekly*: 'At the end of your time there, they have a graduation show at a London theatre – the time when agents and casting directors come and have a look at all the new talent. I realised I would get only two three-minute slots. And if you are in the acting course, then you just do a speech or you perform with other actors. It would be hard to pull off something extraordinary. So I decided to do a three-minute song and persuaded the 'powers that be' to let me make it the show's finale.

'I did one speech, I did my acting bit, and then I did some rock 'n' roll. I chose an old song called 'So Tired', which I did as a Teddy-boy, rock 'n' roll number surrounded by all the girls in sticky-out petticoats, it brought the house down.'

Michael insists he got his first proper break 'because people heard me singing'.

With him feeling so strongly about his Celtic background, fate did produce a most wonderful twist. His newly acquired agent – newly acquired on the back of his graduation stunt – phoned to announce he had secured him an audition in a production of the rock musical *Godspell* and it was at the theatre in Aberystwyth, in his beloved Wales.

For all that Michael was being pushed towards being a dramatic actor, justifying the decision to ignore singing and dancing at Guildford School of Acting, even as a raw recruit to this most precarious of professions, he knew that when an opportunity comes along, in whatever guise, you grab it. That meant him accepting just £85 a week to appear in Stephen Schwartz and John-Michael Tebelak's *Godspell*. But he admitted he 'just loved' the John the Baptist/Judas roles. 'It was bliss. I couldn't believe I was being paid to do something I would've done for nothing although I wasn't paid much.'

The local paper claimed during the run, from 14 July to 25 August 1984, of this production of *Godspell,* directed by Richard Cheshire, that the show 'has so enthralled audiences at the Aberystwyth Arts Centre that already people are going back to see it a second and third time'.

Suddenly Michael was out there, though he was always quick to acknowledge the part played in his development of his tutors and his classmates from GSA. *JustBall.net* reported him saying: 'I look back on my three years at Guildford with affection and a great deal of nostalgia. I couldn't have received a better grounding in the professional theatre and I only hope the future students will grasp wholeheartedly the abundant "aspects of life" that Guildford has to offer.'

But prior to his Aberystwyth break, he did have one moment of minor humiliation. 'I did an audition for the tour of *There's A Girl In My Soup* to play the hippy, stoned layabout drummer,' he told *Star* magazine. 'Unfortunately, I turned up wearing a three-piece, pin-striped suit and tie, was very keen and totally wrong for the part. It was the first audition I'd ever done and I thought you had to dress smartly, like you would for a business interview.'

But *Godspell* was now his focus and his big chance, coming within weeks of him leaving GSA. And it set him off on a wonderful journey that has turned into such an acclaimed career. From the moment he walked out on stage in that historic market town on the coast of west Wales, Michael knew he had found his true vocation. He was asked in 1999 what he wanted to be if he had not gone into singing and acting. He didn't need to pause nor contemplate: 'No, I've never thought I could do anything else.'

It was the dedication to his passion, to his dream, that gave him the single-mindedness that so often has produced great performers, great artists and powerful people, in whatever profession or walk of life. But there was plenty for Michael to overcome. He might have been honing the tools of a potential trade but the obstacles that were to be placed in front of him were not to be small.

Michael, aged 22, knew on leaving GSA that he needed the all important Equity Union card to progress in the theatre industry, and that is exactly what *Godspell* gave him. From there, he secured a season with Basingstoke Rep, and appeared in three productions at the Haymarket Theatre – *Sweet Charity* from 27 September to 13 October, *Lark Rise* from 1 – 17 November and *The Adventures Of Mr Toad* from 6 – 15 December.

Michael is rather scathing about the quality of the productions he appeared in, saying: 'They included the worst-ever production of *Sweet Charity* the world has seen.'

So he decided to take a punt in 1985 after reading an advert in a newspaper and went along to an open rehearsal for *The Pirates of Penzance* at the Manchester Opera House. Unfortunately, 600 other hopefuls had seen the same notice. 'There were three huge rooms – your acting audition, your dance audition and your singing audition. It was a cattle hall, a proper cattle hall.'

But Michael proved to be the 'best of breed'. He was completely taken aback and more than a little ecstatic as he landed the lead role as Frederick for the summer season in 1985 alongside stage stalwarts Paul Nicholas, Bonnie Langford and Victor Spinetti.

Michael told *Women's Weekly*:'I couldn't believe it. When did the starving in the garret happen? It was a dream, an unbelievable experience. My parents were as proud as was humanly possible; I think they were so relieved. They secretly thought I was going to be a bit of a worry, that I was never actually going to find my way through life.'

He added in later years that he didn't know why he was quite so coy about talking about the things that he did as a youngster but admitted that it could be because he was subconsciously trying to protect an image and didn't want people to think badly of him. But he was grateful that his energies were channelled in the way they were, not least because it was a relief for his parents

And his meteoric career achievements became even headier.

Michael had left drama school with two burning ambitions: 'One, I wanted to be in *Coronation Street* and the other was to work with the Royal Shakespeare Company because it is the most respected and revered theatre company.'

Michael revealed that the latter was a goal nurtured by his father Tony, who had reminded him repeatedly after his appearances in *Godspell* and *The Pirates of Penzance*: 'Well, this is great but when you start appearing at the RSC, even as a spear-carrier, that's when I'll think you've arrived.'

It is believed that Paul Nicholas, Michael's co-star in *Pirates* was so taken by the young actor's talent that he made a phone call. The next thing that happened was that sitting in the audience was Royal Shakespeare Company director Trevor Nunn and stage impresario Cameron Mackintosh. With all the drama of the script from some crass movie, the two almost immediately asked Michael, who by this time had shoulder-length hair that was dyed black for 'the romantic look' while appearing in *Pirates*, to audition for the part of Marius Pontmercy in the upcoming debut staging of *Les Misérables*.

But that was only one half of his dream. Michael takes up the story telling *Women's Weekly*: 'I got to know some of the casting people at *Corrie* and they put me in for two episodes. It was the most watched programme on television and I loved it, I've always been a fan. I got to fulfil my fantasy. I'd have been pleased even to be throwing darts in the background at The Rovers. The same week that I did my episodes for *Coronation Street*, I was doing the audition for *Les Misérables* and they just told me I got in. That was like six months out of drama school, so I was pretty chuffed with myself.'

He was cast in the ITV soap as tennis-playing Malcolm Nuttall, regular Kevin Webster's love rival and he once joked to chat show host Gloria Hunniford: 'I was in it for about 30 seconds, with shorts on. That is going to haunt me forever, isn't it? God, don't dig the clip out. I will sue.'

But Michael did not rule out appearing again in the soap, and revealed that he once tried to come up with a plot so the producers could include himself and Cliff Richard. Michael told *My Weekly* magazine in 1999: 'Cliff is also a huge fan and we concocted this storyline in which we were on our way to a gig in Manchester when the car broke down. After we had put it into Kevin's garage for repair, we popped into the Rovers for a drink. Sadly, when we put the idea to Granada TV, they said, "We don't think it is right for us."'

But *Coronation Street* was not Michael's first television appearance. That came in the popular Yorkshire Television game show *3-2-1*, in which he provided the cabaret by singing 'Don't Wanna Give Up On Love'. He not only sported a dreadfully dated hairstyle – which saw him with more shoulder-length curls than you could shake Shirley Temple at – but also wearing an earring. He would have preferred the footage had been destroyed rather than archived so that the likes of chat show host Gloria Hunniford could not re-show it and tease him by saying: 'It is really the most hysterical thing.'

Michael admitted that, while he ditched the earring not long after that appearance in 1985, his hair did 'look like Farrah Fawcett'.

But the serious stuff was his role in *Les Misérables* and Michael knew he had to give it everything. The music was written by Claude-Michel Schonberg and the lyrics penned by and Jean-Marc Natel with an English-language libretto by Herbert Kretzmer. The story, based on the novel of the same name by Victor Hugo and published in 1862, revolves around the tales of a number of characters – including prostitutes, student activists and factory workers – as they struggle for redemption and revolution.

Michael, his family feeling so proud of him, did 12 weeks at the Barbican Centre in London, starting on 8 October 1985, before the show transferred to the West End, where it opened at the Palace Theatre on 4 December. The initial reviews were rather hostile, though all acknowledged that the production was a polished piece of theatre.

Christopher Edwards wrote scathingly in the *Spectator* magazine on 19 October 1985: 'Two things at least are certain about *Les Misérables*. The first is that the critics have expressed alarm, disgust and displeasure that the RSC should lend itself (cynically, they would say) to a trite money-making venture. The second is that the production is sold out, and the auspices for a commercial transfer to all parts of the globe are correspondingly excellent. In these circumstances low expectations are the best ones to hold.'

And Edwards just didn't seem to want to say anything too nice about the production, though he admitted that 'when it comes to modern musicals, my expectations are of the very lowest.' He clearly didn't like the interpretation of the story, but admitted to the *Spectator* it was 'delivered by the cast with enormous gusto and told by the writers with great sententiousness'. He grudgingly concluded: 'If musicals are to your taste, then this one is slicker than many and no more empty than most.'

Whatever the reviews, *Les Misérables* went on to win an avalanche of awards on both sides of the Atlantic, becoming the longest-running musical in the world, the second longest-running West End show after *The Mousetrap* and the third longest-running show in Broadway history. The London version celebrated its 9,000th performance on 10 August 2007.

Michael, in his role as student revolutionary Marius, who falls in love and marries Cosette, was learning all the time. He told Australia's *Illawarra Mercury*: 'The hardest thing about musical theatre is doing the eight shows a week and doing nothing else. You don't have any other life at all. You do the show, you get home, wind down, go to bed. You wake up and your day is then geared around going to the theatre that night. The upside of that is that you are working in a company. It's not just you doing the show – and there's a lot of security and stability in that.'

He was also picking up the tricks of the trade, the little things actors need to know, not least that when you realise your family or friends, or even someone well known, is in the audience, worse still sitting in your eye-line within the theatre, you will feel pressure.

'It does affect you when you know someone special is out there,' he explained. 'At one of the performances of *Les Misérables*, word went around that Paul McCartney was in the front row. He wasn't in the best seats; he was tucked away over on the left. So that night, we all went out and directed all our numbers at him. We were all singing to that side of the stage while anyone in the middle or over on the right only saw us sideways on,' Michael revealed.

But Michael was riding the waves of his inexperience and carrying on regardless. He admitted to the *Guardian*: 'I farted on stage once during the finale of *Les Mis*. It put everybody else off, but I don't think the audience noticed.'

There were other moving moments, which Michael cherishes as memories. He reveals how at one point during his run in the production he was sharing a house with Patti LuPone, the American singer and actress known for her Tony Award-winning performances as Eva Peron in the 1979 stage musical *Evita* and as Madame Rose in the 2008 Broadway revival of *Gypsy* but who was playing Fantine alongside him in *Les Misérables*.

He told one interviewer at the *Telegraph*: 'Patti had split up with her boyfriend. We had sat up all night as I tried to cheer her up and she got through a bottle of vodka. She was absolutely heartbroken. And when we got to the show, she went on and she sang "I Dreamed A Dream" and I've never heard anything so great. Everybody stopped backstage and listened. She just ripped her heart out on stage.'

But Michael's life started to go horribly wrong.

The downward spiral started in the summer of 1985 when he was stricken with a bout of glandular fever. The illness forced him to take off nearly seven weeks from *Les Misérables*. And from there, his world fell apart.

Michael has explained this most painful of experiences in a succession of interviews. 'I never used to suffer from nerves at all. I was very cavalier about the whole thing. I went from *Pirates* into *Les Mis* and I was as green as I was cabbage looking, I didn't know I was born and it was magical because I didn't have a nerve in my body – because I hadn't anything to test me. But I got ill. I got glandular fever and tonsillitis and then I had post-viral syndrome and was exhausted.'

He did not realise the extent of the illness and 'tried to work through it'. But the virus had hit him hard and he was unable to perform properly. The whole episode also gave him a terrible conscience. 'It had progressed into what became known as ME,' he told Michael Parkinson. 'Eventually, I came back too soon. At the time, it was called yuppie flu and nobody knew what it was – they thought it was malingering basically.'

And he added: 'I was drained, and then, I started getting anxiety attacks. For people who have experienced these, they will know. It's quite common. I had my first panic attack on stage. It was just the most appalling feeling I have ever had. Your heart starts racing, you get tunnel vision, you get a pounding in your ears and you break out into a sweat and you get a surge of adrenaline. It is just awful and this all happens in just a couple of seconds.'

The trauma of these attacks bit deep into Michael's confidence. He added: 'You truly think you're going to die. You can rationalise yourself and say, "This is not real, everything is fine." But at that moment, when you have a couple of thousand people out there watching, people on the stage looking at you, you lose control. And that was what was happening to me.'

The situation did not improve. Indeed, the panic attacks became worse and worse. 'It was not just once a night, you know before the show, it was happening throughout the whole show. The people very close to me could see something was wrong, but not the audience. I was just going through the motions. All kind of stuff was going on.'

Michael had always found it difficult to share his problems and this made the situation extremely serious. He said: 'I went into this descent of terrible depression and panic attacks. I would arrive at the theatre, start shaking, turn around and go home. These attacks were not just on the stage. I would get into the tube on the way to work and I would just cross over the station and phone in and say "I can't come in." I didn't know how to deal with it.

'I think because of the whole thing of not being able to open up and share because of the boarding school era I simply wouldn't talk about it. I wouldn't appear vulnerable but it was perfectly clear to everyone that I was cracking up.'

The young starlet who had achieved so much so quickly was in trouble. His parents felt terribly sorry for him, but he lived on his own and he just cut himself off. He added: 'It was a complete breakdown, physically and mentally.

He also told the *Daily Record*: 'I had a breakdown and lost touch with reality. It was a terrible time.'

Michael spent a lot of time on his own in his flat to the point where he did not want to go out of the front door and admits he 'developed agoraphobia'. He told Parkinson: 'I had found a weakness in myself and it played on my mind and just got worse and worse. I just sat in my flat and was miserable.'

'I was in the biggest show ever and I wanted to do it, but I couldn't even get off the sofa. I felt as if I'd let everyone down and that no one understood. I went from this person who could go out all-night partying, and who thought that nothing could touch me, to feeling vulnerable and naked on stage. Those anxiety attacks opened up a whole area of demons in my head. "When is it going to happen again?" "Why are all these people staring at me?" It was the blackest hour of my life,' he explained to the *Sunday Express*.

This was a subject that Michael has been brave enough to talk about in a number of interviews. In 2008, he told *The Scotsman* that he went through 'varying states of lunacy', adding: 'It was getting to the point where I was thinking, "I can't do anything else but I can never, ever go back on the stage." At one point I thought I'd never go out of my front door again. It was a really horrible, weird, mucked-up time. It made me grow up and it made me realise the vulnerabilities that people have.'

Michael admitted that he turned to drink in a desperate cry

for help. Eventually he had to confess to himself that he could cope no longer. He told *Women's Weekly*: 'I phoned Cameron, who had already given me three months off, and he agreed to let me go. I told him that I'd given up the business. I sank to my lowest depths. I was in my mid-20s and was convinced I would never work again, never perform again ever. I had walked out of *Les Mis*, one of the greatest shows and one of the best parts for a juvenile lead, but I told myself that I just could not do this and I had to leave.'

This was in October 1985. It mattered not to Michael at this point that *Les Misérables* was proving such a huge success, and indeed the production, with the role of Marius that he originated, would go on to be staged in 41 countries, in 291 cities and be translated into 21 languages.

Michael was struggling. All the anxieties of his youth returned. One minute he was achieving more than he and his friends from his classes at the Guildford School of Acting had dreamed about, the next he was staring at personal failure.

He admitted that he experienced 'varying states of lunacy', adding: 'I've been right down there and done the things one shouldn't. For nine months, I descended into the lowest, lowest pit. I'd given up a decent life and saw the black side of myself. I stopped caring about anything, including myself. I was drinking heavily, self-destructing.'

His world was shattered and it was hell. Had he run before he could walk? Should he have stayed in rep longer? He knew in his own mind his career had moved forward 'really, really fast'. There were so many questions and virtually no answers.

CHAPTER 3

Something Inside So Strong

From the autumn of 1986 right through until the spring of 1987, Michael was cocooned in his flat, terrified and shattered, a shell of the confident youngster who had burst so bullishly onto the scene in Aberystwyth. 'I just wanted to disappear. I didn't want anyone looking at me, I didn't want to be the centre of attention,' he said.

But two phone calls were to change his life.

The first came from a most unexpected source. Thames Television offered him, out of the blue, the chance to sing live during the *Miss England* show on 8 April 1987. 'They wanted someone to do the cabaret while they counted the votes,' he said.

What should he do? He believed that he had come back too early from his glandular fever-related illnesses; should he give it more time? Michael steeled himself and searched deeply into his vat of emotional reserves that seemed at this time to be so empty. 'It was tacky but it was a moment that I realised it's never going to be worse than this,' he told the *Daily Record*. 'I had convinced myself that I was going to have a heart attack and die on screen or on stage. But if I didn't, then I knew I was never going to get any worse than this. I could only get better.'

So Michael took the assignment, the bravest of brave moves. He believed it was 'kill or cure,' and told Michael Parkinson: 'I went on. I did the show, absolutely terrified, pins and needles down my arms from the tension. But I got through. I didn't die, I did an all right job. I watched it back and I thought, "No one would have known." There were two ways of going – either you give up or you deal with it. I faced the demons and beat them. All I could say to myself was that I would never get that low again. It was a good lesson for me. I worked it out myself. I didn't go and see anyone; I just worked it out myself what my problems were that needed resolving.'

That fact that he confessed to his failings allowed him to start rebuilding the strength to conquer those failings. He told the *Guardian* in later years: 'It was possibly the best thing that could have happened because it made me grow up and it made me realise the vulnerabilities that people have.

'Yes, I get terrible stage fright. I tap my fingers and cheekbones before going on stage to calm down. But it does get easier with time. I get very nervous before a show. If I could click my fingers before going on the stage and not have to go on, I would. I really, really would. But then you get on there, and the secret really is concentration, you get on and you see a crowd. Funny enough, it doesn't happen when I do concerts. Concerts are absolutely fine. It's when I'm acting, when I'm performing on the stage with other actors. It comes back, not often, when I am not well, but I know how to control it.'

The second 'career-saving' phone call came from Cameron Mackintosh's secretary. Michael was asked to come in to sing for Andrew Lloyd Webber, with a view to being part of the second casting of the established West End production *The Phantom of the Opera* as Raoul, Vicomte de Chagny.

Phantom – the music composed by Lloyd Webber with lyrics by Charles Hart and Richard Stilgoe – had opened to huge acclaim on 9 October 1986 in London's West End at Her Majesty's Theatre in Haymarket. The show – just as Michael Crawford, in the title role, was to do – won the 1986 Laurence Olivier Award. Broadway was calling and Lloyd Webber wanted to move it to Manhattan, complete with the main players of the original London cast.

For the record, the show opened on Broadway on 16 January 1988 and in that year snapped up the Antoinette Perry Award for Excellence in Theatre, better known as the Tony Award. By the time the productions celebrated their 25th anniversaries, they were the third longest running West End show and the longest running Broadway show by some margin. Box office receipts globally by 2011 were in excess of £3.5billion.

That was all a world away from 1987 and the fragile Michael. 'I was sitting in the bath terribly hungover when I got a call asking me to be at Her Majesty's Theatre in one hour,' he told the *Daily Telegraph*. 'Cameron knew about the problems I'd had in *Les Mis* and said, "I think this'll be good for you, because it's the biggest show, it's a real hit, but the pressure isn't on you. Come and see if you can." I panicked but I raced down there.'

Michael is not the sort to blow his own trumpet, except of course the pretend instrument with which he had paraded around playing as a three-year-old, so he is just being honest when he claimed: 'I did a blinder of an audition. I got the part.'

Stepping into the London production was Michael's chance to prove, perhaps most importantly to himself, that he had chased away his demons, to show that his recovery from his disintegration in *Les Misérables* was as complete as it could be.

By 15 July1987 Michael was part of the second cast making an audio recording of songs from *Phantom* – the original version released by Polydor Records earlier that year had become the first album in British musical history to enter the UK chart at Number One. Michael opened officially in the role of Raoul, the kind-hearted childhood friend of Christine Daae, on 12 October 1987. This was the start of a strong working relationship with Lloyd Webber that was to reshape Michael's career.

But appearing in *Phantom* was not straightforward for Michael. By his own admissions, he was still drinking heavily, the drinking that was the result of him becoming a recluse.

The role as Raoul, which was originated so successfully in London by the experienced stage performer Texan Steve Barton, was particularly challenging and arduous. But, perhaps in a perverse way, this was what Michael needed to rebuild that confidence.

'I was on stage the entire time. It was very difficult, technically and musically,' he said in an interview with the *Daily Mail*. 'But I was slowly getting back a confidence and enthusiasm for life. I was beginning to have a pride in myself again and I really felt blessed. I was desperate to do the right thing, to make everything work, to be successful. The business can be so consuming, and for the first time since I'd rehearsed with *Les Mis*, I couldn't wait to get into work.'

Michael had learned painfully that it is destined to be part of a performer's life that with every wonderful high you reach there seems to be a corresponding devastating low. So when reverse situations were thrown in front of him in the future, he was equipped to handle them.

He said to *Women's Weekly*: 'My tonsils got infected. When a surgeon said they should come out, I didn't hesitate. Now I feel that the whole extended period of anxiety was the best thing that could have happened to me. It made me a better performer, without a doubt.'

Doing *Phantom* in 1987, through to 10 October the following year, did put him back on the right road, even if it was 'a good three years before I was my good old self again'.

In an interview with the *Daily Record*, Michael said: 'We all have hideous things that happen to us in our lives and it is how we deal with them and get through them and learn from them. My recovery was gradual. The Beta-blockers stop your heart from racing as much and give you a psychological lift. Instead of fearing a wave that is about to crash over you and leave you out of control, you have to find a way to stop the wave and instead say, "I'll surf it."'

What Michael has always retained, whatever is going on inside his head, whatever demons he is trying to overcome, is the ability to enjoy himself with the cast. And while *Phantom* was a personal mental battle, he could still join in the banter when necessary. On the day in October 1987 when his run in the show was ending, all manner of practical jokes were going on.

He told interviewer Billy Sloan in 1994: 'I'm terrible for playing tricks on other members of the cast. There is the tradition that when you leave a show, the final matinee, things get sent up. Little things were happening throughout the show because other people were leaving as well.'

The first incident involved jewellery being put on the fingers of Carlotta, the opera singer. But cast members had linked all the rings with wire so her hands were tied together. Then, when Michael's character Raoul gets into the box to watch the opera, he could hardly contain himself as there was a cast member dressed as a gorilla in the shadows, out of sight of the audience. So Michael was determined to get his own back.

He explained to Gloria Huniford: 'When Raoul comes out from swimming across the underground lake and there is a great big rip on his shirt, I had a tattoo put on there 'Raoul for Christine forever'. And then for the very final scene, there was an alternate girl playing the role of Christine in the matinee, Jan Hartley. The last thing you see is Raoul and Christine going off in the boat while the Phantom has a bit of a breakdown at the front. So I thought gondola, phew, obvious isn't it? I stuck on a chest wig, had medallions and a Wall's Cornetto. I'm telling everyone, "Don't give it away because I was going to send Jan up."'

But Michael was not having it all his own way. 'There I am with this chest wig and the Cornetto dripping in my hand and

I look over my shoulder and I can see the outline of the frock that Christine is in and the wig. As we set off, she starts singing "Say you'll share with me". But the voice wasn't coming from the boat and I look over and Jan is standing in the wings, singing away, not looking because she was going to laugh. I looked down and it was the other girl playing Christine, Claire Moore, who was then there. She had false teeth, eyelashes out here, a fake moustache and a thermometer strapped to her forehead with skull-earring. She was draped so that no one could see her from the audience. I turned round with this chest wig and a Cornetto in my hand and the only line I've got is, "Say the word and I will follow you". And I went, "Say a word, follow you" and killing myself laughing.

'How we got to the end of the show I don't know. I had friends in and they said afterwards, "You could tell it was your final day. The emotion in that last scene was extra-ordinary, you were wonderful." If only they knew.'

And there were other memorable moments in *Phantom* for Michael. He recalled to the *Telegraph*: 'One of the funniest things I've ever seen on stage was in the final lair scene, which is where Christine pulls the mask off the Phantom and reveals him. Once, she pulled off his mask and as she did it, he put up his arm and his cufflink got caught in her wig. So as she revealed his hideous deformed face, he pulled off her wig and revealed her bald cap, the microphone packs and all the wires. She looked worse than the Phantom. It was the final moment of the show, so what do you do other than laugh hysterically?'

The camaraderie of *Phantom*, plus the discipline necessary to handle the rigours of the role, meant that for his full year in the show, Michael had to remain focused.

This put back into his life some basic structures and helped him to curb his drinking. The result was that his self-esteem and confidence grew.

And such was Michael's success in *Phantom* that, within months of his run ending, Lloyd Webber was approaching him to appear as Alex Dillingham, the lead in his latest project, *Aspects Of Love*.

This production, with music by Lloyd Webber and lyrics by Don Black and Charles Hart, centres on the romantic entanglements of actress Rose Vibert, her admiring cousin Alex, his underage cousin Jenny, his uncle George and his uncle's mistress Giulietta. This story had been brought to Lloyd Webber's attention when he was asked in 1979 to write songs for a proposed film version with Tim Rice, with whom he had collaborated so successfully to produce *Joseph And His Amazing Technicolor Dreamcoat* in 1968, *Jesus Christ Superstar* in 1970 and *Evita* in 1976.

Lloyd Webber, on his website, explained that his first attempt at writing the music for *Aspects* 'bore little fruit'. He said: 'So I gave the book to Trevor Nunn, who was delighted with it. In 1983, we presented a "cabaret" of some songs we wrote together for a possible full-length musical. But these songs did not work either. It was a little before the completion of *Phantom* that I realised that I wanted to change direction sharply in my next work, so we decided to try once more.'

Of the 1979 version explained Lloyd Webber, nothing survived. And of the 1983 version, the most substantial melody to survive was the Pyrenees folk song. He said the principal melodies and the great body of the work were penned during his collaboration with Black and Hart.

Lloyd Webber added: 'To offer the work to Trevor Nunn to direct was obvious, since his interest in the book has been every bit as great as mine for almost as long. Indeed, in 1983, he took over the rights to develop the novel as a film. It is, perhaps, worth recording that *Aspects* very nearly did become the first musical of mine that was made as a film without a theatrical presentation but Trevor Nunn convinced me otherwise and thus we are enjoying our first collaboration together about human beings.'

Aspects Of Love presented Michael with the challenge of creating a role instead of slipping into an existing character, as he had done with *Phantom*, but of course he had done the same, the creation bit, with Marius in *Les Misérables*.

He told *Radio Gloucestershire* interviewer Sue Wilson in 2001: 'It's the most challenging to create a role because there is nothing, there is no benchmark. When I created Marius in *Les Mis*, for example, most of it hadn't been written, so you've got the basic outline of the show but you don't quite know what the finesse is going to be, the intricacies, the delicate characterisations, because they literally haven't been written.

'But then when things arrive, because people have heard you sing, they kind of know your character and are almost tailor-made to who you are, how you are interpreting the role. And that's just great, to be able to say you created a role in a show like *Les Mis*. Others base their role on what you did. It's the most exciting thrill, it's the biggest challenge and when it pays off there is nothing better.'

Though Michael had built a name among theatre-goers following his strong performances in *Les Mis* and *Phantom*, when it came to *Aspects*, he was the juvenile lead with the real ticket-seller for the production being seen as movie star Roger Moore.

The veteran James Bond actor, at that point aged 62, was to play the part of Uncle George and everything seemed to be going well in rehearsals. 'Roger was great fun, and very much like the persona he brought to the Bond movies – urbane, stylish, witty, intelligent. We had a lot of fun in rehearsals and he had a good voice,' Michael revealed.

The two men struck up a friendship and decided to be really dedicated and that involved joining the warm-up rehearsals of Gillian Lynne, the choreographer. Michael told Michael Parkinson: 'Roger turned up in tracks that he had obviously not worn before. We stood at the front and Gillian is stretching. Finally, Roger is on the floor and he looks across at me and says, "Is this woman mad? I'm James bloody Bond." And he was gone.'

Unfortunately, shortly after this – and before the production even opened – Roger was 'gone' for good and out of the show. That left a huge emphasis on Michael now that the 'big name' was not on board. He told *lastminute.com magazine*: 'Roger would have been ideal for the part of Uncle George, but I think the problem was he wasn't at all used to the rehearsal process for a musical. It was a completely new experience for him, as I think he had been in only one play in his career, and that had been at the very start.

'Being a movie star and performing in films is a wholly different thing, a different process, from being on stage. It broke his heart to leave, but he felt he should, and though I respect his decision I would have loved him to have stayed and to have confounded the critics by turning in the sort of performance I knew he could.'

That Roger Moore stepped back from the production did not affect *Aspects Of Love* from achieving significant pre-launch popularity. The show was previewed at the Sydmonton Festival in Hampshire on 9 July 1988, and then on 21 January 1989 Lloyd Webber cleverly released the most powerful song from the show, 'Love Changes Everything', as a single, sung by Michael. This was three months before the show was due to open – and the record went on to spent 15 weeks in the Top 100 UK singles chart, reaching Number Two on 25 February 1989.

The publicity for the show was perfect. The BBC reported: 'Advanced ticket sales have already reached £5million and anyone who is naive enough to phone the theatre for tickets is told by the answer-phone to call back in April 1990.'

So *Aspects Of Love* opened surrounded by huge anticipation on 17 April 1989 at the Prince of Wales Theatre after a charity gala premiere on 5 April. Some of the reviews could have been more positive. Lloyd Webber's production set-up, the Really Useful Company, naturally posted on its website only the positives.

Michael Coveney's report in the *Financial Times* included phrases such as: 'a remarkably daring piece of work'; 'Trevor Nunn's very fine production is a rare example of theatrical intimacy succeeding in large-scale circumstances'; 'brilliantly choreographed by Gillian Lynne'; 'the musical direction by Michael Reed and the sound reproduction by Martin Levan is of the highest quality'; and 'you will want to see this show not because of its showbiz hype but because there are new creative forces at work here which may yet define the lyric theatre of the future'.

Jack Tinker in the *Daily Mail* wrote that 'the daring shown here deserves to win our admiration' and spoke of 'a vibrantly intelligent and commanding performance by American Ann Crumb and a perfectly delightful performance from Diana Morrison.'

Michael Billington told the *Guardian* readers that 'The musical texture becomes lively and varied and the stage starts to flood with real emotion. Trevor Nunn creates both images of rapturous gaiety and moments of desolating sadness. Mr Lloyd Webber shows a capacity to reach emotions that other composers do not touch.'

The audiences were raving about Michael's performances to such an extent that he was assuming the status of celebrity, which sometimes has its downsides – and one incident scared him greatly.

This happened when a woman, who had sent him numerous letters and who had tried repeatedly to phone him, suddenly appeared. 'She turned up at my agent's office and we had to call the police,' Michael revealed on *JustBall.net*. 'I thought that was the end of it but one Saturday she came to the theatre saying she had to see me urgently. She screamed, "If I don't see him, I will kill him and then kill myself." I was cowering in a corner, scared stiff.'

The woman opened her bag and a large carving knife appeared. The police rushed to the theatre and the woman was led away.

A rather less daunting challenge for Michael was the need for him to lose some of his puppy fat, as it were, for *Aspects*

Of Love not least because he appeared semi-naked at one point in the production. He was now 27 years old and, perhaps, carrying 'a few extra pounds'. He had felt fat at school and through his rebellious teenage years – and his abhorrence of any physical activity had hardly helped him to mould a svelte-like figure. So he decided to lose weight.

It meant a rigorous fitness programme. 'I realised I had to appear on stage every night in boxer shorts. It soon became apparent that bits of me were wobbling out of time to the music. It was too embarrassing – I had to do something about it,' he revealed to *Top Santé*. 'All adolescents feel unhappy about the way they look, but being overweight is particularly traumatic. What's more, I don't think that feeling of dissatisfaction ever leaves you. My problem is that I love food – good food, bad food, it doesn't really matter.'

Michael, also realising how exhausting the role would be, got himself a personal trainer to devise a programme to help him develop his aerobic capacity. He said: 'As a performer, I need to be able to come straight out of a really tiring dance routine and go immediately into a heavy ballad. To do that without gasping, it's very important for me to work on my breath control.'

He appreciated the value of training sessions but he has never really got to a point where he enjoys them, explaining: 'I grit my teeth and tell myself that, ultimately, this is what I get paid for.'

Throughout *Aspects Of Love*, Michael was building a strong working relationship with Lloyd Webber. The two gelled and shared a mutual respect. Michael told *Radio Gloucestershire* in 2001: 'Andrew is a great mercurial talent. I have a lot of time for him, and a huge amount of respect. You can tell by his music that he is a deeply passionate man.

'I don't think there has been a show – I hope he won't mind me saying this – that I've been involved with him that, come the dress rehearsal when everything goes wrong, the set doesn't work, the sound isn't right, the thing just isn't working, you think it's never going to work, he does not run down to the front of the stage, jump into the pit, pick up all of the music, round on the orchestra and say, "Right, that's it. No one is going to play my music. That's it. I'm going home. It's just not happening." His shows are like his children, and he is desperately protective of them. And I've got a great deal of time for him. The people who really care and think that what they do matters put in that extra bit of effort.'

This is a wonderful example of exactly how dedicated Lloyd Webber is and what a 'hands-on guy' he is. But of course this brings pressure with it. 'That's only because he is a perfectionist,' Michael told the *Daily Record*. 'But so am I. We both wanted *Aspects Of Love* to be as good as possible. In the final weeks of rehearsals, that cast would arrive in the morning to find he had written 10 new changes and thrown in a brand new song. Right up until opening night, he was changing things as he went along. He can be very tough, and incredibly powerful. But that's what makes Andrew such a successful guy.'

Michael managed to make two other significant appearances in 1989 – a Stephen Sondheim tribute concert at the Royal Festival Hall in London on 17 September and his first Royal Variety Performance at the London Palladium on 20 November

– while filling the last nine months of that year with his commitments to *Aspects Of Love*.

The production brought two extremely important 'aspects' to Michael's life. The first was the hit single 'Love Changes Everything', the success of which propelled him into the realms of pop star and all the associated adulation factors that come with that.

Michael revealed to the *Sydney Morning Herald*: 'I honestly didn't realise what an impact the song would have, or what it would come to mean to so many people. When Andrew sat me down in front of a piano and played it to me, he said, "This is going to be a big hit." I realised it was a good tune but I didn't at all anticipate how big a hit it would be.'

Michael describes the show and that song as a turning point for him, explaining that 'they opened up so much to me and to my career as an artist, so I can't be anything but grateful to them.'

He added: 'And if the song means so much to people as it does – they have it at weddings and at funerals – then that is great. It also brought me to a much wider public: people who would never go to see a Lloyd Webber show. When I went on *Top Of The Pops* to sing, that was pretty cool. It was a real 'pinch myself' moment because I didn't even think I'd be making records let alone be in the charts.'

The second 'aspect' from the show, and as if to prove that the song 'Love Changes Everything' really did have such true meaning, was that it introduced Michael to Cathy McGowan.

CHAPTER 4

Someone To Watch Over Me

What happened to Michael in the spring of 1989, just as he was preparing to star in *Aspects Of Love* at the Prince of Wales theatre in London's West End, was akin to the plotline from one of his beloved romantic musicals. And just as with the intentions of all good love stories, the romantic encounter endured.

The meeting between Michael and Cathy McGowan – the iconic Sixties mini-skirted dream-girl who by 1989 was doing television celebrity interviews – came about because of a comment made by Cathy's sister-in-law Angela. The pair had been friends since their teens and Angela went on to marry Cathy's brother John McGowan, who had been a disc jockey in 1965 on King Radio, a pirate broadcasting station operating from a fort in the Thames Estuary.

Angela had seen Michael on the television show *Wogan* in

February 1989 performing 'Love Changes Everything'. She instantly thought the he was a bit of a dish and she insisted to Cathy: 'You just have to interview him.'

Cathy duly put in a request as the debut single was propelling Michael up the charts. Michael revealed: 'I refused the interview at first because I thought Cathy would be a bitch – but when she walked through the door, I was smitten.'

The interview, according to the BBC archives, went something like this:

Cathy: 'This amazing voice you've got. Has it been trained?'

Michael: 'I have always sung. Given my family are very musical, with a great Welsh background. My uncle sings with a male voice choir, that kind of thing. I've always been surrounded by music and I've always sung, but my voice has never been trained. To be honest, when I first started off in the business at drama school I never thought I'd use it. It was just something I loved to do. And to be able to make money doing something you love to do is marvellous.'

Cathy then asked Michael if the thought of having to fill the Prince of Wales Theatre frightened him. Michael replied: 'We have got a huge advance, already about two and a half million pounds and people say it is a guaranteed success, but not at all. There are people who have booked their tickets who have heard nothing and know nothing about the show. They are expecting it to be the best show in London and we are going to endeavour to do that, it is a hell of responsibility.'

Michael went on to reveal that he had first heard 'Love Changes Everything' in the previous May or June, just before the company started work on preparing a version of *Aspects Of Love* for the Sydmonton Festival. He added: 'As soon as I heard it, I thought it was a fabulous tune, fabulous. And then having heard the rest of the score, I could not believe he [Lloyd Webber] has done it again. He has got a magnificent score, wonderful lyrics by Don Black and Charlie Hart – and it is up to us now. We have got to do something with it. It's wonderful.'

From 1964 to 1966 Cathy had been the presenter of Rediffusion Television's path-finding rock music show, *Ready Steady Go!*, whose popularity coincided with the arrival and meteoric rise of The Beatles and everything that went with that.

The Friday evening programme's slogan was: 'The weekend starts here'. Cathy, who had been working for £10 a week in the fashion department of *Woman's Own* magazine, applied for the role of co-host – along with 600 others – and despite her lack of experience managed to land the job. She is said to have clinched the deal in a run-off with Anne Nightingale, who later became a BBC *Radio 1* DJ, by giving the answer 'fashion' to a question from executive producer Elkan Allan as to whether teenagers thought sex, music or fashion was more important.

Cathy, whose raw innocence saw her become agitated on camera when things went wrong, was adored by audiences of youngsters for being so natural and, perhaps, so ordinary. One commentator claims that she may have been the inspiration for Susan Campy from The Beatles 1964 movie *A Hard Day's Night*. In the film, George Harrison tells a producer that Campy is 'that posh bird who gets everything wrong' on a teen television show. The producer replies: 'She's a trendsetter. It's her profession.'

Cathy was dubbed 'Queen of the Mods' by the press, and

singer Donovan in 1965 labelled her the 'young Mary Quant-look hostess' in a reference to fashion icon Quant, who was the leading British proponent of the mini-skirt, an item the slender and attractive brunette Cathy helped to popularise.

In 1965, Cathy said of her magazine job prior to her television break: 'Oh, it was horrid. These people of 40 used to water down all my ideas because they never quite believed me. They looked at me as though I had taken a turn. But now, on television, everybody takes notice of me. It's lovely because I just wear the fashions and they catch on.'

Though she continued in broadcasting and delved into journalism when *Ready Steady Go!* ended, her career waned substantially and never really touched those television heights again. However, she married Welsh-born actor Hywel Bennett in 17 January 1970 at St Bartholomew's Roman Catholic Church in Streatham, south London, close to where the couple both lived and met.

Her popularity by the time of her wedding – she also had a fashion house producing trendy clothes for teenagers – meant that there was a mass of photographers waiting outside the church and Pathe News reported her as having told them about the marriage, at a time when it was more de rigueur to be a Swinging Sixties' wild child: 'There are some old-fashioned ideas that make a lot of sense.'

Cathy has played down her role in the Sixties, saying: 'They are terribly overrated. I wasn't part of what was supposed to be going on. I didn't see any of it. I was working all the time and had everything under control.'

She let her professional ambitions take a back-seat after she and Bennett, who found fame playing the title role in the television sitcom *Shelley*, had a daughter Emma in 1973, though in that year she was part of the board when London's *Capital Radio* was launched. Sadly, her marriage ended in divorce in 1988. In an interview with *Hello!* magazine, Cathy said about Bennett, who was reputed at one time to have had a drink problem: 'I gave Hywel all the support I could when he needed it, as a friend. He has had a lot of courage to come through it. He has got a great career and is a wonderful actor. I couldn't be more pleased for him. But I would support anybody who was down.'

By the late 1980s, Cathy had returned to the spotlight, in London at least, carrying out personality interviews for BBC's *Newsroom South East*. Following her successful chat with Michael in the February 1989 about 'Love Changes Everything', she was delighted to be assigned to interview him again in the April.

The fact that Cathy had managed to persuade Michael to let her have backstage access at the Prince of Wales during the Press Night for *Aspects Of Love* illustrates exactly how far Michael had come in perfecting his recovery psychologically from his dark days in *Les Misérables*. He was able to accept the invitation for a BBC camera crew, doing a news item on *Aspects*, to film him in the lead up to him going on stage. Clearly, the panic, the nerves were under control.

The footage of Michael's second professional meeting with Cathy, seen by millions of BBC viewers, tells a wonderful tale of success and friendship. She interviews a series of celebrities about the show.

Legendary movie producer Michael winner said: 'This is a terrific show. I mean it's my favourite Andrew Lloyd

Webber. It's a wonderful story, it worked terrifically. I was really delighted.'

Chat show host Michael Parkinson remarked: 'Superb. The first act was wonderful. The second one probably not as good, but I love it.'

Documentary maker Desmond Wilcox claimed: 'Wonderful. I cried.'

Stage diva Sarah Brightman insisted: 'I had a great time'

Novelist and politician Jeffrey Archer, when asked about Michael Ball, said: 'Brilliant, he'll go far. He is fantastic.'

And his wife Mary added: 'What an actor. Wonderful.'

Cathy then visits Michael in his dressing room after the show. Both are seen smiling surrounded by well-wishers – including Trevor Nunn, Michael's sister Katherine and his brother Kevin – with Michael in a bathrobe. The pair are hugging and kissing. Michael holds Cathy in his arms for an eternity, or so it seems.

Cathy: 'That was wonderful.'

Michael (laughing): 'This is nice, isn't it?'

Cathy: 'What was it like?'

Michael: 'I can't think, my brain's gone. It was wonderful, terrific. The most terrifying moment when I did the opening chorus of "Love Changes Everything".'

Michael and Cathy are then seen canoodling in the back of a limousine being driven to the first-night party. Cathy tells Michael 'what a great night' before he hands her a coin claiming it is payment for a bet she wagered that the song 'Love Changes Everything' would make the Top Ten in the singles chart. When Michael claims that he has forgotten his ticket to his own party, Cathy promises that she will use her influence to get him in. He says: 'This is really weird, Cathy, really weird.'

It is clear from the footage, as they arrive at the function and Cathy is seen talking to Lloyd Webber, that there is a special bond between her and Michael. Back in the studio the following day, Cathy is talking with BBC *Newsroom South East* presenter Guy Michelmore about the evening.

Guy Michelmore: 'Very nice. A spectacular night out that looked.'

Cathy: 'It was fabulous, Guy. Absolutely wonderful. He's got such a great family, and he's so nice and natural.'

Guy: 'It has to be said, though, the papers gave it what could only be called mixed reviews.'

Cathy: 'Well, I don't understand that. I saw some of those reviews and I don't think they were in the same show that I was in. I thought it was absolutely splendid. I saw the preview and I saw this. It's just amazing. It's a beautiful show.'

Guy: 'It's going to Broadway, I understand?'

Cathy: 'Yes, it is, so we're going to lose Michael.'

The show might have been going to lose Michael to Broadway, but Cathy was not. From that moment on, they were friends, and then good friends, and then an item, and then inseparable.

Michael said that Cathy was absolutely not looking for anyone, adding rather modestly that she certainly would not be after someone like him. He has claimed that he was still rather muddled about life when Cathy came to interview him. But they started talking and she phoned him that night. The couple 'just clicked,' said the *Sun*. But Michael has joked that she stalked him and finally won him. He believes meeting

Cathy was the greatest thing that happened to him and that she completely sorted out his life.'

The age gap – Cathy was born in 1941 making her 21 years older than Michael – did not seem to matter to them, though curiously the difference in their ages became narrower and narrower the older Cathy became. In some interviews, the difference could be put at as little as 14 years, which of course would have meant that Cathy would have been aged 16 when she had been presenting *Ready Steady Go!*.

The truth is revealed on her wedding certificate, which gives her age as 28 on 17 January 1970. The likely explanation over the 'date of birth' discrepancy – as it appears on all her biographical data as 1943 – is that when she applied for the *Ready Steady Go!* job in 1964, she really needed to be a teenager not 22 going on 23. So she did a little bit of subtraction – and stuck with it ever since. And, of course, she has always looked so young, anyway.

But Michael was not worried and said about the age difference, whatever they admitted it was: 'She's a fabulous woman. Have you seen her? She looks younger than I do. She's absolutely amazing,' he exclaimed to *OK!* magazine.

However, every interviewer from 1990 onwards would ask questions, as much as the private Michael would allow, about his relationship with Cathy. He has always insisted that it 'wasn't love at first sight' but 'definitely interest at first sight'.

Much of this questioning about the state of their relationship stems from an incident that upset Michael greatly in the spring of 1990. The society journalist and royal watcher Nigel Dempster reported in his column – which appeared regularly in the *Daily Mail* and the *Mail On Sunday* – that

Prince Edward 'had developed a touching friendship' with Michael while the royal was working for Andrew Lloyd Webber's Really Useful Company as a production assistant on *Aspects Of Love*.

When confronted in April of that year in New York by a *Daily Mirror* journalist, the prince, then aged 26, forgot all about protocol and allegedly protested: 'I am not gay. It's just outrageous to suggest this sort of thing. It's so unfair to me and my family. How would you feel if someone said you were gay? The rumours are preposterous.'

Buckingham Palace, as you would expect, refused to comment, and all that Michael, then aged 27, would say to papers, including the *Chicago Tribune*, was: 'We've only ever spoken five or six times and that was about work. I don't know how people dream these things up. That was ludicrous, although it hurt my family. I just shrugged it off and said, "Well, the story's bullshit, but at least they spell my name right."'

In the wake of this story, Michael was asked about the insinuations that his relationship with Cathy was not genuine. He told *TV Quick* magazine: 'That's total rubbish. I could have let the rumours get under my skin but, no, it doesn't worry me. I'm in a secure relationship and very happy.'

The furore appeared to make no difference to him and Cathy. They 'didn't get together exclusively' until 1991 but then moved in as partners the following year.

Michael has deflected intrusive questioning from journalists including those at *Women's Weekly* by saying such things as: 'We've always jealously guarded our privacy. We don't do first nights. We don't pose on red carpets. We don't let people photograph us in our home. The job is exciting but the madness of show business isn't real life. Real life is when you shut the front door, stick the telly on and open a bottle of wine. I have the love of a great lady. We have our private life and we've always kept it that way.'

However, Michael has never shied away from praising Cathy and what she has brought to his life. 'What makes Cathy special? Oh God, so much. But the bottom-line is she really loves me. I know I can put my complete trust in her. People talk about the age difference – she is 15 years older than me but have you seen her? It simply isn't an issue. I love my home; I love the normality of my life with Cathy.'

The couple bought a cottage in Barnes, south-west London as well as a country retreat to allow them to escape when the work schedules allowed. They added to their lives by taking on board Tibetan Terrier dogs. First there was Yogi, who unfortunately died in 2001, and then a black and white one called Ollie before a third, Freddie, arrived. Yogi might be remembered by some fans as he appeared on stage during one of Michael's open air concerts in 1997 'where he was the big star of the evening'.

Interviewer after interviewer has asked Michael to explain their love. In 1993, he told *OK!* Magazine: 'Cath and I went to New York to see a few shows and generally have a good time. She is the most important person in my life. We hit it off from the beginning. We think the same. We laugh at the same things. And I love how she looks. I don't know anyone who dresses more beautifully. She has incredible style.'

As if annoyed by the constant probing about their relationship, Michael went on to say: 'Look, I'm with the person I love. I've got a great house, the job's going well and it's really stimulating work. New stuff that I never thought I'd be doing. It's difficult to know how you can improve on that. On the other hand, I wake up every morning and think they are going to come for me now; that it was all a joke.'

Michael then told an amusing anecdote to illustrate how as two people they think as one, and that they ponder that sometimes their incredible success might come crashing to an end. He said: 'Cathy and I were having that very conversation on the last night of one tour. The party was going on somewhere else in the building. We slipped back into the auditorium of the Dominion Theatre in London's Tottenham Court Road. We sat there in the total emptiness and looked at each other. Suddenly, Cath pipes up, "Right , I'll get the car started. You grab the takings. And then we'll be off." We felt like Bonnie and Clyde. There's this feeling that we'll be rumbled at any minute. Life couldn't be better.'

In 1994 in an interview with *TV Quick*, he said: 'I go home to Cath and we shut the door and leave it behind. Cathy is so rock solid in my life, there's just no way I could carry on without her. No matter how big a star you become, you have to have an anchor, and my Cathy is mine. I value her opinion probably above anybody else's. And she is completely straight with me. She'll listen to something and if she doesn't like it, she'll let me know. She doesn't spare my feelings. She tells me exactly what she thinks, whether it's good or bad. I wouldn't want it any other way.'

By 1998, Michael told *OK!* magazine: 'When we started going out, we would go out for an evening and end up at my place. I lived in a real bachelor flat in West Hampstead, so she would walk in, a vision of gorgeousness in this fabulous Armani outfit, put on the Marigolds and start cleaning the sink. I think that's when I fell in love with her.'

When Michael collected the Variety Award for Best Recording Artiste in 1999 – by which time Cathy was still only '14 years' his senior, he said in his acceptance speech: 'Then, 10 years ago, the lady who has been by my side since then and who I want to share this with, she's here as well today. So Cathy, this is for us, not just for me.'

Michael had developed a strong comfort zone in which to live his life. He was able to tell the *Daily Mail* in that same year: 'I love my home. I love the normality of my life with Cathy. It is the one, significant, all-consuming relationship that I have and thank God I've got it. Cathy is absolutely vital to me. She has totally changed my life.

'She helped me to do that. Slowly, our relationship developed but I still had my inner demons to contend with. I had given the lovely boy-next-door interview and we'd got the journalist bit out of the way, then we started to phone each other. She'd phone me every day. I very quickly just needed her around to talk to. If you're having that many conversations, you start opening up. I opened up with her and she did with me.'

Michael so much appreciates how Cathy has brought an important dimension to his life. 'I honestly can't envisage that anyone else could have come along and had the effect upon me that she had. I needed a woman who understood enough to be able to take me on. I also needed somebody who I could give to – somebody who found something in me that they needed.

'Cathy made me feel fantastic. She made me feel I deserved what was happening to me. She completely built up my confidence. When I told her I'd never been into certain designer shops, she would say, "What do you mean, you can't go into Armani? Don't be silly." I love froufrou stuff, the idea of nice watches, nice shoes, nice clothes. She opened up a whole new world. She brought out the fun side of me.'

Michael could easily insist that it was love at first sight, but what makes you believe his words is the way that he recounts how Cathy grew on him. He explained in the *Daily Mail* interview: 'To be honest, in the beginning part of the attraction was that I was going out with Cathy McGowan. It was a case of, "Wow, Cathy McGowan's interested in me." Then, over time, it turned into something more intimate and profound.

'Our relationship is something that has grown and grown. That's what love is. A lot of people didn't understand our relationship. Some people disapproved of it, but they didn't know me. I have to have normality.'

And Michael protects their privacy. He wouldn't dream of letting people in their house unless they were friends, explaining that it is 'too precious'. He loves the security that they have together. He loves being away from home knowing that there's something and someone to go home to, someone who gives him a reason to do what he's doing. He added: 'My life is so removed from what it was. This is my dream to have stability, to be almost like I am now – able to understand about relationships, love and family.'

Every time, up until 2012 that is, that Michael was asked about marriage, he would reply along these lines: 'To all intents and purposes, we are married. We haven't thought any more about marriage because we don't need to. We're ecstatically happy and have a great way of life. Neither of us expected it. It's weird that love hits you so unexpectedly.'

Cathy said: 'He's funny and makes me laugh, and he's nice looking, which is a plus. He sings to me all the time. When he's away, I put on his music and think, "Well, aren't I lucky?"'

Michael told the *Sun* newspaper in March 2009 how he had written a song to Cathy called 'Just When' and that he had put it on his latest album, *Past and Present – The Very Best of Michael Ball*. He explained: 'I was in a bad place when I met Cathy. I was kind of self-destructive, unfocused and she made my life better.'

The number included some moving lyrics. Michael added: 'It's the first song I've written for her and she cried when she heard it.'

Michael and Cathy would seem to have it all. The fact that they have never married or had any little ones does not seem to worry them. However, Michael considers that he does have children. His brother Kevin and sister Katherine both have youngsters who he adores. He has also shared the responsibilities of caring for Emma, Hywel Bennett and Cathy's daughter, who was just 16 when her mother met Michael.

When asked by *OK!* magazine about his relationship with Emma, Michael said: 'We decided that I am rather like her big brother or a best mate than her father. I'm the one she comes to first when she's got a problem.'

Emma moved to Manchester in 1995 but returned to London with her boyfriend Dean just months before the birth of their first son, Connor, on 28 April 1999. Michael became godfather to the little boy and when he did his Millennium concert in Kuala Lumpur, Dean and Emma used the trip rather romantically to marry there. At the wedding, Michael sang the Shania Twain song 'You're Still The One', and said: 'It's a beautiful song and has got lots of good memories for us.'

Connor, who calls Michael 'Bally', got a baby-sister Grace Catherine on 30 October 2001. Michael told *My Weekly*: 'I am besotted with Connor. He would say, "Bally more popcorn." He is just gorgeous. I never thought a baby was going to come into my life in any shape or form – let alone one I was going to be so close to. I've thought about fatherhood but not having children has never been a matter of regret. We're surrounded by kids and I have had such an engrossing career.'

But, of course, that brings us back to the question of Michael's parachute jump accident. Undoubtedly, the knowledge of his problem from the resultant surgery was made all the more painful after he found love with Cathy. But Michael explained to the *Daily Mail* in 1999: 'I told her quite quickly about the accident. I think I'd have blown it all again, gone back down, if it hadn't been for her.'

Michael has admitted that he had no other way of dealing with the fundamental problems he had. But he explained that Cathy took that out of him, adding: 'It was hard for her to break me down, to make me comfortable, to make me relaxed. I could be really tactile with everybody in public, but I couldn't do it in private. If she touched me I'd literally tense up and turn away. I was frightened. I'd spent so long compartmentalising my life – putting my problem away in a separate area and doing everything possible to make sure it didn't rear its head.'

CHAPTER 5

Tell Me It's Not True

Cathy and Michael, as their relationship developed, had a particular common love for Angela, Cathy's sister-in-law who had been the catalyst to the pair meeting. The two women had been friends since they were young teenagers and Angela went on to have two daughters with Cathy's brother, her husband John.

But life was to deal the cruellest of blows.

By a strange stroke of twisted fate, tragic news came through in March 1992 on a day when Cathy and Michael could not have been happier, having agreed to take the giant step of buying their first home together – at Barnes in south-west London. But their world of romantic bliss came to a shuddering halt when the call arrived that morning from Frankie McGowan, Cathy's younger sister.

Michael told *You* magazine in 1996: 'Frankie rang in a

terrible state on the day Cathy and I moved into our new house saying, "You're going to have to tell Cathy." It's the worst conversation I ever had in my life. Angela had gone in for a routine hysterectomy operation. She had had smear tests and everything seemed fine. When they opened her up, they found the fourth stage of ovarian cancer. There had been no symptoms.

'Cathy is very emotional and Angela was more like a sister. They had met at 16 and had probably spoken on the phone almost every day since. So what can you do when you love someone and you know that the next sentence you come out with is going to destroy them? I took hold of Cathy and said, "There are not many things I'm going to have to tell you like this. Please, you've got to be strong." Then I did it quickly, but with optimism. "While Angela's alive," I said, "We mustn't give up."'

Early detection of this form of the cancer can see it isolated and dealt with, yet when it is diagnosed at an advanced stage, there is little that any amount of surgery can achieve.

Angela died within four months on 19 July 1992. 'The family was shattered,' said Michael. 'The speed of it all was just so scary. She lost all her weight and all her strength. It was awful.'

The last time she was able to leave her home was to see Michael singing. 'I was doing a tour and the nearest venue was Croydon, so she came to see me there.'

Since they had met, Cathy had always believed Michael was particularly like Angela. Good-hearted and amusing. Speaking to *You* magazine, Cathy said: 'Since her death, I've been looking for Angela everywhere and I've found her in Michael.'

The trauma of losing Angela changed Michael and Cathy's relationship. When they met, they enjoyed all the normal aspects that go with that initial attraction – crazy meals plus huge phone bills. But her death made them look deeper into themselves, perhaps giving them a greater maturity, a heightened understanding of what they had together and a realisation that their relationship would endure almost any set-back.

He told TV chat show host Gloria Hunniford in 1997, with reference to Cathy being a Roman Catholic: 'I found it was great talking to Cathy because her faith is so strong and she has such conviction and she drew such strength from it. I envy that in a way, because of course she had a focal point to her religious belief to help her through it. It's a very personal thing, but it certainly helped her and it helped me knowing that she had that to lean on.'

The whole McGowan family and Michael were stunned by the loss of Angela, and they were shocked to find out about the lack of proper awareness that surrounded the disease. By the first anniversary of Angela's death, Michael, Cathy and Frankie had set up their own charity Research into Ovarian Cancer or ROC.

They had been approached for their support by the Ovarian Cancer Screening Unit, based at St Bartholomew's Hospital, London. The unit was desperately in search of funding to keep their work going and asked if they could help. A partnership was formed, ROC was established and 'no one could have envisaged the success it would bring in the next decade,' insisted its website.

Michael told the *Sydney Morning Herald*: 'When Angela

died, we became extremely angry and put all our energies into finding out why there wasn't more research going into this. We discovered there was one tiny research unit in London that was about to close for lack of funding. We said that we would try to make enough money to keep it going. At that point it was testing 150 women – absolutely nothing for one of the biggest killers of women.'

He hosted the first of a series of concerts for the ROC charity on 26 September 1993 at the Dominion Theatre in London's West End. He told respected showbiz writer Garry Jenkins: 'Cathy and I owe our relationship to Angela. If it hadn't been for her we might never have met. What happened to her ripped the soul out of the family to which I have become very close. John is battling on but, especially during the summer nights, he opens the door of his home and there is no one there.'

The whole incident affected Michael greatly. He added: 'I think it is worse if a mother dies rather than a father. I hope this doesn't sound sexist but, traditionally, it is the mother who is the core of a home and family atmosphere. And for the two girls to lose their mother when they were 15 and 18 is terrible. Angela said she would have died happily as long as she had seen her daughters marry, but she never did.

'We owed it to Angela to do something and all we could do is to channel our energies into something positive. Ovarian cancer is curable in 98 per cent of cases if it is found in its early stages. But at the moment it is never found until the fourth stage, which is when it is terminal. They are developing a blood test that will run in tandem with smear tests and mammograms.'

Michael has been organising fundraising concerts under the umbrella of his ROC charity ever since to bring in money to increase the number of women who can be tested. He told the *Daily Mirror*: 'It is important to keep this research going so that other women do not have to go through what Angela did. They call it the silent killer because it's hard to detect in its early stages. It's not picked up in smear test and most women find out they have got it only when it's too late and it has spread out of the ovaries.'

In 1998, Michael's determination to raise money to fight the disease was reinforced when he lost another dear friend, the actress Mary Millar who played Rose in the BBC1 sit-com *Keeping Up Appearances*, to the illness at the age of 62.

He revealed to *OK!* magazine: 'Mary and I had been in *The Phantom Of The Opera* together. I was floundering a bit and she took me under her wing and we became very close. Mary's case was very similar to Angela's, she was diagnosed too late and by the time she went in for an operation, the cancer had spread out of her ovaries and was attached to her bowel and liver. She died within four or five months.'

Mary passed away on 10 November 1998 and just 12 days later Michael hosted the third of his special ROC concerts at the Theatre Royal in Drury Lane, London – the second was staged on 26 November 1995 at the Theatre Royal, Haymarket, London.

'Mary had planned to come to the benefit concert for ROC at Drury Lane so we dedicated the show to her. I did the eulogy at her memorial service and it brought back Angela's death all over again. The only thing you can do is take that awful anger and grief and try to channel it somewhere positive, which is what Cathy and I have tried to do with ROC. Ovarian cancer is the biggest gynaecological killer, and the charity is raising money to develop a two-pronged test to detect if first women have a susceptibility to developing ovarian cancer, and second, have the cancer itself.'

That 1998 concert raised £40,000 alone – and the ROC managed to pull in £1million during its first five years to 1997.

Eight years after Angela's death, Michael was asked by one interviewer if coping with the loss was becoming any easier. He replied: 'They say that time heals everything, but there are moments where something will remind me of her and I'll catch my breath. The feeling of, "Angela would have loved this." Christmas time as well as birthdays can be very difficult for the both of us, as well.'

There was a fourth concert hosted by Michael for the ROC on 1 September 2002 at the London Palladium, and by 2004 great strides forward had been made by the charity. Michael at that point gave an interview with the *Sydney Morning Herald* saying: 'Ovarian cancer is not very trendy but because of my profile at the time, because I'm a bloke talking about it, going on chat shows talking about ovarian cancer, it got a lot of interest in the UK and we began to make serious money. We eventually got 150,000 women being tested and we were given a grant for £22million from the Government.

'Predominantly my fans are women who are susceptible to this disease and this was a way they found out about this, about the simple blood tests that could catch it in the early stages, and the support groups. It's not all nutty fanaticism.'

Cathy told *You* magazine: 'Being involved with Michael doing something so tangible has channelled my grief.'

CHAPTER 6

New York State Of Mind

M ichael, by 1990 with his life stabilised by the presence of Cathy, was beginning to think his future might lie as much in being a concert solo singer as in his current situation appearing as a stage musical performer, despite his achievements with *Godspell*, *The Pirates Of Penzance*, *Les Misérables*, *The Phantom Of The Opera* and *Aspects Of Love*. But he, like every other actor, had dreamed of walking out onto a stage on Broadway so when the chance to take his character Alex Dillingham to the Big Apple with *Aspects*, Michael kept the focus very much back on his stage career.

Andrew Lloyd Webber announced that many of the original cast would also join the transfer from London's West End to the Broadhurst Theatre. So Michael left the London production in January 1990 ready to open on Broadway three months later on 9 April.

Michael flew in 'the whole family' to the United Sates for the first night and he relished his time in New York. Well, most of it. He told Terry Wogan at the time: 'I like New York, but I miss the green bits. We have got Regent's Park, we have got Hyde Park but they have got Central Park, which is sort of a different shade of grey and brown from the rest of New York. I live in a place called Greenwich Village, which bears as much resemblance to a village as Twickenham. It's a bit more like London than any other part of New York and it's quite fun. But no one here can make tea. The tea-bags they dunk in water. It's vile.'

The opening night to *Aspects Of Love* proved, as you would expect, a wonderfully glitzy occasion with an array of stars attending to see if Lloyd Webber could weave the magic wand again. Michael told Terry Wogan in a live broadcast the morning after the opening night: 'It was an incredible evening, unbelievable. They stood up, they cheered. They have been a wonderful audience all together. It's great. I've had about two hours sleep and I've got to go now and do the show again.'

He was ecstatic and had clearly been partying, admitting: 'I danced with Liza Minelli, can you believe that?'

Michael explained how the audience was vastly different in New York to the one he had experienced back in Blighty. He said: 'They sort of chat during the show. They think it's like watching a TV show. They laugh more, they chat, when they want to go to loo they go out to the loo, they don't give a damn really. They just enjoy themselves. The tradition is different on Broadway than it is in the West End, which tends to be more serious.'

Wogan asked Michael: 'After the show, the tradition is that

you all go off to Sardi's somewhere, don't you? And sit and get drunk and wait for the reviews. Was it like that?'

Michael replied: 'In our case it was the Rockefeller Center, the top of this amazing building with views all over New York. They had bands playing, and amazing food, it was quite an evening, unbelievable and there we waited for the reviews.'

But the reviews were not worth waiting for, well not the important one, anyway. Michael explained to the *Daily Record*: 'Frank Rich, he's the guy who writes for the *New York Times* and has never yet written anything nice about Andrew Lloyd Webber and this hasn't been an exception, bless him.'

Rich, who was nicknamed the Butcher of Broadway for his scathing penned criticisms of shows he did not appreciate, wrote aggressively: 'Andrew Lloyd Webber, the composer who is second to none when writing musicals about cats, roller-skating trains and falling chandeliers, has made an earnest but bizarre career decision in *Aspects Of Love*, his new show at the Broadhurst. He has written a musical about people. Whether *Aspects Of Love* is a musical for people is another matter.'

And Rich did not leave it there as he laid into Lloyd Webber, claiming that he 'continues to compose in the official style that has made him an international favourite, sacrificing any personality of his own to the merchandisable common denominator of easy-listening pop music'.

And he damningly added: 'Though *Aspects Of Love* purports to deal with romance in many naughty guises – from rampant promiscuity to cradle-snatching, lesbianism and incest – it generates about as much heated passion as a visit to the bank. Even when women strip to lacy undergarments, the lingerie doesn't suggest the erotic fantasies of Frederick's of Hollywood so much as the no-nonsense austerity of Margaret Thatcher's Britain.'

Rich laid into Michael's role saying that one of the lines from Alex's 'Love Changes Everything' song was very pertinent because it expressed the thought that love can make 'a night seem like a lifetime'.

The reviewer even taunted Lloyd Webber over his songs by claiming that 'the composer's usual Puccini-isms have been supplanted by a naked Sondheim envy. The first song for the two young lovers, "Seeing Is Believing", echoes "Tonight" in *West Side Story*, and a later duet for duelling male rivals recalls "A Little Night Music" (as does much of *Aspects Of Love*, its staging included).'

Rich lambasted everything about the production, insisting that 'the sexless casting of the principal roles by the director, Trevor Nunn, only adds to the musical's icy emotional infantilism', and he particularly upset Michael himself by writing: 'Mr Ball's Alex cuts a preposterous figure as a libertine. A beefy juvenile who would fit right in with the Trapp Family Singers, Mr Ball bares his chest for no worthwhile aesthetic or prurient reason, but not to the point of dismantling the chest mike from which emanates his entire personality.'

Those connected with the production, which had proved so popular with audiences in London, were astonished at the ferocity of Rich's barbed criticism. Michael told Terry Wogan: 'Nearly all the others have been raves, but he sharpened his knife and he stuck it in. I can't wait to meet him. But I'm framing Clive Barnes's review on my wall. His was fantastic. He can come for tea.'

Barnes, of the *New York Post*, had praised the whole production, saying things such as 'what a smile-producing celebration' and 'there are very real charms in this tuneful and blitheringly delightful show'.

However much he enjoyed his experience on Broadway – the show was nominated for six Tony Awards though it didn't win any – the financial figures for *Aspects Of Love* were not good. When it closed on 2 March 1991, after 377 performances and 22 previews, the entire $8million investment was lost, this, according to the *New York Times*, made it 'perhaps the greatest flop in Broadway history'.

The criticism by Frank Rich stayed with Michael a long time. He told interview Billy Sloan in 1994: 'The review was incredible. Even though we were playing to packed houses, Rich really put the boot in. And I got it in the neck. He said I sounded like a member of the von Trapp family from *The Sound Of Music*. It hurt. I wanted to bomb him. But revenge was sweet. Andrew bought a racehorse and when the stable asked, "What do you want to call it?" he replied, "Call it Frank Rich." It's a real donkey and it has never won a race.'

After such a poor review, Michael would be entitled to have been excused from shying away from any in the future, yet he admitted in later years: 'I do read reviews, but I shouldn't. Even a good one is destructive – it makes you self-conscious. As an artist, you can't trust critics; you must put your trust in your director and yourself.'

Yet despite the *Aspects Of Love* experience on Broadway, Michael did not at this point rule out spending more time in the States. When questioned by *Women's Weekly* he said: 'New York is completely exhilarating but, at the same time, so exhausting. If I'd spent any longer than nine months there, I would have gone barmy. But there's such a big market in the US and I want to explore that. Then there's Europe, Australia, the Far East – the big world.'

Once *Aspects Of Love* came to the end of its run in the spring of 1991, Michael returned home and took a long, hard look at where his career was going. And the decision he was to make would see him steer clear for six years of musical theatre, the very thing that had brought him his initial successes.

He told Devon's *Herald Express* in 2004: 'It was a conscious choice to turn my back on musicals for a while. I was offered a contract for a solo album. At this time, I was thinking a lot about the careers of other people I've worked with. There were mountains of offers from musical theatre but there was nothing I wanted to play.

'There were performers who were doing lead roles, going from *Les Mis* into *Phantom* and then *Miss Saigon*, and then maybe back to *Phantom*, but they didn't have the recognition – the show was the star. I thought that there had to be a way to break out of that, to actually make a name for yourself. All of us want our name above the title, and the only one who had done it was Elaine Paige. She did it through making records to bring her to a wider public and through the TV exposure that resulted.'

Michael had been voted the Most Promising Artiste in 1989 by The Variety Club of Great Britain, and that seemed to have provided him with an extra burst of motivation. Cathy was also instrumental in giving his career a new direction. He explained to the *Financial Times*: 'Only four per cent of the country visits the theatre – that is a lot of people but you need to look beyond that. Cathy convinced me that a hit record meant people outside the world of musicals were aware of me.'

So he signed the record deal with Polydor and started work on a debut album with a view to developing a singing career. He embarked on a small concert tour of four shows in 1991 as a trial in Bristol and Wales – though his first proper solo concert was a charity event to raise money for the restoration fund of the St Laurence Church in Bidford-on-Avon, where his parents lived. He gave two performances on Saturday, 15 June – with Cathy acting as the presenter.

Michael said: 'At first, it was a bit strange and frightening to be up on the stage on your own, without co-stars and without the help of a director.'

But he has always been one of his own biggest critics and he was honest enough to admit: 'I hated the way it was going – it was like karaoke, I didn't know what I was doing and didn't have the right people around. It was shockingly bad but I got through it and people came.'

In 1991, Michael had performed a preview of *Sunset Boulevard*, playing Joe Gillis, at the annual Sydmonton Festival on Lloyd Webber's estate in Hampshire during the summer and was also invited again to appear for a second time at the Royal Variety Performance on 30 November at the Victoria Palace Theatre in London. But more significantly for his career, Michael received an offer from the BBC that gave him a real dilemma.

CHAPTER 7

One Step Out Of Time

The stage success Michael had enjoyed in the first seven years of his career, from 1984 through to 1991, gave him a certain celebrity status within an industry in which those involved live and die on reputations. Towards the end of 1991, with him focusing on his solo singing career after being hurt by the failure of *Aspects Of Love* on Broadway, he was faced with a tough career decision. He explained: 'An opportunity came from the BBC to do *Eurovision*.'

Michael would be 30 years old in 1992 and his career was racing forward. The *Eurovision Song Contest* was, and still is to many, the most unfashionable piece of television in Britain if not in Europe, though sometimes viewers would get the impression that people from the other competing countries really did care about the whole production or festival or whatever it was, and is, meant to be.

The official website claims the event is 'one of the most typical European traditions and without doubt Europe's favourite TV show'. Perhaps more honestly, the site reports: 'After more than five decades featuring some 1,100 songs, the contest has become a modern classic, strongly embedded into Europe's collective mind.' The writer of that had forgotten to add: 'For better or for worse.'

True, since its debut on 24 May 1956 the event had become one of the Europe's longest-running television shows, albeit only once a year. But it had apparently helped to sideline more budding singing careers than it had cleared the tracks for them to go full steam ahead to stardom. The oddities of the competition start, for some, with the geographical movements of various countries – that is to say, some might put Morocco in North Africa and others place Israel in the Middle East not in Europe at all. You could call it continental drift but perhaps more accurately musical chairs.

That aside, it is not simply losing the *Eurovision Song Contest* that can kill a potential career, winning it can do exactly the same. And this 'kiss of death' has become more poisonous over the years. In Britain most people have heard of our early winners – Sandie Shaw (1967), Lulu (1969), Brotherhood Of Man (1976) and Bucks Fizz (1981) – poor old Cliff Richard could manage only second with his *Congratulations* 'classic' in 1968 – but what about Katrina And The Waves, who took first place in 1997?

Ireland, the most successful country in the competition's opening 56 years to 2011, had managed to win it seven times. Dana's 'All Kinds of Everything' in 1970 did wonders for her profile and Johnny Logan holds the accolade of being the only act to win it twice, with 'What's Another Year' in 1980 and 'Hold Me Now' in 1987. But the other winners from the Emerald Isle all during the 1990s – Linda Martin, Niamh Kavanagh, Paul Harrington and Charlie McGettigan and Eimear Quinn – are far from household names.

In 1991, the BBC's selection programme *A Song For Europe* propelled forward from an array of acts an 18-year-old called Samantha Janus as Britain's entry for the contest that was to be held that year in Rome. At 15, Janus had left home 'as a self-confessed wild child for a life in squats', which of course involved drinking, smoking and taking drugs. But Samantha turned her life around and enrolled in the Sylvia Young Theatre School in London, thus giving her some credibility when it came to developing a career in the entertainment business.

But her romantically heroic comeback in life cut no ice with *Eurovision* judges and her song, 'A Message To Your Heart', finished a lowly 10th, managing to reach only Number 30 in the UK singles charts.

So when it came to the following year, the BBC decided to revert back to the selection process that decided the entries from 1964 to 1975. This meant that a singer was picked internally by dear old Auntie herself and the public would vote on which song would go with them to the *Eurovision* finals. The lucky artist selected for 1992 was Michael Ball.

At first he said 'no', but he had a rethink. Suddenly, and inexplicably to some, perhaps even many, he believed the whole idea could be just perfect for him. 'I thought, "Let's see if we can make this work to my advantage,"' he said.

What was a young artist with his stage credentials doing getting involved? But Michael had made up his mind and would try to complement his theatre successes with a solo singing career, which rather surprisingly had gone nowhere after his 1989 hit single 'Love Changes Everything'. A second single released later in that year of 1989, 'The First Man You Remember', disappeared without trace.

Yet even he joked, with the sort of humour that everyone seemed to reserve for *Eurovision*, before the contest: 'No, it's not going to destroy my career. There are a lot of things other than *Eurovision* that can do, but not this. No, if I come last I will blame the great British public for picking the wrong song. And if I come first, it will be totally down to me.'

He strode forward boldly and sang eight songs on prime-time BBC television, terrific exposure for him, in the show *A Song For Europe 1992*. The number he performed seventh, 'One Step Out Of Time', emerged as the winner 'by an overwhelming margin' – with more than 60,000 telephone votes to the Beeb separating the first and second places.

And maybe he had it right to get himself involved in the venture after all – because when he belted out the song – composed by Paul Davies, Tony Ryan, and Victor Stratton – on 9 May 1992 in Malmo, the third biggest city in Sweden, at the MalmöMässan, he was effectively performing in front of 600 million viewers, as BBC show host Terry Wogan pointed out.

One commentator wrote about the song: 'It was a mid-tempo ballad, relating the singer's comfort with being "one step out of time" in relation to rejecting the reality around him, instead pining after his former lover. Not accepting that his relationship is over, and spurning the disapproval of his friends, he wishes to put "his love on the line" one more time, imploring his former lover to just let him know what he had done wrong.'

The song, which had been the pre-contest odds-on favourite with the bookmakers, was performed 16th on the night, after Austria's Tony Wegas with *Zusammen Geh'n* and before Ireland's Linda Martin, who sang 'Why Me?'. But there was no fairytale ending.

Belgium, Austria, Denmark and Germany awarded the United Kingdom their top mark of 12 points yet in the final count up Michael, on 139, was in second place – 16 points behind Linda Martin, who received the maximum marks from only three countries. This would be the third of four second-place finishes the UK suffered between 1988 and 1993. Malta, who had only rejoined Eurovision the year before, came third out of the 23 participating countries that year.

Yet Michael had done appreciably better than Janus the previous year, thus justifying the BBC's remodelled selection process. He claimed some time later to the *Illawarra Mercury* in Australia: 'I lost because Cyprus gave me no points. I think we had some political argument going on with Cyprus at the time. At least it means that I would never be saddled with *Eurovision Song Contest* winner next to my name.'

In fact, Cyprus gave Michael six points and it was Greece, Portugal, Norway and Yugoslavia who each failed to award the United Kingdom any marks. Three of those countries received no marks from the British panel of judges, which surprisingly was alone in awarding its top mark of 12 to the Iceland entrants, Heart 2 Heart singing 'Nei Eoa Ja', who finished seventh.

Michael added in various interviews over the next few years

comments such as: 'We didn't take it very seriously then. It's great entertainment. It's lovely to watch the rest of Europe give us a good kicking and that's what it is. It's a fun piece of TV and it should never be taken seriously. I do what everyone else does, sit there and slag off the music, slag off the dresses and slag off the political voting – it's hysterical, it's so political. Maybe it will turn and it won't be a joke in the future. If we were to win it again and the singer has a hit with the song, maybe it would get its credibility back.'

When asked by *OK!* magazine whether he would do *Eurovision* again, Michael replied: 'I would rather stick needles in my eyes. I have to say, I love watching *Eurovision*, but I don't enjoy being judged with a television up my nose. Besides, I've been there, done it and really do have the T-shirt. I don't need to do it again.'

And on another occasion he claimed it wasn't him who entered but 'someone pretending to be him'. He added: 'And if I find out who it was, they're in real trouble.'

Yet Michael is no fool and when he could be pinned down to being serious about the contest, speaking to *The Stage* he said: 'The *Eurovision* experience is an amusing footnote to my career. It did mean that people got to see me singing a different style of song away from musical theatre, as myself, and were appreciative of it. I do have really good memories of *Eurovision*. It came at a time when I was trying to break out of the musical theatre mould, and what better exposure can you get than that? Many people came to know me through the *Eurovision Song Contest*.'

Indeed, since that Malmo performance, he has gone on to release album after album that have virtually all gone Gold or even Platinum. For all the ridicule, his plan to place himself in the British public's consciousness as a mainstream singer and performer was a success. The single 'One Step Out Of Time' peaked at Number 20 in the UK singles chart, staying in the Top 100 for seven weeks.

But what *Eurovision* did for Michael was to prompt the release of his debut album, *Michael Ball*, and spark a UK concert tour, which proved to be a sell-out. The album included the songs: 'One Step Out Of Time', 'It's Still You', 'Holland Park', 'Secret Of Love', 'As Dreams Go By', 'Who Needs To Know', 'Simple Affair Of The Heart', 'If You Need Another Love In Your Life', 'Beautiful Heartache', 'No One Cries Anymore', and 'Love Changes Everything'.

The success of his album and the profile *Eurovision* had given him triggered a huge following for him and he embarked on his first solo UK concert tour, which concluded at the London Palladium. By the night of his 30th birthday on 27 June 1992, the album had gone to Number One.

Impresario Cameron Mackintosh took to the stage in west London – Michael played the Hammersmith Odeon on the Saturday night, but by the following night he was playing the Hammersmith Apollo as the same venue had changed its name – to present him with his first Gold Disc. It was, Michael admitted, 'the start of a whole different career for me'.

And this success was especially sweet for Michael because earlier in that year he was annoyed greatly when snubbed for a production he really wanted to perform in. Nicholas Hytner was directing a revival of the Rodgers and Hammerstein classic *Carousel* – and Michael was very keen. '*Carousel* has been the only role that I was really cross I didn't get seen for and would loved to have done,' he said. 'They did it at the Royal National Theatre and they wouldn't even see me for it, and I was really pissed off about that.'

He ended 1992 with the accolade of being invited to do a third Royal Variety performance – though this one was particularly special as it was the Queen's 40th Jubilee – at London's Dominion Theatre on 7 December.

The success of those past 12 months meant that Michael could launch himself into 1993 confident as arrangements were made for a second UK tour, and again all 30 dates were to be sold out. All the time, he was growing a larger and larger fanbase, predominantly women, who were taken by his sweet tones and boyish looks.

One commentator wrote on *Justball.net*: 'He is bringing his capacity audiences to their feet, night after night, venue after venue. And how did he achieve this? With a fabulously expensive display of strobe lighting and pyrotechnics? With laser beams and a decibel level to alert the local authorities? No, as a matter of fact, what had Michael Ball's adoring audiences clamouring for more was an unashamedly old-fashioned mix of well sung music – everything from pop to light classics – slick dancing and a liberal dash of genial good humour.'

Michael told *OK!* magazine: 'I quite deliberately try to provide something for everyone. From what I can gather, people really want to feel they have been entertained – and you do that by giving them as much as you can. I love country music. I love pop. I love opera.'

It was during the early part of 1993 that Michael had the chance to sing with New Zealand opera legend Dame Kiri Te

Kanawa in front of a capacity audience at the National Indoor Arena in Birmingham. He said: 'I couldn't compete with her as a singer, as a technician. Her ability to hold notes, her breath control, her vocal range – it's the best, simply superlative. But we found a way of working together, a way of giving each other our individual strength, if you like. And she is so down-to-earth, totally unpretentious.'

He recorded the album *West Side Story*, taking the role of Tony and performing with Barbara Bonney and the London Philharmonic Orchestra, but he also moved his career another important step forward.

Michael told *Women's Weekly*: 'I consider anything that comes through my letterbox.' And he went on to explain: 'The artists I really admire – Barbra Streisand, and all those great old performers, such as Frank Sinatra, Sammy Davis Junior and Judy Garland – juggled different talents. I think there's a different set-up in America, there isn't the pigeon-holing. If you can act, terrific. If you can sing as well, that is even better, and if you want to write, brilliant.'

So perhaps it was not surprising when he made the break-through into television. Yes, he had appeared before on the small screen, not least from the resurrecting of his career with that performance on the *Miss England* show in late 1986 and, of course, his exposure to 600 million watching *Eurovision*. But now he had been handed the chance by Carlton TV of his own television series, entitled simply *Michael Ball*, to go out from 8 July 1993. It was only six episodes of a chat show-style format, but it was a major opportunity for him to try to display his versatility, to reveal the sort of person he was behind the voice.

And Michael revelled. 'It is nerve-racking, quite frankly, when I think about the sort of people I'm singing along with. I have chosen big stars who are the greatest in their field. Ray Charles is the king of soul, Tammy Wynette is obviously the queen of country music, Montserrat Caballe is the greatest soprano there is, and you cannot name a better pop star than Cliff.'

The show was not a huge success in viewer terms, nor did Michael particularly dazzle, but it did give him crucial exposure to his by-now diehard fans, ensuring that his second album *Always* – which was released on 29 June, two days after his 31st birthday – leapt up the UK charts and reached Number Three in September 1993, staying in the Top 20 for 10 weeks.

That success brought him an exclusive contract with Sony music for his next album – and it also ensured that the first of his concerts for his Research into Ovarian Cancer charity, in memory of Cathy's sister Angela, in the September had all the exposure necessary to make it a success.

Always contained the numbers: 'A Song For You', 'A House Is Not A Home', 'If I Can Dream', 'Cry Me A River', 'You Don't Have To Say You Love Me', 'Someone To Watch Over Me', 'On Broadway', 'Tell Me There's A Heaven', 'Always On My Mind', 'You'll Never Know', 'Stormy Weather' and 'You Made Me Love You'.

Michael said through his record company at the time: 'This album represents several months of searching, reassessing and fun. Searching for the right songs – the songs that I love to sing and have a special meaning for me. Re-assessing how they should sound now, and how I could put my own stamp on them. And fun, because that's what it was to record them. The reason it was fun is in no small part due to the people involved in its making. Their kindness, patience, and inspiration made it all possible. Therefore, to everyone at Westside Studios, to all the fantastic musicians and singers, and the gang in the office, and of course to Cathy and everyone on the "home front", I say "Thank you" and "I love you."'

With another successful year under his belt – 1993 was rounded off with an eight-date sell-out Christmas tour – Michael beamed: 'I'm with the person I love. I've got a great house, the job's going well and it's really stimulating work, new stuff that I never thought I'd be doing. It's difficult to know how you can improve on that.'

Such was the demand and enthusiasm for the *Always* album that Michael released his third offering within a year when *One Careful Owner* came out 1 August 1994 and that, like the first two albums, also gained Gold status. It included the classic songs: 'Wherever You Are', 'From Here To Eternity', 'The Lovers We Were', 'Take My Breath Away', 'Leave A Light On', 'When We Began', 'My Arms Are Strong', 'I Wouldn't Know', 'All For Nothing', 'In This Life', 'Give Me Love' and 'I'll Be There'.

Michael went to Scotland in July 1994 for a whistle-stop tour to launch the single 'From Here To Eternity' from the album *One Careful Owner*. When he arrived in Glasgow, he was ambushed by a swarm of female fans clutching autograph books and cameras. He was taken aback and said: 'I had no idea this would go through the roof, but when success comes along, you just go for it. Since I appeared in the West End, I've got used to people hanging around outside the stage door. And the more exposure I've got, the bigger my fan club has become. And, of course, most of the members are women.'

But Michael assured journalist Billy Sloan when asked about his fanbase being mostly female: 'I don't take this sex symbol lark seriously at all. How can you? I've had girls hiding in my hotel bedroom and following me around in cars. The usual stuff. Most of my fans are very respectful, kind and know what the limit is. There are a couple who go over the top, and I have to sort them out. I've never been in the position where I've been so keen on some girl that I had wanted to get into her life. I always try to be polite and respectful – as long as people are polite and respectful towards me.'

Michael's celebrity was growing and growing, triggering the offer of a second series of his own Carlton TV 'chat and music' show to go out from August 1994. Again the names came. Montserrat Caballé was back singing with Michael – as was Shirley Bassey, Cher, James Brown, Lulu and Joe Cocker. 'Sometimes I stop and think, "Good grief, just look at me singing with these people."'

But presenting, at this stage of his career, did not come easy to Michael, with his nerves still an issue. The late Godfather of Soul James Brown was 'scary as hell' to Michael when he turned up in a fleet of six limousines with a huge entourage of heavies and with a little truck for small talk. The troubled music legend had not long finished a three-year jail sentence after publicly waving a shotgun around in Atlanta, Georgia, while high on drugs and demanding to know who had used his private bathroom.

Michael told *Wales Online*: 'I was so anxious about meeting him I refused to come out of the loo, but I finally I managed to go out and introduce myself. I walked over to him, sheepishly held out my hand and said, "Mr Brown, my name is Michael Ball and I'll be singing with you later." He just looked at me and replied, "Never mind that, gimme the key of D" before launching into a version of "I Feel Good". It went on for ages and he started to ad-lib, coming out with all these different rock stars' names at the end of each riff – Chuck Berry, Elvis Presley, Marvin Gaye and so on. I tried keeping up with him but I had to throw the towel in when all I could think to come up with was Karen Carpenter.'

And that was not his only terrifying moment while recording the show. Michael performed with Cher and, halfway though their song, he grabbed the American music and movie star and hoisted her up into the air. 'Cher screamed at me to put her down,' he told the *Daily Record*. 'She had no knickers on and didn't want everyone to see up her dress.'

But the chat show came to an end after the two series in 1993 and 1994 – and he admitted in 1999: 'I wasn't too keen to do more in case I came to be regarded as a light-entertainment host rather than a singer. And, if I'm honest, I don't think that I was very good. I didn't understand the medium of television and I didn't make the most of the guests who came on. I was out of my depth.'

However, the solo career decision was progressing strongly and developing well. Michael was being pursued by an army of loyal female fans and he was picking up various smaller awards, such as being voted one of the men that women would most like to marry in a survey by the magazine *TV Quick*.

This popularity sparked a third UK concert tour while the

release of a compilation album, *The Best Of Michael Ball*, brought a fitting conclusion to what had proved to be another year of plaudits.

Those attending his concerts were now being offered a full range of Michael Ball branded merchandise, from the glossy programme to sweatshirts at £22 and posters at £4. His performance at Hammersmith in December 1994, which closed his 17-date tour, received a glowing review from Alan Jackson in *The Times*. He wrote: 'The atmosphere was part West End theatre matinee, part office party. There were older ladies in tweed coats and sensible shoes, younger women with tinsel in their hair and astonishingly high heels, and occasional couples – some hand-holding Mr and Mrs Marrieds – enjoying a night away from the kids.

'While many musical theatre stars sound arch and slightly ridiculous when attempting more mainstream material, Ball is able to carry off a range of styles with enthusiasm and an eager-to-impress charm,' journalist Alan Jackson wrote in *The Times*.

The difference now was that such acclaim was giving Michael the confidence, obviously with the enormous help of Cathy, to be able to switch on and off from his work. He claimed: 'My idea of heaven is having friends round on a Sunday and cooking up a storm.'

Michael had perfected the balance between his professional world and what went on behind closed doors. 'I'm normally quite forthright and able to talk about things but I feel very protective about my private life, I really do,' he told *Women's Weekly*. 'All I do is to provide entertainment, a bit of light relief in troublesome times. That's what I give and I don't think it means everybody then has an automatic right to pry into things that I'm not giving away to the public.'

He admitted that on stage he still suffered from the nerves that had wrecked his *Les Misérables* days – but he knew how to respond to these reactions without panicking. He added: 'I get so nervous I've no control over my bodily functions – and I really don't like listening to myself. I always think, "Oh, for God's sake, you could have done that properly." My concentration is total and I never go on stage thinking, "This is easy, I'm going to slay them with this."'

In 1995, the ever-industrious Michael kept his solo music career speeding along. He earned top billing in three major open-air concerts in Exeter, Woburn Abbey and, along with the BBC Big Band, at Ludlow Castle in Shropshire. He sang at the opening ceremonies of the European Youth Olympics in Bath as well as the Rugby Union World Cup at Twickenham while also performing for the Queen at the VE Day 50th Anniversary concert in London's Hyde Park.

If he was not out of breath from that lot, he performed a duet with Elaine Paige at the BBC Radio Music Live 95 concert in Birmingham as well as appearing at concerts in Jersey, Belfast and Harrogate, Yorkshire. Additionally, he recorded a Christmas special for Carlton TV, which went out on Christmas Eve with his guests being Dusty Springfield and Michael Bolton.

What particularly pleased Michael was the chance to finally lay the ghosts from his troubled *Les Misérables* past with him being invited to recreate the role of Marius in the Tenth Anniversary Gala Concert at the Royal Albert Hall on 8 October.

This was billed as The Dream Cast and was a concert version of the original stage musical. It was filmed live and proved a huge success on DVD and video when released three years later. The anniversary cast included Michael, Colm Wilkinson, Philip Quast, Lea Salonga, Judy Kuhn and Ruthie Henshall, with the stars being chosen from the London, Broadway and Australian versions of the show.

Additionally Michael, as if to prove that nothing within the sphere of entertainment was beyond him, made his movie debut in 1995 in the film *England, My England*, in which he portrayed the composer Henry Purcell, alongside Simon Callow and Robert Stevens, with Tony Palmer directing. This production, written by John Osborne and Charles Wood, depicted the life of Purcell through the eyes of a playwright in the 1960s who is trying to write a play about him.

This movie did not receive much acclaim and it did not have casting directors knocking down Michael's door as the next new Hollywood idol. However, it was another credit to put on his CV to show how his acting and general entertainment talents could be adapted and stretched.

Speaking to *Radio Gloucestershire* in 2001, he said of *England, My England*: 'It was a fantastic thing to be involved with. It was John Osborne's last script. It was Sir Robert Stephens' last movie. I really enjoyed playing opposite Simon Callow.'

But did this ignite a burning desire within him to do straight acting? He said: 'Because I've always felt my strength is music, my favourite way of communicating with an audience, and trying to move an audience is through music, I've concentrated on that, and haven't really put myself in the eye-line for straight theatre. And I think that when you've done that people would find it harder and harder to cast me in something. I think there would have to be something specifically right for me, for me to do some straight theatre. But you know me, I'm up for anything.'

Michael was asked directly in that interview in 2001 if he would fancy being a movie star and he replied: 'Sure I would. But to make movies in Hollywood, you have to up sticks and go there. My name means very little over there. And even if I was successful there, my schedule is so packed that I don't know how I would fit everything in.'

CHAPTER 8

Wind Beneath My Wings

Michael, by the start of 1996, was simply flying with his solo singing career. His concerts were being sold out with amazing regularity and his albums had developed a wonderful habit of going Gold almost before they had hit the music stores. Television was showing a lot more interest and every interview he gave seemed to highlight the contentment he had found in his life.

What better way to start the New Year than to release an album, with *First Love* coming out on 15 January on Columbia/Sony Music. Michael wrote on his website: 'This album certainly isn't the one we originally set out to make. Our first idea was loosely based on the theme of 'anthems'. But when Nigel Wright, my producer, and I started working and throwing ideas around, we kept being drawn to favourite songs which, although quite often anthemic in style, were nonetheless love songs.

'It became clear that these songs – some suggested by friends, family and fans alike – had a common thread and made a very satisfying whole.'

The songs, with '*Ne Me Quitte Pas*' sung partly in French, included: 'The Rose', 'Let The River Run', 'Somewhere', 'If You Could Read My Mind', '(Something Inside) So Strong', 'How Can I Be Sure', 'If You Go Away (Ne Me Quitte Pas)', 'I'm Gonna Be Strong', 'I'm So Sorry' and 'All By Myself'.

The album went straight into the charts at Number Four but while Michael was fulfilling his solo dream, he still had a yearning to return to the theatre. He had missed the theatrical stage during his by now six-year absence. It was a perfect moment when producer Bill Kenwright approached him with an offer, showing him his ticket stub from the opening night of *Aspects Of Love* that he had attended on Broadway in April 1990. He'd written on it: 'Get the rights for Michael Ball.'

Kenwright wanted him to appear in the British premiere of Stephen Sondheim's play *Passion*, and Michael told *The Stage*: 'It was a bold choice to come back with – and that is precisely why I did it. I had really forgotten the buzz of doing a theatre piece. That first day of rehearsal, of meeting up with everybody you are going to be working with, and the whole rehearsal process – seeing the set model, doing the first Sitzprobe (a seated rehearsal where the singers perform with the orchestra), doing the first previews, getting your dressing room – I really missed that.'

He added that the most marvellous thing about theatre is that it 'is just so not precious, like it can be in the pop and television world, where it is much more hierarchical and you can get isolated. There is more interaction with people, more collaborative things and you understand what people want when they come to the theatre. But it's also bloody hard work.'

Michael was signed up to play the part of romantic army officer Giorgio Barchetti in *Passion*, a musical adapted from Ettore Scola's film *Passione d'Amore,* which was based on Iginio Ugo Tarchetti's novel *Fosca*. The script was by James Lapine, with music and lyrics by Sondheim. The play had run on Broadway at the Plymouth Theatre, after 52 previews, from 9 May 1994 to 7 January 1995.

Publicity material claims the 'central subjects include obsession, beauty, power, manipulation, passion, illness, and love – it is also a partially epistolary play, parts of the story being told through letters. Set in 19th century Italy, the musical revolves around a handsome soldier, Giorgio, who is shattered and ultimately changed by the unconditional and obsessive love of Fosca, his Colonel's chronically ill, bedridden cousin. Throughout the play, Giorgio corresponds with his beautiful but married mistress Clara through letters'.

The whole project appealed greatly to Michael. 'It was about not just wanting to be typecast, about not wanting to limit what I'm allowed to do myself,' he added. 'Part of the reason I did *Passion* was because there had been so much Michael Ball – the personality, the TV series and blah blah – that I thought, if I don't watch it, there will be no way back. People would be thinking, that's not Giorgio, that's Michael Ball and I would hate that.'

He told Germany's *Musicals* magazine: 'I got to work with Stephen Sondheim, whom I think of as a genius. Cameron

Mackintosh had asked me whether I wanted to do *Side By Side* (a musical revue featuring songs by Sondheim) but I didn't think this to be a good idea. Cameron said, "You are giving away the chance to work with the greatest".'

Michael revealed how he then moved on to *Passion*. He added: 'I didn't really like the Broadway production. It was no commercial show. It was much more gloomy, small and a bit frightening. Sondheim had written a new song for me, a solo, "I love Fosca", explaining why Giorgio had fallen in love with her. Well, to be able to work with Sondheim and not having the pressure of making commercial decisions made me accept the offer. This work would really deserve to become a big hit.'

He went on to explain exactly what draws him to a role. He said: 'It has to be three-dimensional. It can be small, as long as it is interesting. Take, for example, Amos Hart in Chicago, this one would frustrate me: the two women always on stage and I always in the dressing room. I don't want to play mini roles anymore. I prefer to appear at galas together with an unbelievable ensemble.'

He was to perform in *Passion* alongside Maria Friedman, an English actress who is a couple of years older than Michael. It was claimed that she put in such a powerful performance as the ugly and reclusive Fosca that it moved Sondheim to tears – and Michael said: 'She transformed herself into a hunched imp who, through sheer force of longing, could make a handsome young man love her.'

Passion did a short provincial tour – at the Theatre Royal in Plymouth from 17 – 24 February, at the Palace Theatre in Manchester from 26 February to 2 March and at the Theatre Royal in Nottingham from 4 – 9 March – before the previews in London started on 13 March. The production opened officially at The Queen's Theatre on Shaftsbury Avenue in London's West End on 26 March 1996. The reviews were extremely positive, so important for Michael on his comeback to theatre after the caning he took from Frank Rich six years previously when *Aspects Of Love* opened on Broadway.

The Times wrote: 'Stephen Sondheim's new musical is unlike any of his previous work: a thrilling and devastating psychological tragedy of a fatal obsession. Once again, Sondheim redefines the limits of musical theatre. Jeremy Sams directs with impeccable style: melodrama haunts but never invades the play. Maria Friedman and Michael Ball star and I mean star. A jewel in the West End's crown.'

The Observer said: 'Michael Ball makes the romantic cypher that is Giorgio interesting by his attractive presence, his ability to indicate fissures in the indifference before the dam bursts and, especially, in his wonderful baritonal tenor voice.'

And the *News of the World* insisted: 'Stephen Sondheim's new musical *Passion* is a killer of a show – full of super-charged emotions. Michael Ball is on powerful form as Giorgio. Don't go along to the Queen's Theatre in London expecting to hear the sort of show-stopping numbers that Michael Ball has brought houses down with in *Les Misérables*, *The Phantom Of The Opera* or *Aspects Of Love*. *Passion* has none of those. You'll end up believing love changes everything but Mr Sondheim achieves this in a more subtle way than Andrew Lloyd Webber. I'm not entirely convinced that a good looking chap like Giorgio would fall for frog-eyed Fosca. But Maria Friedman gives a pretty amazing performance as the sickly temptress.'

The show, despite achieving such acclaim, was on a limited run and closed on 28 September 1996 after 232 performances. Friedman won a Laurence Olivier award for her performance and Michael had once more increased his standing – with his versatility, which he was so desperate to show that he possessed, being laid out for all to admire.

What a perfect way to finish the year with another solo album, his fifth. And this time Michael stuck with what he really did know best a work entitled *The Musicals*.

This was released on PolyGram records on 4 November 1996, to coincide with his fourth sell-out national tour and featured the songs: 'All I Ask Of You', Something's Coming', 'Losing My Mind', 'Memory', 'Don't Rain On My Parade', 'With One Look', 'Show Me', 'I Dreamed A Dream', 'You'll Never Walk Alone', 'East Terms', 'Last night Of The World', 'Loving You', 'Anthem' and 'Love Changes Everything'.

Michael's album dedication said: 'This album marks the end of a year spent back in the world of the musical theatre, after an absence of six years, and I've loved every minute of being back. Choosing the material was the hardest part. There are hundreds of wonderful songs which I could have happily included and no doubt will record at a later date, but each of the tracks on this album has a special place in the hearts and memories of many people, including myself.'

With this album also going Gold, just as his four previous solo offerings had done, 1996 ended with Michael topping the bill at the *Joy To The World Christmas Concert* at the Royal Albert Hall, subsequently broadcast by the BBC.

The year 1997, by Michael's now high standards, proved rather quiet though it started with his video, *The Musicals*

And More, shooting straight into Number One in the UK video charts and managing to stay in the top five for more than nine weeks and the Top 20 for more than a year.

He experienced a busy summer with an appearance at a huge event in St Louis, USA, and he also made a comeback to British television screens when he was asked to launch the Wednesday *Lottery Show* on BBC1 as well as appearing during July on the main *National Lottery Live* show.

Michael was involved in two open-air concerts – one at Bedford Park in North Devon, close to where he was brought up as a child, and then he achieved top billing for *Proms In The Park*, a concert held in Hyde Park, London, in front of 35,000 people in conjunction with the *Last Night Of The Proms*.

The demand from his fans was so huge that he ended the year with a fifth national sell-out tour entitled *Nothing But The Best* and was a guest of honour at the *Hallelujah Christmas Concert* in Birmingham. During an interview in 1997, when asked if his voice was a God-given gift as he had never had formal training, he replied: 'Absolutely, it's a great gift. There's no reason why I should have it, in fact there are 20 reasons why I should not have it. I don't guard my voice particularly. The way I sing, I don't sing from the throat, I sing from my heart, from inside. This is especially when you are singing a song that means so much to you.'

Michael was delighted to do a fourth Royal Variety Performance, on 1 December at the Victoria Palace Theatre in London, as the Queen and Prince Philip were celebrating their Golden Wedding Anniversary. He told chat show king Michael Parkinson: 'Producers phoned me up to say, "We've got a lovely idea. When the Queen and Prince Philip were courting, their show was *Oklahoma* and their song was 'People Will Say We're In Love'. We got Barbara Cook, who is one of the original stars to come along and sing. Would you come and do the other part of the duet with her, would you play Curly?" I said that I would be thrilled. A lovely, lovely thing.

'So we rehearsed it and we performed it, and it went really well. You do the line-up at the end. I really love those sorts of things. You are looking at all the flashing jewellery, going "Oh that's my mortgage." Well, Prince Philip came up and said, "What exactly was that you sang?" I said, "From *Oklahoma* [it's called] 'People Will Say We're In Love'. It's your song, yours and the Queen's song." He said, "Never heard of it all my bloody life".'

The highlight for Michael in 1998, a time packed with concerts and special appearances, was the Andrew Lloyd Webber 50th Birthday Celebration Gala. He appeared singing a moving version of 'Gethsemane', 'All I Ask Of You' as a duet with Sarah Brightman and 'Vaults Of Heaven' before rounding off with his hit 'Love Changes Everything' – for which he was accompanied by Glenn Close, Antonio Banderas, Sarah Brightman, Marcus Lovett, Elaine Paige, Donny Osmond and Tina Arena.

The event at the Royal Albert Hall on 8 April – a huge success with two hours of hits from the noted song-writer's body of work spanning almost three decades – was televised the following week by ITV. Lloyd Webber, whose birthday was actually on 22 March, had been created a life peer as Baron Lloyd Webber the previous year.

Michael said: 'It was a special gala and I think I was the

only one there I've never heard of. It was fantastic being on stage. It was the most wonderful, wonderful evening. Glenn Close, when she made her entrance, was singing this song from *Sunset Boulevard*. It was breathtaking.'

He also revealed that Banderas had borrowed his shirt, moaning a couple of years later: 'He still hasn't given it back.'

Michael revealed to television chat host Gloria Hunniford: 'In the changing room, Antonio is putting on this white shirt but he goes, "Is no good, I don't like it, is no sexy, is no right, what am I going to wear? This is no good. Bring something." So I said, "I've got this really nice shirt I was going to wear after the show," and he goes, "Is perfect." He put on this black Donna Karan shirt, a really nice bit of shirt. And he says "Is now my lucky shirt. Is my singing shirt. You never ever see it again."'

To his shame but also great amusement, Michael revealed that he got so drunk with Irish band Boyzone at a party for Baron Lloyd Webber that he ended up pinching the composer's birthday cake. Earlier that year, Michael and Boyzone singer Ronan Keating had performed together during a three-part series, called *Ball In The Hall*, that Michael had made for BBC Wales at St David's Hall in Cardiff. Other guests included Lesley Garrett and Martine McCutcheon.

Michael also took part in a special *Hey, Mr Producer* gala on 7 and 8 June at the Lyceum Theatre in London, honouring the life and work of theatre impresario Cameron Mackintosh. And during the summer, he performed at a selection of sell-out open-air festivals, such as the Chelmsford Spectacular in Essex and the Liverpool Summer Pops. They were followed by a third hugely successful concert for the cancer charity ROC on

22 November at the Theatre Royal, Drury Lane in London when Michael was joined on stage by a host of celebrities, including Anthony Andrews, Lily Savage, Con O'Neil and the Rt. Hon John Major.

But the real crowning glory for Michael in this year – as his solo singing career went into overdrive – was the success of his sixth solo album, *The Movies*, which was released on 27 October. This included the songs: 'Wind Beneath My Wings', 'Love On The Rocks', 'We Have All The Time In The World', 'People Are Strange', 'My Heart Will Go On', 'Have I Told You Lately', 'Everybody's Talkin'', 'Hot Stuff', 'How Deep Is Your Love', 'I Believe I Can Fly', 'The Way We Were', 'Against All Odds', 'Blue Brothers Medley', Shake Your Tail Feather', 'Think', 'Everybody Needs Somebody To Love' and 'Because You Loved Me'.

But more importantly, this became Michael's first album to go Platinum with more than 500,000 sales in the UK.

CHAPTER 9

Hot Stuff

Michael was becoming ever more feted as a recording artist and the demand for his concerts was ever growing. The popularity of *The Movies* album won him a second Variety Club of Great Britain award at the start of 1999, this time as 1998 Best Recording Artiste. When the tickets had gone on sale for his sixth UK tour at the end of 1998, they sold out within weeks. It meant that the April and May dates would see 74,527 people attend his 25 concerts throughout the UK.

On 7 April 1999, he received glowing praise from reviewer Andy Richards in the *Birmingham Evening Mail*, who wrote: 'When Michael Ball kicked off his NEC show with the *Full Monty*'s 'Hot Stuff', there was no need for him to shed his clothes as well. For his marvellous voice was enough to inflame the passions of the mostly female sell-out audience.

And he failed to disappoint them as he led them through a two-hour plus stunning extravaganza on a "music and memories" theme.

'Backed by a 10-piece band and three hard-working backing singers, Bromsgrove-born Michael was back on his home patch and revelled in delivering a memorable night. There were songs from across the musical spectrum – and a send-up of *The Blues Brothers* monster hit "Everybody". Michael ended the night with his much-loved showstopper, "Love Changes Everything".'

The Theatregoers Club of Great Britain in July 1999 voted Michael the Most Popular Musical Actor over the past 21 years and he was earning himself royal approval – being booked for private shows for The Prince's Trust, hosted by Prince Charles at Highgrove, and by Prince Philip, for a Duke of Edinburgh Awards Night.

The dates just kept coming. He performed a concert in Amsterdam, two shows at the Liverpool Pops Festival and open-air concerts at Castle Howard in North Yorkshire and Longleat House near Warminster, Wiltshire.

In August, he was off to Scotland to give a concert at the allegedly haunted Glamis Castle in Angus. It is claimed Michael dashed off stage, pulled on a kilt and searched every nook and cranny of the imposing building. But any 'phantoms' stayed firmly hidden behind the ancient walls. One local, who spoke to Michael, claimed: 'He was really hopeful of seeing one of the famous ghosts. He was a wee bit crestfallen he didn't bump into a spectre. After all, Glamis is supposed to have a spook in every stairheid.

'Michael searched most of the building and never even

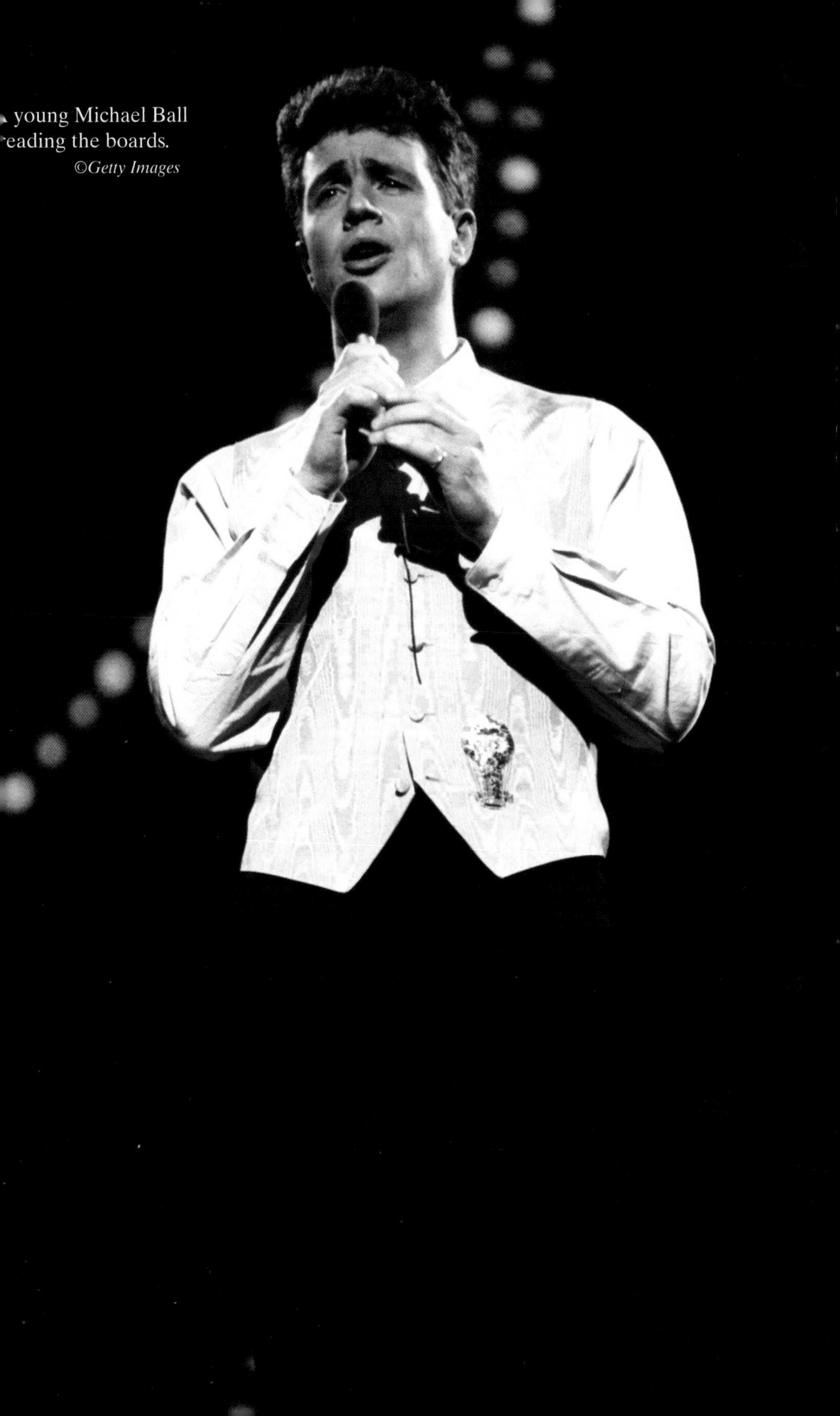

. young Michael Ball
·eading the boards.
©Getty Images

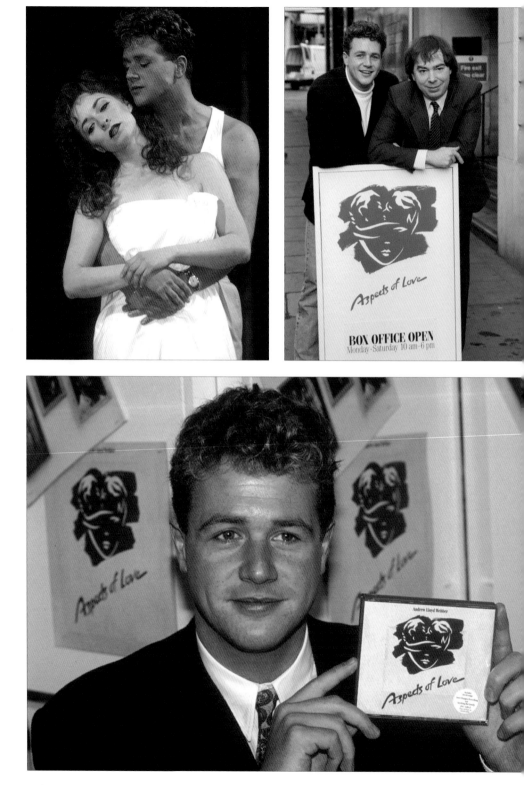

Michael's portray of Alex in *Aspects of Love* won him world acclaim, and the hit song 'Love Changes Everything' propelled him to number two in the charts.

©*Rex feature* and (*Top left*) ©*Getty Imag*

...all made his West End return in 2007, starring as Edna Turnblad in the hit musical *Hairspray*.

above: As Edna. From left, Mel Smith, Leanne Jones, Michael and Ben James-Ellis.

© Getty Images

below: Out of costume at the *Evening Standard* Theatre Awards, 2007. From left, Patrick Stewart, Leanne Jones, Michael and Ben James-Ellis.

©*Getty Images*

Michael and partner Cathy
McGowan in 2011.   ©Getty Images

Michael has worked alongside some top names in the business.

Above: At the Olivier Awards in 2011 with Imelda Staunton, choreographer Matthew Bourne and Angela Lansbury.

©*Getty Images*

Below: *Les Misérables* 25th anniversary concert. From left, Cameron Mackintosh, Nick Jonas, Samantha Barks and Michael.

©*Rex Features*

With the Laurence Olivier Award for 'Best Actor in a Musical' for *Hairspray*, 2008.

In 2010, with only 10 day's notice, Michael replaced Michael Crawford as Count Fosco in the musical *The Woman in White*.

©*Getty Images*

Musical royalty. Michael
with the one and only Liza
'with a Z' Minnelli.

©Getty Images

caught a glimpse of one. Perhaps the ghosts were so impressed with his singing that they decided not to frighten the life out of him. I'm sure if they had known he wanted to see a ghost they would have been happy to oblige. It's not like they are shy, they regularly frighten residents and staff at the castle.'

Ireland and a few pints of Guinness beckoned for Michael in September 1999 – with all four dates being sold out. 'The audience blew me away after the first song,' he said. 'At the end, I did not want to come off the stage because I was enjoying myself so much. Playing to an Irish audience is unique and I know the moment I get on stage I want to stay there for ever.'

He has a particular affection for The Point in Dublin, having played previously in the city in 1997. 'Dublin's my favourite city right now,' he told one Irish newspaper. 'I know how important it is to have a fanbase and each week we get hundreds of people who want to join up and get on the mailing list. It's great to know how many people in Ireland enjoy what I do. What I enjoy are the parties. I always end up in Lillie's Bordello. They know how to have a right good knees-up.'

Michael was asked by *My Weekly* why he was working so hard and replied: 'It's partly down to that old entertainer's fear that your last gig will indeed be your last gig. But I also really enjoy new challenges. Having said that, because I'm doing so much more this year as well, the tour was a real killer. I've still hardly caught up with myself.'

Having put the finishing touches to two new albums and a Royal Albert Hall video, Michael was delighted in October 1999 to be invited to be involved in the opening and closing ceremonies of the Rugby World Cup staged in his beloved Wales, at Cardiff's Millennium Stadium.

He told the magazine: 'I doubt I have ever sung in more arousing circumstances. There was an absolutely tremendous atmosphere in that stadium. My dad has an events marketing company, which worked on the ceremonies, so it was great to be involved with him.

'I walked out for the opening and there were 72,000 people and I don't know how many million watching on television throughout the world. That is so huge, and so beyond comprehension, that you are not actually nervous. You feel like you are just one little part of a huge event. I really can't explain that. And when they all start singing "Bread Of Heaven" with you, you have got 72,000 backing singers, you just feel all the confidence in the world. I just thrive on it. It was a fantastic feeling.'

Michael had never had children but he had always appreciated those of family and friends that he was close to, so when any chance presented itself to do something for youngsters, he was particularly keen to do whatever he could. He was given the opportunity by the BBC to anchor the *Pebble Mill* lunchtime show in November 1999 and he used this to boost further the coffers of the *Children In Need* initiative.

Between 1980 and 1998, more than £250million had been raised for *Children In Need* by the superb efforts of everyone, with Terry Wogan working his magic at the helm. When it came to the 20th anniversary, Michael was talking about a target of £25million from the one night.

He told viewers: 'It will be the last one of this Millennium so from that point of view we are hoping that we raise a record amount. This is very much a time of reflection, to think how fortunate so many of us are. We are bound to be reflective about what has been before and about the future. We have all either got children we know or children in the family and we all want to give them the best possible chances.'

Each year the Midlands, where of course Michael was born and brought up for the first three years of his life, was now raising up to £500,000 out of a national total of around £11million ,on the *Children In Need* night out – a figure that invariably nearly doubled once all the pledges were in.

Michael said: 'Home is my four walls but what affects your life is bigger than the four walls you live in. Yes, there is a danger of people being "charitied" out and that's a shame. Yet *Children In Need* is a great example of being committed to making a change and putting money to a good use. We all waste money so much. All of us are guilty. If we can just give a little bit back and know it's in the right direction, so much the better. And there is an obscene waste of people's potential. Just give a little back.'

Michael dedicated the first of two albums he launched on 10 December 1999 to his grandson 'Connor, the monkey boy', who is Cathy's daughter Emma's little lad. *The Very Best of Michael Ball (Live At The Royal Albert Hall)* video/CD included a number of medleys as well as the songs: 'Hot Stuff', 'Everybody's Talkin'', 'Love On The Rocks', 'Something Inside So Strong', 'Someone Else's Dream', 'My Heart Will Go On', 'Empty Chairs, Empty Tables', 'One Step Out Of Time', 'Everybody Needs Somebody To Love' and 'Love Changes Everything'.

He was asked by the *Birmingham Evening Mail* when it came to the album – a collection of covers of songs by the likes of Neil Diamond, Glen Campbell and Barbra Streisand – that surely he would get greater satisfaction from singing his own compositions? He replied: 'Yes, I would but it doesn't matter where a song comes from as long as it is great material. Some of the greatest writers have written for me. I could never compete with that. It would be nice to see if I could do my own songs but I was almost paranoid about it. I never had the guts to do it. I will never be a good enough songwriter to be able to do all of my own stuff.'

There was a festive album, *Christmas*, also released on 10 December – subsequently re-released the following year – which included a collection of standards. Both those 1999 albums – his seventh and eighth – were to go Gold within three weeks of going on sale.

The launch of the live video and CD saw the year end on an added high. His video went straight in at Number One, and chalked up more than 140,000 sales in the UK.

Michael was to see in the Millennium with an outdoor concert in Kuala Lumpur, which he then turned into a well-remembered family holiday. But he had mixed views about the future generally. When asked what he would do if he was Prime Minister, he joked that he would emigrate. But more seriously he said: 'Actually, I wouldn't be really happy and I wouldn't be despondent, either. I would see an opportunity for Britain to continue as a world leader, as a good example for other countries thanks to the democracy that we have.

'There are certain areas that we are really strongly lacking in – it shocked me earlier this month, for example, to read about how [our] "success" rate in treating cancer compared with other countries. I always just assumed that we had the best health service and were at the cutting edge. To find out that we are not is an embarrassment. If I was Prime Minister, I certainly wouldn't be complacent by any means. I would know we had the resources, both human and medical, in order to help make people's lives better and there are some great things happening.'

With the dawn of the 21st century, Michael announced a seventh UK tour, with all 27 dates selling out within six weeks. In July 2000, while he was working on his upcoming album *This Time It's Personal*, he received a request from Public Broadcasting Service in America to do a short promotional tour to help promote his *Live At The Royal Albert Hall* video, as part of the station's 'pledge drive' in August. The project proved an overwhelming success and had the audiences clamouring for more as well as significantly boosting the sales of the video.

This spurred Michael to embark on further video initiatives, and in September he recorded a one-off performance at the Café de Paris in London's West End to an audience of just 300, a vast cry from the 75,000 people in total he had performed to early in the year on his UK tour.

But the toll of the concerts was having an effect on Michael, who just would not let up on the hectic gig schedules nor did he seem to be losing his enthusiasm for producing more and more albums. But he admitted in that year to *OK!* magazine: 'I'm three quarters of the way through a tour and I'm tired but it's going really well.'

He explained how he got back home to London early on

Monday morning for the first time in five weeks, adding: I was very pleased to see Cathy and my dog and to have my first home-cooked meal in ages – bacon and eggs at two o'clock in the morning, it was lovely. When I do get a very rare day off, I'll completely chill out. I love watching telly and doing absolutely nothing – not even thinking.'

But the respites were never very long for Michael. He added: 'Unfortunately, the coach comes to take me to my next venue that little bit too soon. Life really just revolves around being at home whenever I can because I spend so much time on the road or in hotel rooms. When you come off stage, you're physically tired, but buzzing with adrenaline. Normally, I'll invite some of my friends around for a party backstage, but because I've usually got a show the next day I can't party that hard, so we wrap it up at about midnight. Then I'll go home and assess the day with Cathy and a single malt.'

Adjusting to these sort of irregular hours does take some getting use to and Michael, since those disastrous days not looking after himself well enough when he became poorly during *Les Misérables*, has made sure he keeps a weathered eye on his health.

He added: 'When you're on tour, your body clock gets turned upside down because you go to bed late and don't wake up till midday. My life has always been like that, I got used to the weird hours from doing long runs in theatre – but Cathy hates it. She is getting used to it, after all we've been together nearly 10 years. We're home birds really, but we do love the movies and try to see everything that comes out.'

Michael would also enjoy seeing friends in shows but stressed that he and Cathy were 'pretty low key and not premiere types'. Simply, he would rather be with family and friends than out on the razzle. He sees it as his job which he would rather not do it in his spare time.

But he added: 'I love performing and have a great fanbase, most of whom have been following my career for donkey's years – ever since *Aspects Of Love*. They are a broad spectrum of people, and I love meeting them all and having a chat after the show.'

Michael finished the tour in Dublin. Gloria Hunniford, on her *Open House* chat show in 2000, asked him if it had taken three weeks for him to get out of the city, he replied: 'Oh, my God, it took me three weeks to remember it. I swear it. I don't know how we did.

'I was dying on my legs, but we did. It was a great show, a really great show, fantastic reaction and I have a lot of friends over there. So I actually came out of the pub at 9.30 in the morning. I went with a lovely single malt out into the middle of Grafton Street, in broad daylight. I have the Irish record now. Previously, it was Tom Jones, who went along till 7.30am. So he has got two hours to go.'

Gloria asked him if he thought that the musical in general is 'sort of a bit dodgy at the minute in the West End'. He replied: 'Yeah, I think that the West End is tired. I think I was very lucky. I was there right at the beginning of that whole renaissance of British musical theatre. We led the way in the world, and I think it has kind of gone back the other way now and the things that are successful are *Mama Mia* or the Disney shows.

'I read the other week that Cameron Mackintosh had decided he wasn't going to produce a new musical because he had tried with things like *Martin Guerre*. There isn't the excitement and I do worry about it. I do not know where the new talent is and the old shows like *Les Mis* and *Phantom* are running and will run forever and ever. But you know they are creaky. We need new things.'

New things to Michael were not, at this point in his career, stage shows but albums and he was on with his next one, his ninth, with *This Time ... It's Personal*, which was released on 30 October 2000. This included the songs: 'Walking In Memphis', 'If Tomorrow Never Comes', 'You're Still The One', 'The First Time Ever I Saw Your Face', 'Just When', 'The Song Remembers When', 'I Don't Want A Lover', 'You Bring The Best Out Of Me', 'Never Coming Back', 'The Greatest Man I Never Knew', 'Think Twice', 'No Matter What' and 'The Dimming Of The Day'.

He told Ms Hunniford: 'There are songs that are very personal to me. Previously I've done songs that fell into a genre. They are either all songs from movies or all songs from musicals; they had a theme and this kind of had a theme, but the theme is what's in my heart. The catalyst was the song "Walking In Memphis" because I love listening to the American sound. I needed a hook for the album and I heard the song on the radio with Marc Cohn singing it. That's the power of the music, it transported me. I was imagining myself singing it not listening to it. I was the guy walking down Beale Street (Memphis) and all the sounds and smells and tastes and sights all came to me. For some reason, it sparked in me to look for other material.'

Michael also named the song 'If Tomorrow Never Comes' as the first song that really got him into that kind of sound.

He told how he heard it when he was in New York, for the first time when he was in New York, doing rehearsals for *Aspects Of Love*. It was a cold January and he said he 'was really terrified' as he had never been away from home before.

He added: 'I didn't know anybody. I was in New York in a blizzard. I was really lonely and this song – I had never heard of Garth Brooks before – 'If Tomorrow Never Comes' came on the radio. I burst into tears and phoned home. I phoned to tell everyone I loved them. That's the power that these songs have. They transmit, when they are done well, an emotional power. It can make you do something – it can make you think about where you are at that period of your life, and you act positively.'

Another number on the album gives another wonderful insight into the emotions that Michael derives from music. He revealed how 'The Greatest Man I Never Knew', a Reba McEntire song about a father and his son, made him think about his relationship with his dad – and he told how he was able to draw on his experience with his dad when he was in his teens before they became close. 'I can empathise with this song,' he said. 'There are loads of people who are unable to say that they love you when they should and having recorded that song two of the musicians went straight out and phoned their dads.'

Michael ended the year by heading 'off for some R&R' – rest and recuperation – but not before he oversaw the re-release of the previous year's *Christmas* album as well as a single, 'Amazing Grace', which he put out in aid of *Children In Need*.

But there was one very significant twist to come before 2000 was finished.

CHAPTER 10

If Tomorrow Never Comes

Michael's debt to Cathy was so much greater than simply her being the catalyst to him completing his professional, and personal, recovery after the horrors of *Les Misérables*. And as if her love, companionship and guidance wasn't enough for Michael, two days before Christmas 2000 – only a matter of months after they felt they had completed those finishing touches that made their house in Barnes, south-west London, their own home – Cathy literally saved his life.

The couple had been out for the evening at a party-come-work function and arrived home just before 1.30 in the wee small hours. They took themselves off to bed and Cathy 'went out like a light', according to Michael. But he couldn't sleep. 'So I went downstairs to my study, I poured myself a little single malt whisky, as you do, and I was downstairs for about an hour and a half,' he said.

Michael, who also took a dose of the Night Nurse cold remedy, remembers returning upstairs but, on seeing Cathy asleep, decided not to disturb her so he took himself off to the spare room – which had originally been Emma's bedroom.

But at 4.40am, Cathy suddenly woke up choking and coughing. She was disorientated. She realised there were fumes. She felt around in the darkness and discovered Michael was not in the bed. She rushed over to turn on the lights but they didn't work. There was panic and fear. The enormity of the situation hit her. She realised the room was full of thick, black, choking smoke.

Michael told chat show host Gloria Hunniford: 'Cathy is now really freaking because I am not there. She runs through the pitch black and the smoke, down to where my study is and opens the door. Flames come out. She can't get physically in there but thinks I'm in there, having fallen asleep in the chair. She is shouting but is getting no response. She is convinced I am dead, that I've gone in the fire.

'She then, God bless her, ran out into the street, screaming. She stopped a bus, I think, that was going past and someone called the Fire Brigade. Then she thought maybe I am in the spare room. She ran back into the burning house, through the smoke and the flames and she could not see a thing. She came up to the spare room and was feeling around and felt I was in the bed. I had passed out with the fumes. But thank God she did. I was comatose.'

Michael, completely oblivious to the situation, woke up and wondered why exactly Cathy was hitting him. And then she was hauling him out of the bed. He claimed it was 'real hero stuff'. And he added: 'I came to and realised we were in serious trouble and ran down. I thought it was a dream or that she was just exaggerating. I came down and, well, did a stupid thing. I opened the door of the study. And it just all came out. I said, "Right, get out." But she runs back up to grab Yogi, the dog, who is spark out with the fumes. And we went. The Fire Brigade then arrived, who were fantastic.'

When Michael looked over at Cathy, he saw lines and black streams below her nostrils through inhaling and exhaling all the smoke and fumes. He said: 'She was in a real state of shock, but I did not have the state of trauma she had because in her head for that moment I was dead. She was just inconsolable – but then came the relief when she found me.'

Michael explained to the TV audience: 'If Cath hadn't smelt the smoke, I'd be dead. I did almost die because the spare room was directly above the study and the poison gases were rising, which is why I hadn't woken up. There is absolutely no question she saved my life. She did. She was extraordinary. It's that instinct for survival and what is quite clear if your house is burning down, you save the people you love.'

The fire had been started by an electrical fault in the study and 'the house was a write-off.' But Michael added: 'I don't relive it and I am not terrified that a house will go up in flames again.'

Yet all Michael's gold discs had melted, his old photographs and programmes were destroyed. The CDs, videos and TV footage were also all stored in the study. He said: 'But we were absolutely fine – it did put things into perspective and made me realise that stuff wasn't important. All our memorabilia was lost, as well as the furniture and carpets. But it didn't really matter that the stuff couldn't be replaced. No one was hurt and we were alive. You carry your memories with you.'

It was Christmas and Michael had to work something out or they would be homeless for quite a while. So the next morning he went out and found a house to rent. 'Everyone began helping,' he told the *Daily Mail*. 'A local shop lent us some furniture and hampers of food arrived. Friends and family rallied round.'

And once the fans heard about his plight they began searching archives for footage of Michael and Cathy so they would have as much memorabilia as possible. And the record company replaced the discs that were lost. 'It really brought out the best in everyone,' he said. 'It put life into perspective, giving us a good shake-up and making us really treasure what we have. And if I ever needed a demonstration of Cathy's love, there it was. It made me feel very lucky.'

Months later, Michael could joke about the whole experience. He told host Gloria Hunniford in October 2001: 'When the Fire Brigade were arriving, I was out there, in my pants and a jacket that Cath, who was in her nightie, had thrown around me. We were watching our house go up in flames and I am going, "Has anyone got a fag, excuse me?"

'So this one bloke, bless him, finally gave me a cigarette. And I said, "Have you got a light?" I swear this is true. And he went, "Well, no, we are not allowed to carry things like that." I said, "Well, where can I get a light?" And he went, "In your house."'

The following morning Michael and Cathy were outside looking at the devastation caused to their home. He explained: 'We were sitting in all the rubble, and I'm now chain-smoking.

It was filthy, black and horrid, really, really soul-destroying. But I lit up a fag in this rubble and Cath goes, "Where's an ashtray?" It's true.'

And graciously Michael apologised to her for flicking his ash on their newly burnt out home.

The house was renovated and furbished but the couple did not want to move back in and bought a Victorian abode not so far away in the middle of Barnes. Michael was happy that he and Cathy had survived although he was upset about his memorabilia. Yet in the years ahead, one interviewer asked him what was the best Christmas present he had ever received. He explained: 'I had never kept anything like a scrapbook and, one Christmas morning, I came down and found three enormous folders. Cath had gone back to my old school, drama school, my first jobs, my friends and family and people I had worked with and, without me knowing, found all these old photographs and reviews to remind me of what I had done, right up to the present day. I was so moved, because she had done so much research and it was such a thoughtful, brilliant thing to do.'

As an aside, Michael also revealed to *Women's Weekly* that Cathy was responsible for the worst present he ever received. 'It was a Gucci, patent leather document holder-cum-manbag,' he said. 'She had decided this was going to be the trendy new thing, and it was the worst thing I've ever seen in my life. Cathy still maintains it was fabulous.'

Perhaps, in light of the fire, it is a touch ironic Michael has always had a battle with smoking, ever since those days at Plymouth College when, as a 12-year-old, he would nip behind the bicycle sheds for a cigarette. Stage-hands were well used to seeing him, throughout his career, standing in the wings and having a quick smoke. He went through a number of attempts at trying to kick his 30-a-day habit.

In 1992, he thought that patches had helped him cure his smoking. 'The night before I wore my first patch, I went out with some friends and smoked myself silly – the idea was to make myself feel really sick,' he said.

Well he might have made himself sick but not sick of smoking because he was soon back on the weed again and by 2000 he was really putting his mind to attempting to stop, not least because he thought it was affecting his health and his singing, and because he wanted to help Cathy's daughter Emma to quit, too.

He boasted in that year to the *News of the World* that he had not had a cigarette for four months, claiming: 'I have cracked it and feel so much better. My voice sounds a lot better, and I also notice that I feel refreshed and fit. I have never felt better.

'I had been trying to quit for years but I just did not have the staying power. But now I have the motivation. I just look at how healthy I am. Trying to quit smoking is one of the hardest things I have ever done. I know a lot of my pals who are trying to give up the weed, like my friend Marty Whelan from *Open House*, whom I have known for years. He is trying to quit smoking. I hope he succeeds. It will give him a new lease of life.

'But it's not easy when you are in the entertainment industry because you are surrounded by bars and clubs and the first thing you do after getting a drink in is to light up.'

And about a month later in October 2001, he was boasting

to Ms Hunniford about his achievements. She admitted: 'I couldn't believe this. In the past, I've been side-stage and you are stubbing out the cigarette as you are going on to sing, which is almost unheard of for a performer.'

Michael replied: 'I am not proud of it. Actually, do you know in a curious way I think I was smoking perversely. I used to go, "Well, I have never had singing lessons and I am smoking like a chimney and it does not affect my voice". I have not thought that since giving up in May. My stamina, as far as my voice goes, is so much better. There are notes there that I did not have before.'

Unfortunately, his near life-long habit returned and got the better of him again. By 2006, he was telling another interviewer that he was not in a particularly happy mood that day, explaining to Portsmouth's *The News* he said: 'I'm climbing the walls. I've just given up smoking. I'm nearly eating my foot with frustration – and I'm piling on the weight.

'I'm doing the Allen Carr Easy Way, which is a lie. You have counselling sessions but you do it cold turkey. I haven't touched one for two weeks. And I'm determined to give up now. I gave up once before and my voice definitely got clearer, and I had more stamina. I do feel better for it already. I'm replacing it with other things though – such as food. I've got an oral fixation right now.'

And by March 2011, he was proudly able to tell *Daily Express* journalist Cheryl Stonehouse that he had not had a cigarette for five years. With the comfort of feeling he had at last broken the cigarette spiral of hopelessness; he was able to talk completely freely about it.

He said: 'Playing on Broadway has to be every stage

performer's dream. Yet when I was offered the chance to take my role as Count Fosco in *The Woman In White* to New York my biggest concern was whether they would let me smoke in the dressing room. There is a kind of arrogance or maybe it's a kind of bloody-mindedness that goes hand in hand with smoking.

'I hope most people who know me would say I'm no *prima donna* and I have never gone about making ridiculous demands, but I do look back at my 30 years as a smoker and cringe at the way I behaved to make sure I got my fix. I can hardly believe it now but on Broadway I actually said to the theatre manager, "Well, if I can't smoke you'll just have to fire me."'

Michael admits for for the entire run, he sat in his windowless dressing room chain-smoking – and the place stank. This, in New York, where smoking is almost as dreadful as shoplifting, he joked.

It took a pact with his stepdaughter Emma, also a heavy smoker, to kick the habit for good and put both their healths back on the road to recovery.

Michael admitted that smoking had really got a hold of him. He had to have his fix so much that when booking non-smoking hotel rooms he would put shower caps over the smoke detectors. He had smoked when he had horrible chest infections even though 'my lungs and vocal cords were my living'. His manager Phil Bowdery, who is vehemently anti-smoking, would throw his hands up in despair and say, 'You know what you're doing to your talent, you know it can only get worse.'

But all the lecturing in the world did not persuade him to give up smoking until 2006. And it was the impact on his health that finally made him quit. In the *Daily Express* interview, he added: 'In my early-40s, I began to see some worrying effects on my health. I was increasingly unable to reach some higher notes at all and my feet itched and throbbed because my circulation was so poor.

'It was killing my stamina and that was no good for a career that depends on being able to perform live for up to three hours on stage eight times a week. I was catching every passing bug and every cold went straight to my chest. There was a day when I looked in the mirror and thought to myself, "Now you're starting to look like a smoker. Anyone who sees that complexion will know the dull grey skin comes out of a fag packet."'

Emma had owned up to being a smoker and she and Michael would puff away together to such an extent that Cathy sometimes had to leave the room. So the pair decided, after Michael's failures with patches, medication and will-power, to go to an Allen Carr face-to-face session. 'And both of us stopped that day,' he said. 'About two weeks later, I thought I was weakening so I went back for a top-up session. That was about five years ago. I have never looked back. Not so much as a crafty puff. Neither has Emma, and we have both made her mother happy.'

And in 2011 he told the *Daily Express*: 'The health benefits have been enormous. The difference now in my voice after four years without a cigarette amazes me. I get very cross when I think how much better I could have been singing through my 30s. This winter when I have been turning up for shows to find half a dozen people are off with flu I've been amazed I haven't picked up anything.

'Eight shows a week are a pretty good workout anyway but I also take my vitamins and eat good food. Perhaps too much, because the downside of not smoking has been putting on weight. But even carrying a few extra pounds is worth it for the return of my health. My circulation is better, my skin looks alive and I have bags of energy.'

Packing up smoking finally did see Michael pile on the pounds. This did not matter when he landed the role as the plump mother Edna Turnblad in *Hairspray* in 2007 but the problem still aggravated him. He said in 2009: 'I look enormous on television. It is harder to lose it when you are older and when you don't really have to, given the show that I was in. I have always battled with my weight. I am not thrilled about it and I am very self-conscious.'

He has fought constant battles to shed the pounds and in 1997, when he admitted to being 13st 7lb – not excessive for a man who is 5ft 11in tall – he was accused in the media of spending £4,000 on liposuction to remove the flab. He rubbished this claim, joking the only money likely to have been spent on that department would have gone into bar tills.

Michael has been through spells of doing daily workouts but in 1998 he told the *Rosemary Conley Magazine*: 'I see myself as a fat person. I've battled with my weight for most of my life. It has been constantly up and down. I can put on a stone in a month, no trouble at all. Even looking at photographs of myself at my slimmest and fittest, I literally don't recognise myself. I think, "That can't be me." I can totally relate to people such as anorexics, who have a distorted self-image.'

Now aged 36, Michael explained that his approach to

fitness tended to be cyclical. When he was not working he liked to party hard. But that saw him put on some weight. Then he would do a blitz to shift it. He added: 'I put on quite a bit making albums. What happens is that you are in a dark studio for hours on end. You never see daylight, so people bring you things, all the bad comfort things – pizzas, curries, chocolates, pints of beer. And if I can't decide what to do in a song I think, "I'd better have a Mars bar, that'll do it. But then you get home in the early hours, tired but not sleepy, slump in front of the TV and you snack.'

That is when he would put on weight. But he would then realise he had to do promotion for the album and he would panic to take the weight back off again.

He added: 'So I make a conscious decision. I stop drinking for a month. Beer is a biggie for me – I love a couple of pints. I eat low-fat, starting with a big healthy breakfast, and then I go to the gym for a couple of hours. I go four or five times a week and do 20 minutes on the bike, 20 minutes running, using the heart monitor, and then lots of stretching exercises.

'In some exercises, I'm like a ballet dancer, and in others I'm like a 90-year-old. Then I'll have a steam and a relax and think about ways I can treat myself for being so good. I enjoy it. It's essential to enjoy exercise. It's no good punishing yourself, which is what I used to do. I'd go on a starvation diet, go mad and over-exercise, lose the weight, then watch it pile back on.'

CHAPTER 11

Alone Together

Michael, despite the traumas of the house fire, made sure that the show carried on as he headed for Australia in the New Year of 2001. It was a one-off concert, and he was relishing the challenge because his latest album, *The Musicals*, had just gone Gold in the UK. After playing Star City's Lyric Theatre in Sydney on 10 March, he said: 'I just loved the place and I can't wait to get back.'

On his return to the UK, he started to plan another new album – it would be his 10th. He also made an appearance in the Midsummer Classics at the Royal Albert Hall in London as well as headlining a number of solo sell-out concerts, including two in Harrogate, an appearance at the Liverpool Summer Pops and a couple of open-air performances in Essex, at Audley End and at Chelmsford.

He also managed to perform with Lesley Garrett CBE, one

of Britain's most talented opera singers and principal soprano at the English National Opera. She was seven years his senior but the two gelled immediately with a wonderful sarcastic rapport between them, in which they would tease each other unmercifully about their different music forms.

Lesley would snipe: 'You're such a natural, talented, wonderful, instinctive musician.'

And Michael would remind his illustrious partner that the song 'Love Changes Everything' required him to hit two high B flats, eight times a week, twice on Wednesdays and Saturdays. And he would add: 'None of this opera bollocks where you maybe show up twice a week.'

Lesley admitted – on the popular ITV gossip daytime show *Loose Women* – that Michael and her were guilty of getting rather drunk one evening. She told the programme, on which she was a guest panellist from 2006 to 2011: 'I got into terrible trouble with Michael once. We were at a wrap party and he led me astray. We ended up singing "*Nessun Dorma*", I think. The next day, my family was going to Thailand on holiday and I threw up at every stage of the journey, even in the bins at Heathrow.'

But she told the *Guardian* in 2009: 'Michael is responsible for me becoming involved in musicals. We met backstage at one of his shows and hit it off straight away. I asked him to come on my show and sing some opera with me, and he agreed but only if I, in turn, sang some songs from musicals with him. I got hooked and did more and more. When I heard a whisper that *The Sound Of Music* was coming to town, I asked what he thought. He was so supportive and has encouraged me all the way.

'Personally, Michael is heaven on a stick – if you want a good night out then you couldn't do better than an evening spent in his company. He's the funniest person on the planet, he is very sensitive and hides that behind his humour. I admire him as well as love him.'

But the real cherry on the musical cake for Michael in 2001 was a most surprising stage show. He was developing a greater and greater confidence to challenge himself musically, though he was careful not to give out an aura of over-confidence.

But he was offered the challenge to embark on a two-hour solo cabaret song show at the Donmar Warehouse in London's Covent Garden, a small venue that was growing in cult status. He said: 'This is the most frightening thing I've ever done. There is something about the audience being in your face that meant that at no point could you fake it, or relax or be in your own space. It truly was like nothing I'd ever done before.'

Movie actress Nicole Kidman had brought an almost notoriety to the tiny 251-seat not-for-profit West End theatre with her scantily-clad performance, when she was wearing anything at all, in the debut of *The Blue Room*, which ran for just over seven weeks in the autumn of 1998. The play was directed by Sam Mendes, the Donmar's artistic director, who had asked David Hare to adapt Arthur Schnitzler's 1900 play *La Ronde*. It was 'essentially a series of sketches in which one person couples with another who couples with yet another and so on until the circle closes' and involved Ms Kidman daringly playing a young tart, an au pair, a married woman, a model and a grandly self-dramatising actress.

All very arty and befitting of a true theatre venue, which had been established in 1953 by producer Donald Albery who named the venue using the first three letters of his name and those of his friend, the prima ballerina Dame Margot Fonteyn.

Mendes, who won an Oscar for directing the hit movie *American Beauty*, had approached Michael, who had said: 'I would love to be involved.'

How exactly musical-centric Michael fitted into this sort of theatrical bracket was puzzling to most people and even more so when it was realised that he was part of the fourth *Divas At The Donmar* season. But that mattered not a jot – not to Michael's amazingly loyal fanbase, who would turn up anywhere, anytime to take in one of his concerts, and not to those managing the theatre, as they would have a sure-fire winner on their hands.

To have priority booking to see a production at the Donmar, you needed to be a member, a 'Friend' of the theatre. When the sexy Ms Kidman agreed to perform, within touching distance of the audience, 'the rush to become a member was predominantly male-driven,' reported the *London Evening Standard*. 'Some 400 new Friends suddenly signed up, contributing a welcome £25,000 to the Donmar coffers. This time it is the women who cannot wait to call themselves a Friend of the Donmar, of which there are now around 1,800.'

Donmar executive producer Caro Newling revealed, only days after Michael's appearance was trailed: 'The priority booking period began only this week and we have already had 150 people joining so that they can take advantage of it. It is clear that Michael Ball has a huge following and we are obviously delighted at the response. When Nicole Kidman appeared here, a lot of people joined as Friends and have since remained Friends. We hope that happens again.'

Michael was using the occasion to try out a range of new

material, accompanied by only a piano, not an orchestra in sight. He joked that he was the male equivalent of a 'diva', which could be termed as a 'duvet' or 'dude', but in a way his appearance did make sense.

'It is experimental theatre, it is exciting, it is a terrific space to work at,' he told Gloria Hunniford. 'Everyone is around you, sitting so close, but it was an opportunity for me to do something really different. I said my prerequisites for the show were: I'm not going to have any safety net, I'm not going to sing any song I've ever sung before.'

Jonathan Butterell, who worked with Michael on the stage play *Passion*, devised and directed the production, to be entitled aptly *Alone Together*, while his trusted friend Jason Carr was musical director for the show that was to run from 17 – 29 September.

Michael added to Gloria: 'I actually put in a couple of lines of dialogue after the second song. It would take people a while to realise it wasn't Michael Ball in cabaret, it was a theatrical event. So I put in just a couple of lines to make that clear, that we were going on a journey of a performer told entirely through song. And that each song would emotionally link into the next. I couldn't speak to the audience, I couldn't sing a song I've ever sung before and only have a piano. And it was just so liberating. It was fantastic.'

He performed David Bowie's 'Life On Mars' after opening with 'Blue', the song by Joni Mitchell, who had always been his favourite female singer-songwriter. The show also included a nine-minute medley of 30 Al Jolson songs and it ended with the Radiohead song 'Nice Dream' and the jazz standard 'My Solitude'.

Michael explained that Mendes would persuade people to come to the venue and risk everything. For nothing, basically. But it worked for Michael. He devised a show, a theatrical piece, and called it the scariest thing he had ever done, adding: 'We rehearsed for about a month before I finally first walked out in front of the audience. I could see the whites of their eyes. Every nuance, every gesture, every word is magnified a hundred times. That really, really, really scared me. I thought if I can do this and get through this I don't think anything else will become anything like as scary. But it just worked for me. It was a catharsis.'

Patrick O'Connor in the *Daily Telegraph* review wrote: 'Michael Ball enters from the back of the theatre, and some of his devoted admirers give a little gasp of surprise. Here, he is so close, with nothing but a bottle of designer water as a prop. There is no preamble, no speeches about the audience being wonderful, or any introduction to the songs. It's straight in with "No, Don't Look at Me", from *Follies*.'

The review enjoyed the pace of the show saying: 'What makes this evening into more than just a star trawling through the highs and lows of 100 years of musical theatre is the shyly self-deprecating twinkle that he brings to the whole event. Some of the effects that Ball uses are still calculated for a space a lot larger than the Donmar. In "Padam, Padam", Norbert Glanzberg and Henri Contet's 1951 hit for Edith Piaf, the shouts and foot-stamping could be toned down.'

But it was basically praise all the way for Michael with O'Connor adding: 'Still, it's a finished artist who can make something new of "There's No Business Like Show Business", sung here very slowly, almost as a lullaby until the inevitable wow finish. Towards the end of the first half, Michael Ball lights a cigarette to punctuate a nostalgic reflection on the disappointments of youth. A section of the audience seemed to find this hilarious for reasons that were not clear, but a concentrated stare from their idol quietened them down.'

And he concluded by observing that this was 'not an evening designed to flatter the tastes of the fans who come in specially embroidered jackets and T- shirts, but a real attempt to get to the heart of each song'.

So Michael had risen to the challenge and won a legion of 'Friends', not least for the Donmar. Many felt aggrieved that he was not nominated for a Laurence Olivier Award for the production. Such was the success and popularity of the short run that Michael was asked if he would transfer the show to one of the larger, more traditional West End venues, but he declined, saying: 'I didn't feel right doing it. It was so specific for that space. I didn't quite see how I could make it work in a larger auditorium.'

There were also moves to take the whole concept to New York, but this was autumn 2001 and the 9/11 catastrophes were so fresh in everyone's thoughts that people's minds were elsewhere. The lasting legacy of *Alone Together* was the DVD, video and CD.

Michael was now enhancing greatly a reputation as a polished all-round performer. A one-off concert at the Symphony Hall, Birmingham, in mid-December 2001, drew this praise from Bob Downing of the *Evening Mail*: 'There are few who can match Michael Ball when it comes to musical theatre. The singer has the gift of stepping into the roles of so many characters when he performs songs from these successful musicals. It was easy for him to slip into the role for "Empty Chairs And Empty Tables" from *Les Misérables* for it was a show that made him famous. But his exceptional duet with Claire Moore from *The Phantom Of The Opera* saw him not just sing those lyrics but get right under the skin of them and deliver them with artistry. His powerful voice is a feature of his stage act and the delivery is of the highest order. Michael Ball is simply a magnificent performer.'

His celebrity was growing and growing and everyone wanted a piece of him – stage, television and now even radio with him undertaking a series from September 2001 for BBC Radio 2 called *Ball Over Broadway,* in which he travelled to New York to examine the various theatre shows staged there.

Michael remarked: 'What struck me there was the difference. I was there 10 years ago doing *Aspects* and it was a dodgy place, New York itself, and going to the theatre wasn't that pleasant an experience. It was the life and the vibrancy of the productions. *The Producers* is the best thing I've ever seen, from the second they struck up the overture, "Springtime For Hitler", I don't think I stopped laughing for two and a half hours.'

Despite the radio diversion, as pleasant as it was, Michael relished his by now annual album releases. Each time he attempted to produce something just a little bit different – and his *Centre Stage* offering, released by Universal on Hip-O Records on 17 September and including a duet with Lesley Garrett, tried exactly that, being described as 'an absorbing mix of emotions and rhythms'.

The album was a compilation of songs from musical theatre, featuring songs such as: 'Every Story', 'Can You Feel The Love

Tonight', 'A Boy From Nowhere', 'Lift The Wings', 'Not While I'm Around', 'The Phantom Of The Opera', 'Music Of The Night', 'The Winner Takes it All', 'Seasons Of Love', 'Bring Him Home', 'Tell Me On A Sunday', 'Immortality', 'Send In The Clowns' and 'It's Not Me'.

One commentator wrote: 'An interesting choice is "Send In The Clowns", from Stephen Sondheim's *A Little Night Music*, which is normally delivered by the leading lady in the show. Ball once asked Sondheim why so many of his best songs are reserved for women, to which the great songwriter replied that mostly the songs were not gender specific but merely reflected a character's situation. He encouraged Ball to record any songs he found appealing.'

Michael said in a *HMV Choice* interview: 'I did an album of musical songs about four or five years ago. When I was putting those together that's when I realised there are about 5,000 other songs I could have included. So talking to friends, and with fans giving me ideas, and also in that intervening five years a whole lot of new songs have come along from new shows, I wanted to put together another musical album.'

So Michael headed out of 2001 in a good place, not least with *Centre Stage* going Gold. So he did not really need reminding that the following year he would be approaching the age of 40, with all the fears and disillusionment that can bring. He joked: 'Yes, everything will be falling off soon'.

But he was insistent that the Donmar Warehouse experience and his thirst for trying new ventures was no mid-life crisis, explaining: 'I think as an artist, you have to keep trying new things. You can't keep doing the same things.'

CHAPTER 12

Truly Scrumptious

Michael was undoubtedly enjoying his singing career. His 10 solo albums had all gone either Gold or Platinum and he had played to sell-out concerts everywhere, building a huge, and loyal, fanbase. But the time had flown by and he realised towards the end of 2001 that he had appeared in only one stage musical, *Passion*, for a period of only just over seven months, in the past 11 years. And this was the area of the entertainment business that had drawn him in and given him his big break. Surely, he did not want to be remembered for 'exiting stage left chased by a singing ego'.

No, his roots were calling and during his *Diva At The Donmar* run, a most surprising visitor had turned up in his dressing room after one performance. Enter Barbara Broccoli OBE, the daughter of James Bond producer Cubby. She went on to produce the cult spy movies with Pierce Brosnan and

Daniel Craig in the 007 role. But now she was telling Michael: 'We want you to play Ian Fleming's greatest hero.'

He was stunned into silence but later explained to the *London Evening Standard*: 'I thought, Brosnan's out, Ball's in.' Yet life is not always what it seems. And he added with a huge grin: 'Then she explained, she wanted me for Caractacus Potts in *Chitty Chitty Bang Bang*.'

The original *Chitty* book had been published in 1964 having been written by the aforementioned Mr Fleming, the writer who created Bond. Cubby Broccoli, who had turned 007 into a series of blockbuster movies, had also produced the popular 1968 *Chitty* movie, which was adored by children. Now in 2002, with Barbara as producer, this tale was to be turned into a stage musical. Brothers Richard and Robert Sherman, who had written the Academy Award-nominated music and lyrics, were to write six new numbers.

Michael realised this could be the challenge that subconsciously he was looking for. 'I was making myself a name. It's a double-edged sword. It's good for prestige and money,' he said.

There were also the warming memories from his childhood. 'There were three musicals that were my staples as a kid,' he told the *London Evening Standard*. '*Mary Poppins, The Sound Of Music* and *Chitty Chitty Bang Bang*. I even had a toy Chitty that used to go into battle against FAB1, Lady Penelope's Pink Rolls-Royce. The chance to lead the cast in my favourite childhood fantasy film was too good to turn down.'

The proposed show, which was reported to be costing £6million, brought a series of technology demands for the producers and some personal ones for Michael, not least the two months of dance classes to prepare for his role as Caractacus Potts ready for the spring of 2002 at the London Palladium, just off Oxford Street.

'We were working from nine in the morning until 10 at night for weeks on the technical side of things,' he said. 'Normally, with a show this size, you would have out-of-town try-outs – but we had gone from the page straight to the biggest stage in London.'

Fleming had taken his inspiration for his children's novel from a series of aero-engined cars, christened Chitty Bang Bang, which had been built and raced by Count Louis Zborowski in the early 1920s at his Higham country house estate at Bridge, near Canterbury, in Kent. Fleming had become acquainted with Higham Park and the tales of the cars when he was a guest of its owner, Walter Wigham.

The story is based upon the fortunes of an amazing flying car. Inventor Caractacus renovates an old jalopy after gaining money from one of his previous crazy ideas. The Paragon Panther was a four-seater touring car with an enormous bonnet. Once restored, it is named for the noises it makes but then it develops some amazing qualities of its own, not least that it can fly. That worked a treat in the movie, yet how could that be brought to the stage?

Well, as Michael, who was to star with Emma Williams as Truly Scrumptious, assured audiences prior to open: 'Yes, it can fly.' He added during the run: 'When we climb into Chitty and fly out over the audience's heads, the response takes the roof off. I've never heard a crowd roar like that. I haven't done a musical for six years but I guess you could say I've now found the right vehicle.'

Did Michael worry about having £6million riding on him? 'It's not just on me, the show is a collaboration,' he replied. 'You just can't think about it.'

Of course, the downside of live theatre is that not everything went to plan with the gleaming winged car rising up through the main stage on a spectacular hydraulic crane. Michael told the *Weekly News*: 'The car was £750,000-worth of high-tech gadgetry and it worked like a dream throughout rehearsals, the four preview shows and the grand opening night. Then, on the second night, it wouldn't work at all. It just goes to show that money isn't everything. In fact, we used to have less trouble with the props when I did that run in Aberystwyth.'

Michael brought his own touches to the role that Dick Van Dyke had created for the movie version. He added: 'I never really thought there was much spark between Truly Scrumptious (the leading lady played by Sally Ann Howes) and Caractacus in the film, but our Truly is much more feisty and spunky. She is a mechanic and enters on a motorbike wearing jodhpurs and a leather jacket.'

But the flying car was not Michael's main concern and the demands of originating a West End role was something that he had experienced in both *Les Misérables* and *Aspects Of Love*. What was very different for Michael was the dancing. He had hated the thought of strenuous exercise when at Plymouth College and Guildford School of Acting, where he avoided the dance classes. Now that was back to haunt him.

But he said to *The Stage* newspaper: 'It was a great challenge – I had never danced before on stage. After we did "Me Ol' Bamboo", the place went mental. It was another picture to take in my head so I didn't forget it. I had led a troupe of cracking dancers in this fantastically fast number on the stage of the London Palladium.'

And he learned a few little secrets about dancers. He told chat show king Michael Parkinson in March 2002: 'There is a thing called a dance-belt. I was doing this training just wearing boxers and my sweat pants. And I was getting a bit sore because everything was jiggling around. I thought about this and all these dancers. You see them when they are wearing their tights and they got all kinds of action happening. I thought, "This isn't right, surely?" So they said, "Oh, you got to get a dance-belt."

'So I went to this dance-shop and it's like going in to buy a dirty mag. I said, 'You got any dance-belts?' And they got these things up and it's like flossing your bum. It's all padded and fabulous at the front, but then this thing goes right up the back. And I tried these things on. I wore it once. Couldn't be doing with it, now a pair of Speedos is what I wear.'

So Michael admitted that dancing was, perhaps, not his forte. Would he take another dancing role? 'Not if I have anything to do with it,' he joked in a Q & A session with fans. 'I don't think it's my natural thing. But I love moving around the stage. I'd love to be able to dance, I really would. If a show came up that required it, of course I would do it – or have a stunt double.'

But the gala opening, on 16 April 2002, was an exciting if not tense occasion for Michael and the rest of the company. The reviews poured in and most were glowing.

John Peter in *The Times* wrote: 'Ah well, Adrian Noble was right after all. Recently, the artistic director of the Royal Shakespeare Company, where he draws a six-figure salary, explained to an astonished Jeremy Paxman on *Newsnight* why he had gone off to direct *Chitty Chitty Bang Bang* just as his reorganisation of the RSC plunged the company into turmoil. People with young children, he said, with innocent effrontery, were under a lot of pressure to make money. I have to report that the man has done it. *Chitty Chitty* should run and run and run, and make lots and lots of money.'

And what exactly was it that he liked so much? 'It is a big, joyful, enchanting show. Where Ken Hughes's famous 1968 musical film, with music and lyrics by Richard M Sherman and Robert B Sherman, was insufferably twee, this production, adapted by Jeremy Sams, is fresh, warm-hearted, thrillingly inventive: in a word, magical. You cannot fool children: they can spot fake magic from a mile. The night I saw the show, the children's joy was obvious. No fidgeting, no chattering, only rapt attention. The show is cast to the hilt, with Michael Ball as an attractive, open-faced Caractacus Potts, clearly potty about his children, and Anton Rodgers as his batty old dad, who likes to receive visitors in his jimjams.'

Kevin O'Sullivan described the show in the *Daily Mirror* as a 'sure-fire hit' and added: 'No doubt about it: the car's a star. A superstar in fact. It cost £6million to stage *Chitty Chitty Bang Bang* at the London Palladium – a staggering amount in West End theatre terms. But just to see that amazing flying automobile was worth every penny as far as the ecstatic first night crowd were concerned.

'A glittering contraption of gold, glass and varnished wood, it defies both belief and gravity. I am tempted to say it 'literally' flies – with four passengers on board – this extraordinary theatrical vehicle appears to soar through the air. The sell-out audience gasps while I – your cynical critic – strained to work out how on earth the thing got off the ground. And for most of this breathtaking two-and-a-half hour spectacular I remained in a state of awe-struck confusion. Right at the end, I finally spotted the secret. But I'll wager I was one of the very few who did.'

But O'Sullivan was qualified in his praise of the cast, writing: 'Michael Ball is the large cast's only genuinely impressive singer but the marvellously simple songs of Richard and Robert Sherman – the duo who also penned the songs for *Mary Poppins* – don't require operatic talent.'

Not everyone found something positive to say about the production. Indeed, Sheridan Morley, actor and broadcaster son of Robert Morley, was scathing when he wrote: 'The famous flying car is the only reason for seeing this dire and dismal apology for a musical. *Chitty Chitty Bang Bang* has been bolted together from leftover bits of more interesting material – a bit of *Mary Poppins* here, a little *Peter Pan* there. But however terrible was the 1968 film, and believe me it was, nothing could have prepared us for the mind-numbing awfulness of the stage version. There is nothing funny in *Chitty Chitty Bang Bang*, largely because the director Adrian Noble is to comedy what Shakespeare was to line-dancing. The spectacular effects here, such as they are, are reminiscent of a Palladium pantomime circa 1955. There is not a single number in the second half which deserves to have got past rehearsals, let alone as far as a first night. Recently a musical at the Shaftesbury was forcibly closed by local police for making too much noise. This one should be closed for its failure of taste.'

There is no pleasing some people but Michael loved the *Chitty* experience, surrounded by flying cars, dancers, children and animals. He told chat show host Parkinson at the time: 'Yes, there were 30 kids, there were 15 dogs. That's kind of part of the joy. I've never been so popular in my life. Jools Holland came up to me, Dave Gilmour came up to me, Mica Paris, all saying, "Listen, we're bringing our kids to see the show." And that's the joy, because there are kids in it. Kids wanting to come and see it. All of us lot who are 30-something grew up listening to it. So it's truly fantastic.'

The show did not close until 4 September 2005 by which time the production was the longest running show ever at the London Palladium, grossing more than £70million in its three-and-a-half-year run. Michael left in 19 July 2003, admitting in an interview with *Teletext*: 'It was a wonderful show but hard work. I discovered doing *Chitty* how much I missed being part of a company, yet I was hardly ever off the stage. I was knackered. It was not hugely demanding on my voice but the physical energy levels required for the part are enormous.

'It never becomes a chore, but it takes stamina to do a 16-month run, to do that kind of length of time, because you're doing the same thing night after night. The only thing that is different is the audience. Sometimes audiences are better than others and you can be having a run where you are thinking, "No, the same old show." And sometimes the audience will lift you to think, "I really love doing this tonight."'

Another interesting aspect of the growing confidence and stage maturity of Michael was that he had developed into a genuine leading man – seamlessly taking on all the responsibilities that go with that. He recognised this by telling one interviewer at *The Stage*: 'The leading man has to lead the company, to set the example and tone of the production and to energise everybody. When people are in the fifth week, you have to say, "Come on, let's go and do something fun" and keep up the energy, as well as working on your own performance and taking the brunt of all the press.'

Michael knew that he would be at a loss as to what to do with himself after *Chitty* because 'I love working, I love to keeping going, I love to keep acting.' So all the way through the show, he had been planning his 11th solo album – 2002 having been one of the few years since he embarked on his solo career 10 years earlier that he had not released a record.

So he retreated back to the studio through July and August in 2003 to ensure that the album *A Love Story* was ready for release on 29 October. It featured the songs: 'You Had Me From Hello', 'This Guy's In Love With You', 'What Are You Doing The Rest Of Your Life?', 'Time In A Bottle', 'She Makes My Day', 'You've Changed', 'What Makes You Stay', 'God Give Me Strength', 'Didn't We', 'I Wish You Love', 'I Wish I Were In Love Again' plus 'Me And My Shadow'.

In October, Michael headed off to Ireland for a two-day promotional trip for the upcoming dates at Belfast Odyssey Arena, where he would sing in front of an audience of 5,000. He told the *Belfast News Letter* about the new album: 'This is the first of its kind for me, the concept of the album is that it will tell the journey of a love story through various musical idioms.'

For Michael, choosing the songs was the hardest part. He quizzed everyone he knew about the songs that meant something to them, whether it be when their relationship went bad, the song they played at their wedding or songs they like to dance to. He collected a catalogue of songs and then he asked himself which songs spoke to him.

He explained: 'I wanted to tell a story of a love affair. From meeting someone, from saying hello to them and falling in love with them right the way to courtship, the committing to somebody – the great honeymoon period in the relationship and the bit where all the cracks start to appear. Then it goes horribly wrong. And then you come to the end of it.'

He went on to joke: 'And at the very end I go out on the pull with Antonio Banderas.'

The pair, Michael and Banderas, actually did a duet for the album – *Me And My Shadow* – having struck up a friendship after Spanish movie actor Banderas 'stole' Michael's shirt during Andrew Lloyd Webber's 50th birthday bash at the Albert Hall in 1998.

Michael had also interviewed Banderas – the third husband of movie actress Melanie Griffiths – for a new series of his BBC Radio 2 show *Ball Over Broadway*. But the plan to record with the actor took a rather unusual twist, with Michael explaining: 'I got to New York and, bang, the lights went out.'

He had been caught up in the Northeast blackout of 14 August in 2003 – a power cut, or outage as they say Stateside, that affected 45-million people in eight America states and 10-million people in Ontario. It was said to be the second most widespread shutdown in history.

Michael told Irish television interviewer Gerry Kelly: 'Actually it was fantastic. It was the most exciting thing. I was in Times Square, when the whole of the eastern sea-board went up and initially everyone is really scared. We thought, "Is this an attack?" because everyone is very conscious of 9/11. When we realised it's all going to be okay, a party descended in New York.

'It's hard to describe it. There is always a noise going on, always a background hum. There are always lights flashing, there are air-conditioning units, there is traffic. But here, there was no sound. There was nothing. Just people. Cars weren't driving because the traffic lights were gone. Everyone was giving away food because all the freezers had gone. It was just brilliant. It brought out the best in everyone. I was trying to make this record. Our studio wasn't working, but we eventually managed to find one that had all the computers up and running and we recorded the song.'

CHAPTER 13

What The World Needs Now

The success of the album *A Love Story* and Michael's achievements on the musical stage with *Chitty Chitty Bang Bang* meant that he could march with confidence into 2004, a year that was to provide him with the challenges of Australia, America, Ireland and one-off concerts in London and at Windsor Castle.

In March, Michael was off on his travels for his first proper tour Down Under; five sold-out concerts that would include performing at the prestigious Sydney Opera House. And he knew that after the tour he would be off to Byron Bay – the beachside town in New South Wales that is the easternmost point of mainland Australia – to put his feet up for a well-earned break.

Michael had given a one-off concert in Sydney in 2001 and said: 'I've been trying to get back ever since but other work has prevented me from doing so. Now I've got the time and I can't wait.'

What was nice for Michael was that his growing fan entourage seemed to be following him everywhere and 12,000 miles was no exception for at least 70 of his faithful following. He told an Australian press conference: 'I'm lucky to have fans who come to all the shows and follow me out. There are certain fans who come to everything I do. And fans here will look after them, take them out so they are not afraid or isolated. They are really nice people. All of them are women. Well, the diehards are women. They will drag their old man along sometimes because it's difficult for women to travel. But none of them is weird. None of them follows me home. Nobody is trying to jump me in hotels or anything. It's just a really healthy outlet.

'And it is always nice to know you have got people on the inside because I truly don't know what to expect from the Australian audience. I'm going to try things out, to see what a typical Australian audience likes. It's nerve-racking. But that's why I'm doing it, I like the challenge. I have been touring for the past 12 years in the UK, so I know what I'm doing there but Australia is an unknown factor.'

As it turned out, Michael did not have to fly halfway round the world to find loyalty from admirers. The tour was to begin in the New South Wales seaside city of Wollongong at the WIN Entertainment Centre, then move to Sydney before arriving in Brisbane's QPAC's Concert Hall. But one fan, Margaret de Boer, who established the Australian and New Zealand Michael Ball Fan Club and held meetings with other enthusiasts dubbed 'Ballfests', could not wait in her hometown of Brisbane to see him perform so made the 1,000-mile round trip to take in the other venues as well.

Margaret, who first saw Michael perform in 1992 on television when her mother phoned to ask if she was watching him, said: 'We'd never heard of him then but we just loved his voice.'

And the Australian reviewers also liked him with Ken Lord in a Brisbane newspaper writing: 'This was a sneaky one: Michael Ball, superstar of the London musical theatre, and not that well known outside of it, played one night at the South Bank Lyric. After a languid first half, Ball went to bat in the second half, slamming into the showbiz songs that elevated his fame. Stonkered into euphoria by his consummate vocal power the audience ran emotionally amok. By the end of the night the spunky star had yanked 2,000 bodies out of their seats, holding them aloft through lengthy ovations: 24-carat star shine is as rare as it is awesome. A true stunner.'

Michael relished the experience, especially Sydney Opera House, saying: 'One of the best nights of my life was performing there – the place was sold out and it just erupted. I loved Australia – the wine, the food and the scenery, which is spectacular.'

He also managed to fit in a holiday in Australia and travelled north to the Whitsunday Islands in Queensland. He recalled being out with friends, explaining to the *Liverpool Echo*: 'A group of us were on Hamilton Island and there was a karaoke machine in the bar. The girls were desperate to do backing vocals, so I did "Delilah". They didn't know who I was in there and the guy at the bar said, "You've got quite a good voice, you should do something with that." I said, "Oh no, I'm quite happy in IT."'

On his return to the UK, Michael was cast in a special radio production of *Sunset Boulevard*, an adaptation of the 1950 movie directed and co-written by Billy Wilder. Michael was to play the William Holden role of Joe Gillis – which he had done similarly in a one-off appearance at Lloyd Webber's Sydmonton Festival in 1991 – while Sixties singer Petula Clark portrayed fading film star Norma Desmond, a role originated by Gloria Swanson in the Hollywood production. This was performed on 23 and 24 April at the Cork Opera House, Ireland, with the music provided by the BBC Concert Orchestra – and it was televised on 2 May.

Michael had always attracted interest, albeit rather muted, from across the pond and in the spring of 2004 he flew Stateside for a concert at the Abravanel Hall in Salt Lake City, Utah, performing with the Mormon Tabernacle Choir. It is not clear exactly why but he was then given the freedom of the city by Mayor Rocky Anderson.

Proud of the patriotic heritage his mother Ruth's side of the family gave him, Michael did not have to think twice when asked to headline Llangollen's International Musical Eisteddfod on 11 July 2004, following the previous year's guest Shirley Bassey. But despite his wealth of experience on stages all around the globe, he told the North Wales *Daily Post* before the event: 'I am quite nervous. It is serious kudos doing it, and there is real pressure. I really want to do my best and it makes me even more nervous that most of my family are coming up from South Wales – Mountain Ash will be empty.

Michael has performed in many outstanding musicals over the years.

above left: On stage as Sweeney Todd at the Chichester Festival Theatre in 2011.

©*Rex Features*

above right: *Chitty Chitty Bang Bang* opening night with Emma Williams, 2002.

©*Getty Images*

below: Appearing in the *Rocky Horror* tribute show in 2006. © *Rex Features*

Musical talent. Michael and the Bee Gees. ©Rex Featues/IT

The Original 1985 Company.

The making of a musical legend.

Above: On stage during the anniversary performance of *Les Misérables*. ©*Getty Images*

Below left: Celebrating with Christopher Biggins at the *Les Misérables* after party.

©*Getty Images*

Below right: On stage in *Les Misérables*. ©*Rex Features*

Over the years, Cathy McGowan has been a constant support in Michael's life.

Michael has always supported musicals and theatre performances, even when he's not in them!

Above right: With musical legend, Elaine Paige, at the *Avenue Q* press night. ©*Getty Images*

Above left: The late Stephen Gately, Anthony Head and Michael at the *Rocky Horror* tribute show, 2006. ©*Getty Images*

Below: With the producers of *Matilda: The Musical a*t the Dorchester Hotel, Park Lane for the Sky Arts Awards. ©*PA Photos*

bove: In costume ready to perform *Chitty Chitty Bang Bang* at the London Palladium.

elow: Relaxing in costume.

On stage: Michael has had huge success with his solo music career.

©Getty Imag

'Doing the show is such a prestigious thing, especially for anyone with Welsh blood. You want to be invited to perform at the Eisteddfod and to be asked to do the gala event is very special. This will be my first Eisteddfod, and where better to do it? It is incredibly flattering but is a huge amount of pressure – I hope to do half as well as Shirley Bassey did.'

The week-long Llangollen festival has been staged every summer since 1947 and is 'one of the world's most inspirational cultural festivals', attracting around 4,000 performers and around 80,000 visitors to the beautiful tiny Welsh town, with a resident population of around 3,500, in Denbighshire on the River Dee in north-east Wales.

Michael, of course, relished every moment and the fans loved him. All the warmth of his Welsh roots came flooding back. The confused "Wenglishman" definitely knew where he stood that day.

In September, Michael grabbed the chance to reprise – as part of the Singular Sensations season – his *Alone Together* one-man show, which had brought such a different dimension to his career when he debuted it at the tiny Donmar Warehouse in London's Covent Garden three years earlier. The size of that venue had spooked Michael as much as anything and he later revealed: 'There was one woman who tried to touch my leg and there were, at certain moments, audible gasps. They didn't know who I was being. Was I being me? Was I telling a story?'

But the Theatre Royal Haymarket in London's West End would be different, he hoped. 'It is bigger and has a different feel but still has an intimacy about it, and I'm looking forward to it.'

He had learned a lot from playing the Donmar and its 251-capacity audience, but there was a shock in store for him. He told the *Daily Express*: 'People use mobile phone cameras during performances now and suddenly you get a flash in your face in mid-song. But the worst thing happened to me at the Haymarket. I was opening with the first song and there was a voice from the audience, "Michael, Michael…" This woman ran to the front of the stage and said to me: "I can't find my seat and my son is in the one next to me and he won't answer me." So I had to stop and the lights were put up and the son had a look of, "Oh God, let me die." It was awful.'

Fortunately, the run at the Theatre Royal, from 28 September to 9 October, was not all as fraught, and Michael was starting to grow into handling the smaller audiences. He said in an interview with *lastminute.com magazine*: 'When you are in a vast stadium, with say 80,000 people, then it's rather ludicrous – and you can't be nervous about that. When you're on a small stage, eye to eye with the audience, then you have to open up to them, there is just you, your voice and a piano, so you have to be completely honest with them. And that is great both for you as a performer and for the audience.

'I have fans who come to my concerts and to any musicals that I'm in, and they have a certain idea of me, but also a more distant relationship in terms of the staging. When they came to the Donmar, it was a very different experience for them, as it will be in a way at the Haymarket. They realised that I was giving them a very personal evening of songs, that they needed to connect and relate to me and the material in a more intense way, rather than sitting back and relaxing to the tunes.'

The audiences again appreciated *Alone Together* and the

reviews were a balance of good and not so good, but all praised Michael's courage in putting himself forward.

Clive Davis in *The Times* wrote: 'Given that he could easily continue to milk the *Phantom* market for the rest of his days, Ball deserves credit for rising to the challenge of a programme that makes serious demands on its audience. The stage is stark and empty; apart from a bottle of water and a single cigarette, there are no props. With no narrative to guide us, and with none of the usual conversational cues to mark shifts in mood, a heavy burden falls on the singer's shoulders. Sometimes, to be honest, it does seem too much for him.

'When he brought *Alone Together* to the Donmar Warehouse three years ago, the venue's confines went a long way to generating a distinctive sense of intimacy. In the Haymarket, some of that atmosphere is lost, and Ball's boy-next-door persona cannot easily fill the void. We still sense his vulnerability on the songs written for the wee small hours.'

Michael had performed in front of a full house at London's Carling Apollo Hammersmith earlier in the year and this was released on video and DVD on 8 November as *Michael Ball Live In London*. He explained that he wanted to record one show only, adding to the *Herald Express*: 'Sometimes after a show, you are never entirely sure how it went, but for this one everything just worked. The audience were so into the performance, the guy filming it had just one chance to catch it and really understood what it was about, the band played at the top of their game and I was on good form. When I went into the editing suite afterwards I felt like I was a member of the audience. I was chuffed with it, I think it is one of the best crafted and best constructed tours I have done.'

On 18 November, Michael made another brave career decision when he stepped out into the medieval setting of Windsor Castle in Berkshire – before the Queen and President Jacques Chirac as part of the centenary celebrations of the Entente Cordiale – as Jean Valjean in a one-off production of *Les Misérables*. Would all the terrors that blighted his first West End experience in 1986 return? It is easy to say, 'It is Her Majesty, how could I refuse?' but if you are risking the collapse of your career again, many would make a polite excuse and head for the sanctuary of never having a knighthood.

But that is not Michael's style and he came sailing through the Windsor Castle experience. 'We did it in the Waterloo Room, which was hastily renamed the Music Room. Every member of the royal family – plus the heads of state of England and France – were a few feet away from all of us in rags singing about revolution.'

And just 10 days later, he was performing for the Queen again at the opening of the Cardiff Millennium Centre. He said: 'Performing for the royals or even some celebrity can really lift your performance.'

Michael had released his the 39-track album *Love Changes Everything: The Essential Michael Ball*, on 25 October and told *The Stage* newspaper: 'I've been in the business for 20 years and it felt kind of right to go and look back at what I've done over all those years, but also to add a few new things as well so that it's not purely recycled stuff. At the same time, I'm thinking, "Do we really have to put *One Step At A Time* on it?" But, of course, we do.'

The work was coming in thick and fast. Though his latest album, his 12th, didn't go Gold, a flop by his standards,

Michael appeared at Edinburgh's Usher Hall on 4 December for a live show of songs from stage musicals recorded by BBC Radio 2 for their Christmas Eve concert to give a fitting end to the year.

CHAPTER 14

If I Could Only Dream This World Away

E very year brought something new for Michael, whether it be good or bad. And 2005 was no exception. While he had mentally mapped out for the next 12 months the prospect of another album, a new concert tour, perhaps a little more television exposure, he was suddenly faced with a new opportunity.

Another stage maestro called Michael, this time Michael Crawford who like our own 'Bally' had spent his childhood in the south of England, was suddenly struck down by illness while playing the role of Count Fosco in Victorian melodrama-set-to-music *The Woman In White*. The production was an adaptation of the book of the same name by Wilkie Collins and which was published in 1860, being described as an epistolary novel, a work written as a series of documents.

Crawford had originated the part of the grossly obese character, from its opening on 15 September 2004 at the Palace Theatre at Cambridge Circus in London's theatreland, and it proved to be another Baron Lloyd Webber success story. But now Crawford was struggling badly with flu-like symptoms, feeling completely drained and it seemed to be a direct result of the 'fat-suit' he had to wear for his performances.

At first, his illness was a mystery, but in time it was diagnosed that he was suffering from the debilitating illness ME, myalgic encephalopathy, which was thought to have been triggered by a viral infection. And he went through hell. Years later, in 2011, he said in an interview with the *Daily Mail*: 'I thought my career had come to an end because I no longer had the energy, or even the inclination, to work again. I'd be totally exhausted by mid-afternoon, and I could barely climb the stairs at home. It was particularly alarming because all my life I'd enjoyed doing all my own stunts in shows, taking on every physical challenge. Yet suddenly, I'd become like a very old man. I knew something was wrong but I had no idea what.

'It got so bad I had to pull out of the show but no one seemed to know what was wrong. What I thought had been flu turned into a physical meltdown. I went for all sorts of brain and body scans until ME was finally diagnosed. I was told by the doctors that it was all down to the Count Fosco suit.'

What had happened to Crawford was that the suit made him sweat so much that he had become dangerously dehydrated, causing him to lose too many nutrients from his body. The water he had been taking on board was not enough to replace them. 'With no nutrients to sustain me, I had become vulnerable to a virus,' he told the *Daily Mail*. 'My immune system had broken down and this led to ME. Ironically, I'd helped design that rubber costume, and it had been like stepping into a sauna for three hours every night. I look back on it now and realise that creating that suit was one of the worst ideas I ever had.'

When the doctors ordered Crawford to rest in late December 2004, understudy Steve Varnom stepped into the role, and of course the fat suit – and he soldiered on until February. But Baron Lloyd Webber and director Trevor Nunn wanted a more recognised name to keep the box office receipts ticking along.

Michael picks up the story in an interview with *Broadwayworld.com*, saying: 'It was really bizarre. I'd been to see the show, just after Christmas, on 29 December I believe it was, just as a punter because I wanted to see Maria Friedman and because I know everyone involved in it basically. I really enjoyed the show. I saw it with the understudy. At that point, I think that Michael Crawford had just been out of it for a day or two.

'Cut to the beginning of February, and I was actually on the beach walking my dog when I got a call from Maria saying, "I don't know how mad you think this sounds, and they've asked me to call because we're friends, so there'll be no hard feelings, but we've got this situation where Michael's out of the show and it looks like he's not coming back for a significant amount of time, if at all. We're kind of up shit's creek without a paddle. Do you think that you could come and help?"'

Michael had at that point a crammed diary and asked if he could think about Maria's suggestion, promising to call her back. But it took him only 10 minutes to do the verbal arm-wrestling with his mentor Cathy before he was dialling Ms Friedman's number. 'I thought it would just be so much fun, and so out of left field for me to do it,' Michael told *Broadwayworld.com*. 'They had an immediate need, and they asked me if I would step in as quickly as possible. It was the biggest compliment that they had faith in me.'

You would have thought one of the big problems in taking on the role, knowing how Crawford had been affected, would be Michael remembering his own dreadful experience, with identical symptoms, that he suffered while doing *Les Misérables*. And though he had wonderful memories of the Palace Theatre as the place where as a youngster he had marvelled at *Jesus Christ Superstar*, this was also the venue where he had been performing *Les Mis* when he suffered his own 'meltdown'.

It would mean those same surroundings, with all their harrowing memories. It would mean him arriving at the same tube station where he sometimes would simply have to turn around and go home again.

But, such was the confidence that Michael had now developed, he was not going to be denied the chance to step into such a leading-man role. It meant that he would have only 10 days of rehearsals for *The Woman In White* before 'going live', and he would also have to delay his latest album until the autumn. But Michael felt the chance was more than worth it.

He told respected theatre journalist Michael Coveney:

'Count Fosco was a wonderful opportunity. You get to flirt with people on the stage and in the audience. The challenge is finding ways of revealing his nastiness obliquely until it becomes apparent that he is the evil mastermind behind it all.'

Not that Michael had too much time to reflect on his performances as he was already signed up to take over as the guest host on ITV's *This Morning* programme, on screen for two hours live daily. He explained to that New York theatre magazine: 'I worked it out so I could get four shows under my belt – Thursday, Friday, and a two-show Saturday – and then I would do the *This Morning* show and Fosco at night for the next week. It was a pretty intense schedule, but that's exactly what happened. I would do the show at night and then get up at 6am to do the TV show. I was getting about two hours sleep a night.'

The rehearsal period, prior to this crazy double-day schedule that Michael had devised, was also intensive. He added to *Broadwayworld.com*: 'I wouldn't go and see the show again because I felt that it was better that I came at it fresh – and since Maria and I had worked together so much and were such good mates, it was like shorthand. Trevor Nunn was directing another show, so I just had an hour or so conversation with him around a piano, and he came to the dress rehearsal to give me some last-minute tips. I said, "I need to know where to make my entrance, where to make my exit, where's my quick changes, and just put me in and let me free." I won't say that it was easy, but it really came together, and I was ready to go on.'

What Michael also liked about being asked to do Count Fosco was that he felt that had he been cast originally in the show there was a good chance that he would have been given the part of Walter, the handsome romantic lead. 'But this was nothing anyone had ever seen me do,' he said to *Newsday*. 'I'd never been a villain, never been allowed to be funny or evil or to wear a fat suit. It was wonderful to do something unpredictable.'

And he was delighted to team up again with Maria, his co-star in 1996 in Stephen Sondheim's *Passion* in which she had played the freakish spinster Fosca, who was consumed with lust for Michael's character Giorgio. In *The Woman In White*, she played Marian Halcombe, the plainer and cleverer of two sisters exploited for evil ends by the sinister nobleman. So this was now Fosco meets Fosca. Michael joked to Michael Coveney: 'This is my revenge on Maria – it's the revenge of the false eyebrows. I'm getting them this time.'

He also relished the new depth to which he would test his voice as Count Fosco, and he gave Coveney 'an impromptu performance of the powerful *bel canto* he will unleash in the big number'. Michael told Coveney: 'I have never used this part of my voice before, though I did sing "Papageno" with Lesley Garrett on television. It's wonderful singing Andrew's music. He has a melodic genius that goes straight to the heart.'

The fat-suit, which had almost literally turned into a body bag for the unfortunate Crawford, was made from light plastic and foam and weighed 3lb. When Michael was wearing it, his chest size increased to 58 inches and his waist to around 50 inches. To avoid the problems that Crawford encountered, Michael drank three litres of water before putting on the costume, anticipating that he would sweat off at least one litre of fluid while on stage. Three suits were needed as each one would take three days to dry out.

But it was all worth it. During the weeks from February to April in which he played Count Fosco, Michael won a new legion of theatre-loving friends not least those fans who had enjoyed his solo singing concerts but who had not really seen him on a proper theatre stage.

And the reviews were strong, not least from Mark Shenton, who wrote in *The Stage*: 'When *The Woman in White* premiered in the West End last September, I wondered aloud just why the producers had gone to the trouble of hiring Michael Crawford – one of the biggest, and no doubt most expensive, names in musicals – and then buried him unrecognisably in a fat suit. I even suggested that they could have had Christopher Biggins and saved on the transformation budget. But with Crawford's prolonged indisposition from the show, a significant coup has been magnificently achieved by having Michael Ball stand in for him.'

And Shenton went on to praise Michael for ' gloriously completing his journey from juve and romantic lead to ornate, hilarious character actor'.

And while playing a character within a fat-suit might stifle an actor's ability to put personal expression into a role, Shenton could only praise Michael by saying: 'Instead of disappearing into the costume, he inhabits it like a comfortably added layer.'

On leaving *The Woman In White*, with regrets as he adored the part, Michael got back to the schedule of preparing for his summer tour. But first he starred at *The Night Of 1000 Voices* on 5 May 2005, at the Royal Albert Hall in London, an event that was dedicated to the late Caron Keating, daughter of his long-time family friend Gloria Hunniford.

Caron, a television presenter like her mum, had died the previous April at the age of just 41 after fighting breast cancer for seven years. She and husband Russ Lindsay had two sons, Charlie and Gabriel, who were just seven and nine when she passed away. With his experiences in losing Cathy's sister-in-law Angela to cancer, Michael was more than pleased to perform.

He then headed for New York to record another series of his popular *Ball Over Broadway* for BBC Radio 2. It was a labour of love for Michael, who was developing at the same time a strong perspective of the theatre scene on both sides of the Atlantic.

'I go there for a week and go to shows every night, and every matinee,' he told *Broadwayworld.com*. 'I love going to the theatre, and I'm not doing it as a critic, that's not my job. I interview critics, stars, producers, writers, because I'm not qualified to be a critic. I can give an opinion just like everyone else, but I'm not there giving reasons, diagnosing the entire show, that's other people's jobs. I'm saying, "This is what's on, and here's what different areas of the business feel about it." Nobody's going to come up to me in the street and yell at me, "How could you have said that about me?"'

What came out of the radio programme was that one of Michael's most loved shows is *Gypsy*. 'It is one of my favourite musicals of all time,' he added. 'I've seen Tyne Daly, Bernadette Peters and Bette Midler in the lead roles, and of course I've seen the movie with Rosalind Russell. But if I could go back in time, it would definitely be to 1959 when the great Ethel Merman starred as Rose and Jack Klugman was Herbie. That production was nominated for eight Tony awards but didn't win any – isn't that extraordinary?'

This time, however, he did not stay long in New York as he had to put the finishing touches to his sell-out UK concert tour, which would open in Blackpool and close on his 43rd birthday.

After the tour was over, Michael treated himself to a break – lasting just one day – before he started work on the album, not least because he had to head back to the Big Apple in August to prepare for two challenges. The first was that Baron Lloyd Webber had been so pleased with Michael's performance in *The Woman In White* that he wanted him to reprise the role of Count Fosco on Broadway and the second was another venture into unknown territory for him.

Michael had been approached to make his New York City Opera debut in Gilbert and Sullivan's work *Patience*, his first appearance on a Broadway stage since *Aspects Of Love* in 1990. He was following the successful trail of a number of British stage stars who had been appearing in NYCO musicals and operettas, performers such as Jeremy Irons and Juliet Stevenson in Stephen Sondheim's *A Little Night Music*, and Elaine Paige, who 'wielded a mighty rolling-pin' as Mrs Lovett in Sondheim's *Sweeney Todd*.

When Michael was asked to give eight performances, starting on 10 September 2005 through to 5 October, as the extravagant Reginald Bunthorne in the comic operetta *Patience*, he insisted that he auditioned first for the role as he had never done opera before. He concluded: 'I got a measure of them, they got a measure of me. The offer came out of left field. And the prestige for me to be part of the New York City Opera, playing on that stage at Lincoln Center, what a joy. I couldn't say, "No".'

Patience or *Bunthorne's Bride* – the sixth operatic collaboration of 14 between W S Gilbert (libretto) and Arthur Sullivan (music) – is in two acts and was first performed at the Opera Comique in London on 23 April 1881 before moving to the 1,292-seat Savoy Theatre on 10 October 1881, where it was the first theatrical production in the world to be lit entirely by electric light. The opera is a satire on the Aesthetic Movement of the 1870s and 1880s which stressed how aesthetic values were greater than moral or social themes in literature, fine art, the decorative arts, and interior design.

Bunthorne is considered by many to be a send up of the dramatist Oscar Wilde. Michael did his homework thoroughly, calling actor friend Stephen Fry, who told him that Wilde had loved the way he was portrayed and even agreed to do an American tour as a kind of pre-publicity for *Patience*. It was on arriving at US customs in New York that Wilde was said to have famously announced: 'I have nothing to declare but my genius.'

Michael told one interviewer that he considered the closest characters to Wilde were rappers such as Eminem, but he backed off from the fanciful idea of doing the lyrics in the style of rap.

Michael was asked prior to his performances if he thought the humour of the 19th-century operetta would translate to a New York audience in 2005. He told *Playbill*, the US monthly theatre-goers magazine: 'I think there's absolutely no difference to how we regarded things then and how we regard things now. There are still those performers and artists who strike on a new art form or mode that attracts their fans, while the majority of us maybe say, "I'm sorry, but isn't that The

Emperor's New Clothes?" There will always be charlatans who do things just to get acclaim and adulation. So I think it will speak to an audience as clearly today as it did then.'

But coming on the back of his performance as Count Fosco, Michael, in his extensive interview with the magazine's Eric Meyers, added: 'In *Patience*, Bunthorne is the only one who doesn't get anyone at the end. Just deserts, you might say. That is part of the appeal of it for me. Throughout my career, I've usually been the romantic hero, the juvenile lead, the guy who gets the girl. So now, to do in quick succession these two challenging and funny character roles, maybe it will mark a sea-change in what I do on stage.

'Bunthorne is also a high baritone, which is what I am. And I already come with the British accent, so that won't be a problem. The costumes were wonderful – outrageous, campy, over the top. So maybe that is the new market I'm going to be cornering – campy, over-the-top characters who have a nasty side.' And he joked: 'What are they trying to tell me?'

Michael added at that point: 'For sheer joy, nothing I think will beat Reginald Bunthorne in *Patience*. I have never had so much fun on the stage in my life, it was outrageous what I got away with and I'm so glad I did, it was hysterically funny. I've really been blessed.'

And the critics loved his performances. Mark Denton in the *New York Times* wrote: 'The principal attraction of New York City Opera's current production of Gilbert & Sullivan's *Patience* is the presence of Michael Ball in one of the leading roles. Ball, who is bound for the NYC debut of Andrew Lloyd Webber's *The Woman in White* at the Marquis Theatre next month, hasn't been seen on these shores since *Aspects Of*

Love in 1990. He is, you will discover, a bona fide musical theatre star: his baritone is lush and effortless, his bearing is charming and charismatic and sexy without even trying, and his way with a comic line is superbly funny. Ball is, in short, a splendid leading man, of the sort in very short supply these days. *Patience* doesn't give him nearly enough stage time to satisfy his fans, but he's very good in it. When he's around, the energy level of this lesser work by comic opera's masters trebles or quadruples.'

Frank Scheck in the *New York Post* said: 'Someone at the New York City Opera must be accruing some serious frequent-flier miles on British Airways. The company has recently specialised in recruiting West End stars rarely seen on our shores to star in productions. Their latest coup is Michael Ball, now staring in Gilbert & Sullivan's *Patience*, a lively revival filled with madcap humour. Ball is the best thing about the production, a co-production with Glimmerglass Opera. His obvious delight in his silly characterization is infectious and, tellingly, his non-operatic voice delivers the clearest enunciation of Gilbert's convoluted lyrics.'

Tazewell Thompson, who directed *Patience*, admitted: 'I had no idea what a huge star Michael is. Fans are coming from Japan, Australia, London and Rome. But he has been a real team player.'

An interesting aside, giving further insight to Michael as a character, is his reaction to the bombings in London on 7 July 2005. The day after those atrocities, he was called by *Playbill* writer Myers to give that *Patience* interview. But he told the journalist: 'I've never been so proud to be British, and to be a Londoner. I'm right in the centre of the city right now, and there is an extraordinary sense of calm – people are going back to work, the theatres are back open, and everyone's getting right on with their lives. Our emergency services were so well prepared, and reacted so quickly. And you know, it has been very comforting having (New York) Mayor Giuliani here, who let us know that during 9/11, his thoughts turned to Londoners during the Blitz, and how they persevered. The two cities you don't pick on are New York and London. You want tough, we'll give you tough.'

Patience had not even completed its short run when Michael had to start rehearsals for *The Woman In White* on Broadway. Before the show opened, Michael had just one week off to travel back to London to promote his 13th album *Music*, which was released on the 17 October. This included the tracks: 'Music', 'The Show Must Go On', 'Fields Of Gold', 'You Raise Me Up', 'Everlasting Love', 'Bridge Over Troubled Waters', 'And I Love You So', 'Desperado', 'Life On Mars', 'I Am Loved' and 'Sometimes When We Touch'.

He said on his website in his album notes: 'It has been such fun selecting, refining and recording this selection of what are in my opinion some of the finest examples of contemporary music and song. I hastily exclude my own collaborative effort from this group but I did want to include something new to the selection. I hope you will forgive my self-indulgence.'

Michael, his schedule becoming ever more hectic, was promoting the album right until the very last second. After his final round of television appearances, he was put on the back of a motorbike to get him to Heathrow airport on time so he could get his plane.

But for all the plaudits Michael received for his short but

glorious run in *Patience*, taking *The Woman In White* to Broadway's Marquis Theatre, opening on 17 November, turned out very differently.

Michael had become appreciative of New York and New Yorkers, from his days in *Aspects Of Love*, from doing his BBC Radio 2 programme and from his time in *Patience*. The work ethic of Broadway performers is something that impressed him. 'Everyone is really, really focused,' he said to *Broadwayworld.com*. 'From the bottom up, there is a real sense that, "We have a really serious job to do and we're going to get it done." And you work, you work hard to get it right. It's a little more laid back in the UK, so I think that it's nice to inject a bit of fun into an American cast – to bring humour and lighter moments, sending things up a bit – which is kind of our style to diffuse a situation. For us, it's nice to be surrounded by this focused energy.'

Michael had found that *The Woman In White* had grown on him, so he was extremely buoyant at being given the mantle to lead the show across the Atlantic to Broadway to star again alongside his friend Maria. He continued: 'It was a great honour for me, because I think that there was probably an element of gimmick casting in England, as I'm far better known there than I am in the United States. To be asked to do it on Broadway, I kind of felt very proud, because it was entirely on the merit of the performance, and what I can bring to the piece – as opposed to "let's get a name in".'

It did not matter to him that he had to spend two hours in make-up before each performance, with him explaining: 'And I can't take it off between shows on matinee days.'

He told *Newsday*'s Blake Green in November 2005: 'I sweat

hugely under the fat-suit. I have to constantly take in fluids to keep from becoming dehydrated. It really inhibits your movements – just getting out of a chair is different. It's all about dexterity. You have to seem light on your feet, dainty almost. There would be no charm to the man if he was just a lumbering oaf.'

Michael accepted the make-up process though admitted that is was 'really, really tedious'. This involved getting all the hair put away and preparing the skin before the prosthetic double chin was put on, which then had to be blended. 'The problem is that I'm getting these breakouts from the glue for the beard and the moustache,' said Michael.

He also explained how he was not only getting a bright red chin but he was also getting scratches from the animals involved in the show, joking that he thought he was , 'falling apart' and 'needed danger money'.

'The fat-suit, with all these clothes layered on top is hot, uncomfortable and produces an unbelievable amount of sweat but it really does give you the character. I stay in it for the whole show, because it takes too long to get out of it. Between shows, I take it off, but I can't get out of the make-up, so I'm in here wearing a double chin, and sweat pants. I look a little weird, and I don't think that I could go out to a sushi bar dressed like that.'

Michael nicknamed the suit 'Bernard' as he claimed 'it looks just like one of those plucked turkeys' that Norfolk farmer Bernard Matthews had advertised on British television. But he simply relished the role of Count Fosco. 'He's just horrible, without scruples, I love him to bits,' he said. 'He is a really evil, fat bastard.'

The wax-moustachioed Fosco, in cahoots with the villainous Sir Percival Glyde, takes a medicine bag with him everywhere – 'the better to sedate you with, my dear' – and a menagerie. It means that behind the scenes, with their own special dressing room facilities, were a white rat, a mouse and several cages of chirping birds. The door to their room had a sign that warned: 'Do Not Put Your Fingers In The Cages'.

Michael suspected the birds were stand-ins for the people Fosco would like to keep in cages. The rat speaks for itself, though in real life 'Beatrice is really quite sweet,' said Michael. His only real complaint was: 'Oh, sometimes they do pee.'

What Michael did, when he took over from Varnom in London in the February, was to reinvent the character with his own interpretation and, to his enormous credit, this depiction was to be used by those who followed him in the role.

He told *Broadwayworld.com*: 'I feel like I've got the character. I've found the humour, and I always wanted to find more of the dark side of the man. I don't think that when I saw it that his sinister side, his complete manipulation and his brilliance, really came out. He appears at first to be just this "boll weevil" but underneath the cogs are working, and he is working everyone and everything out.'

Michael saw the comedy as being inherent because he saw Fosco as a huge character who was 'very precise and very delicate, with these great numbers, and of course with the rat'. He explained how he didn't want audiences to like Fosco, adding. 'He's one of those characters that when he walks in the room he takes over the room, and you want to say "I wish I knew someone like that, but I wouldn't want to meet them in a dark alley." In a salon full of people at a cocktail party, he would be a lot of fun, but on a one-to-one basis when things are a bit dodgy, you would not want to know him.'

Not content with making the role darker, Michael also changed the look of the prosthetics and wig. 'The one thing that I thought, when I saw pictures, was that the face was not real, and one acts with one's face, and with one's eyes, to try to get across what you're saying,' he explained. 'I wanted to design the prosthetics a bit differently. Of course he has got to have this double chin. I've got these dimples so I thought if we literally take the line along the jaw-line, and include it with the dimples, that they would turn into this chin, then it's all my face.'

Michael's attention to detail, leaving aside the moustache and the beard, meant that he didn't want stick-on eyebrows as they cramp his own expressions. He also was particular about the immaculately dressed Fosco's hair, wanting it swept back to illustrate how he saw himself as a romantic hero. Michael added: 'He's kind of like some of those tenors in operas that are much too fat to play the romantic lead, but they still play the romantic lead. Also, by having the hair back, the face and the eyes become more present. That was my idea behind the look for him.'

With Michael doing his *Ball Over Broadway* series, he was certain that he knew 'what was out there and what people are wanting to see'. He added: 'There is a definite leaning these days towards comedy, towards pastiche, but I hope that there is a place for something like this, which is romantic and witty, and requires you to think. You have to be pulled into this story for this to work. From what I'm hearing from people, they are either going to be loving the whole experience,

185

and getting into the journey with the characters, and being surprised, and not seeing the twist comings – or they are going to go "Give me *Spamalot*."'

Whatever fears there were about whether the show would be a success or not, there was one thing that was certain, Michael's army of fans would roll on up and they did. He said prior to opening: 'They are coming, and they all came over for *Patience* too, in organised fan trips. What is amazing is how many American fans there are, more than I realised, coming in from all over the country. Washington, Seattle, Baltimore, Philadelphia, Chicago – I didn't know how many were out there. It's just brilliant, and they are kind of going, "We've got him now, we've got him." And I'm happy to be here.'

But for all the smooth transition Michael had made in taking over the role in such a rush in London's West End, the Broadway production did not go to plan.

Maria Friedman suffered the trauma of needing to take a break from the previews after lumps were discovered in her breasts and they were diagnosed on 31 October as cancerous – just 18 days before the official first night, which was scheduled for 17 November 2005. It meant she needed surgery – and she needed it immediately.

The previews went ahead with the understudy Lisa Brescia but amazingly Maria made it back for the opening, just nine days after she had a lump removed. Michael told *Broadwayworld.com*: 'It was a very special night to have her back. She had a really serious, nasty op, plus having to deal with having cancer, and waiting for test results. Just the physical thing of having that operation is not nice, but a week later she's in a corset with her doctor strapping her in – it was just amazing. She is old school – the show must go on.'

Michael believed the whole experience brought the company together, insisting that if something like that was going to happen, you could not be in a better job.

But the reviews were not good. The audiences might have taken to the production but the critics were far from impressed.

Ben Brantley wrote in the *New York Times*: 'Bravely flouting centuries of accepted scientific theory, the creators of *The Woman in White* have set out to prove that the world is flat after all. This latest work from the poperetta king Andrew Lloyd Webber seems to exist wilfully and unconditionally in two dimensions. It's not just that this import from London has rejected a conventional set in favour of computer-animated projections that make you feel as if you're trapped inside a floating upscale travel magazine. It's that everything concerned with this reshaping of a landmark English mystery novel gives the sense of having been subjected to a similar process of flattening and compression. Plot, characters, words and most of the performances in this tale of love, deception and unspeakable secrets in Victorian England emanate the aura of autumn leaves ironed into crisp immobility between sheets of waxed paper.'

Brantley went on to say that *The Woman in White* had the misfortune to open on Broadway so close to the Stephen Sondheim production *Sweeney Todd*, which he said 'draws you straight into an anxious fever dream' with the songs seeming 'to come from within you'. He added: 'By contrast, *The Woman in White* feels as personally threatening as a historical diorama behind glass. It's not a terrible show, but it's an awfully pallid one. The difference between it and *Sweeney Todd* is the difference between water and blood.'

David Rooney, writing in *Variety*, praised Maria and wrote that 'Michael Ball animates every scene he graces; his corpulent, twinkle-toed Count Fosco is a gleefully wicked caricature that injects a welcome shot of vibrancy.' But he added: 'For all its villainous men, imperilled women, palpitating hearts, murder and madness, however, the melodrama feels sadly hollow.'

The fact that the critics branded the show a flop, whatever they thought of Michael, hurt him deeply. A song from the show claimed 'If I Could Only Dream This World Away'. How Michael wanted to do that. He was more than comfortable with the performances he was giving, but the reviewers were ruining it all. He loved the role of Count Fosco and had brought a significant new dimension to it – but Broadway is not an easy hunting ground. He described it as one of the low points of his career. And it was as if the show was jinxed. By mid-December, Maria needed further surgery.

As Christmas came, Cathy and he spent it in New York away from their families. He said: 'I had only Christmas Day off. I usually cook Christmas lunch. We had to eat in a restaurant. It was miserable.'

Things were not going well and matters did not get any better.

CHAPTER 15

Trying Not To Notice

Whereas Michael entered 2005 in such a strong place, the situation was the exact opposite going into 2006. The past 12 months had seen some memorable highs but the problems with *The Woman In White* on Broadway took the sheen off all that. His confidence was tottering and, as had happened in the past all those years ago with *Les Misérables*, this seemed to manifest itself in poor health. Just as had happened to Crawford, the toll of wearing that fat-suit was telling on our Michael. He developed flu and was ordered to take a break. He said: 'I was getting a succession of viruses then going onstage and cooking myself.'

Shortly after recovering from the flu and making it back into the show, he was again struggling, this time with a more serious complaint, a throat infection. His doctors had no option but to order him to take a complete vocal rest for at least several weeks. Michael listened. He recalled to himself how his health problems had escalated back in 1986 when he tried to return too early from glandular fever. This time the advice was that he could even go so far as damaging his voice permanently if he did not step back.

The producers were told that Michael was to stand down – and Maria was also having to absent herself from various appearances because of her cancer. But still the cast and company were shocked when, the day after Michael explained that he would have to drop out, it was announced the whole show would close in just fours weeks, on 19 February 2006, three weeks earlier than the original 12 March run-date. The end came after 109 regular performances and 20 previews, with producers citing officially Maria's frequent absences, as well as the negative reviews, as 'difficult obstacles to overcome'.

Michael was in a huge reverse situation – and not for the first time in his career. But on this occasion, he knew how to cope and had the support structure in place within his personal life.

As the song from *The Woman In White* said, he was 'Trying Not To Notice'. He flew back to England to recuperate in spring 2006, knowing that he could bury himself in his music and his concerts with the pastoral backing of Cathy rather than have any chance of sinking into a mire of solitude, self-doubt and loneliness as had happened back in 1986.

He planned a new album release for the autumn, a five-date UK concert tour – one of which would be in Basingstoke where he had been in Rep as a youngster – and a series of one-off concerts. These included playing the role of Frank-N-Furter in *The Rocky Horror Picture Show* anniversary concert on 3 May

2006 at the Royal Court Theatre in London – complete with wig and high-heels.

In August, he gave a powerful rendition of 'Goldfinger' in a gig to celebrate Anthony Newley for BBC's Radio 2 – and in December he teamed up with Petula Clark again for a couple of numbers during one of her concerts. He also accepted an invitation to be a judge for BBC Radio 2's *Voice Of Musical Theatre 2006* show.

On 7 October, Michael was invited to perform at the Queen's Theatre in London's West End at the 21st Anniversary Celebration for *Les Misérables*. And, of course, there was the album. One of the highlights of 2005 was his album *Music* being awarded a Gold disc but now came *One Voice*, his 14th solo album. This included the songs: 'One Voice', 'Hero', 'The Living Years', 'Where Do I Begin', 'Since You've Been Gone', 'I Don't Wanna Talk About It', 'I Don't Wanna Miss A Thing', 'If You're Not The One', 'Lyin' Eyes', 'Everybody Hurts' and 'Home'.

Michael, in his dedication attached to the album, admitted: 'It's great to be home.'

In November, the *Chichester Observer* reported that Michael was a guest at a Christmas fair in aid of the St Richard's Hospital cancer day-unit appeal at Goodwood racecourse, close to his West Wittering home and also near where mum Ruth lived at Singleton. His presence helped the annual event to attract about 1,100 shoppers and raise a record £22,000 for the appeal. Michael said: 'It's our local hospital, I have used A & E many times and it's great. The hospital is a vital part of the community and it's up to people in the community to do whatever they can to support it.'

That made it particularly pleasing for Michael less than two years later, on 4 February 2008, when the work started officially on the cancer day-unit at the hospital, after the fund soared past its huge £3million target. And he was invited to cut the first turf.

As Michael threw himself into various activities in 2006, he was determined to end the year on a high to help blank out the way 2005 had finished up. He and Cathy had felt 'bereft of seasonal joy' having to spend Christmas in New York with *The Woman In White* branded a failure. They promised themselves that this year would be different.

Michael, who went on to complete two *National Lottery Show* appearances on 27 December and 30 December, really got into the festive mood when he was given the chance to fly from Manchester to Lapland in Finland to accompany 87 children with life-threatening illnesses to meet Santa Claus and his reindeer, a trip organised by Stockport-based charity When You Wish Upon A Star.

He told *Hello!* magazine: 'I met people from the charity when I was doing a concert. I talked to them for ages and said, "If there's anything I can do to help just give me a ring." Then they asked if I would like to come with them on the trip. I feel really honoured that I've been able to do so.

'The children's laughter and their singing around the fire are memories I will always carry with me. Watching their faces, relishing the pleasure you can give them, the magic and the joy. The trip was all about that – and, yes, a tear or two. There were moments when I found it heartbreaking. I think if you're going to visit the real Father Christmas in Lapland, then it should be through the eyes of kids. The children I went with were very ill and I think that the trip was as important for their parents. To see their kids having a moment of proper childhood, away from hospitals and injections, was just fabulous for them.'

The excursion – on which the youngsters were accompanied by other celebrities such as *X Factor* boy band Eton Road and *Coronations Street* stars Wendi Peters, Nikki Sanderson, Danny Young and Helen Flanagan – saw the party travel through the Enchanted Forest on husky-pulled sleds and motorised snow mobiles to get to Santa's Village. The children then boarded reindeer sleighs before meeting Father Christmas and Rudolph.

Michael added: 'It was humbling to see these kids sitting on his lap and telling him how much they had been looking forward to meeting him.'

He was particularly moved by a lad of 14 who, because of growth problems resulting from a brain tumour, appeared only around nine years old. Michael described him as 'the brightest, wittiest, wisest little soul I've ever met'. Another little girl, Emily, who was wheelchair-bound, decided she would be his girlfriend for the day.

Michael added:'We all moan about our lives, but there wasn't a single moan from these kids all day long. I wouldn't have missed their company for the world. I'm lucky. I've got a lot to look forward to, but the future for many of the children I went to Lapland with is uncertain. Yet I think the joy the trip has given them will sustain them more than anything else. One little chap told us on the way home, "This was the best day of my life." How do you top that?'

CHAPTER 16

Mama, I'm A Big Girl Now

What a difference a year makes. Michael roared into 2007, having recovered all his old verve and *joie de vive*. Shortly before the end of 2006, he was able to announce his 10th UK tour coming up in the spring, as well as his return to the stage schedule for June as he had signed to appear in English National Opera's production of *Kismet* in London's West End, another wonderful directional change for him.

The direction given to him on 23 January was not quite as wonderful, though, with him being ejected from the American Bar at The Savoy off the Stand in central London for giving an impromptu concert with the late tragic Amy Winehouse and fellow singer Jamie Cullum. The unlikely trio, full of enthusiasm and spirit, had descended on a vacant piano after the South Bank Awards in The Savoy Ballroom and managed to hammer out eight numbers before 'enough guests complained to warrant their unceremonious eviction'.

The stuffy hotel management ordered the trio back to their rooms, leaving Michael to say: 'I'm not as bad as I was, but I still like to party – even though we were kicked out of there.'

The year had started with him co-judging the second series of the ITV reality television show *Soapstar Superstar*, which went out from 5 – 13 January after Michael spent a week in Manchester filming the series.

One of the show's contestants was pretty *Emmerdale* star Hayley Tamaddon and Michael was so taken by her singing talents that he invited her to perform with him in Blackpool in March and at his Manchester Apollo concert on 7 April. He told the *Manchester Evening News*: 'I really liked Hayley and I promised her she could come and sing at one or two of my shows. What I noticed was her great voice and personality. I believe she has got a very bright future in the music business.'

He was also impressed with *Coronation Street* actor Antony Cotton, saying: 'I wasn't surprised at all when he won. He is a showman and a great entertainer and harnessed his honesty and vulnerability really well.'

It was in March 2007 that Baron Lloyd Webber in the *Daily Telegraph* defended his decision to use television talent shows to find new stage hopefuls, warning that the position of the West End theatre as a world-class stage could be threatened because of a shortage of talent for musicals. He was speaking out as it was revealed that a bricklayer, a clothes shop assistant, a cement administrator and two schoolboys were among the 12 finalists of a talent show to find an actor to play the title role in a West End revival of his 1968 show, *Joseph And The Amazing Technicolor Dreamcoat*.

Baron Lloyd Webber said he could name only two British-born actors, Michael Ball and John Barrowman, who were capable of stepping into lead roles. And he added: 'There aren't that many female stars in musical theatre.'

His latest talent show, a 12-part series entitled *Any Dream Will Do*, started on BBC1 on 31 March, and followed *How Do You Solve a Problem Like Maria?*, a similar exercise from the previous year that resulted in Connie Fisher, a telesales girl from Cardiff, winning the role of Maria in the London revival of *The Sound of Music*, produced by Baron Lloyd Webber.

During March and April, Michael completed an extensive 23-date tour, starting with two nights in Belfast before a number of shows in the north of England and the Midlands. He then headed for Glasgow and Aberdeen before returning for concerts in London, Birmingham and Nottingham. Nostalgia saw him perform in Plymouth, where he had gone to school, before rounding off with gigs in Ipswich, Northampton and finally Cardiff.

The serious business of the year for Michael, or so you would have thought, should have come with him agreeing to display his singing talents on the same stage as English National Opera's band of vocal players in a production of *Kismet*.

This was to open on 26 June and run through to14 July at the London Coliseum in St Martin's Lane – the prestigious venue that had previously been the home of the Sadler's Wells Opera Company but was bought for £12.8million by English National Opera in 1974 to be used as their home.

Kismet was first produced on Broadway in 1953 and was

successful enough with the America public and critics to win a Tony Award the following year. It is a musical adaptation of the 1911 play by Edward Knoblock with the story based in 11th-century Baghdad, now the capital of Iraq, 'concerning a wily poet who talks his way out of trouble several times while his beautiful daughter meets and falls in love with the young Caliph.'

Michael was taking the role of Hajj, originated on stage by Alfred Drake and on film by Howard Keel, a roguish, wise-cracking street poet who, in the course of one day, rises from beggar to prince. This seemed like a terrific challenge for Michael to work with an opera company – but reality was very, very different.

The reviews were scathing – with one of the kinder adjectives used to describe the show being 'pantomimic'. The condemnation of ENO, which received hefty funding from the Arts Council, was damning.

Critic Kate Bassett held no punches in the *Independent on Sunday* when she wrote: 'Tell me it's not true. Tell me I'm not watching this unbelievably dim-witted and culturally insensitive musical in a major production by the ENO. The Coliseum has been managerially rocky of late, but Gary Griffin's dire staging of *Kismet* has patently been programmed by a bunch of lemmings leaving nothing to chance. At a time when Baghdad is tragic headline news, the company has crassly chosen to revive this cod Ali Baba-ish rom-com from 1950s Broadway. It's sub-panto.'

Another reviewer, Dominic McHugh, tried to gloss over the cracks, insisting that for all its faults it was 'very entertaining'. He added: 'Michael Ball grabs every note and every word of this Broadway classic by the throat, belts out every number with awe-inspiring power, and commits unstintingly to the production. The results are often overwhelming. Indeed, nearly every member of the cast shows the utmost commitment, so that while the silliness of *Kismet* sometimes works against them, the musical values are nearly always very high.'

But Michael knew a different truth and he managed to rise above the embarrassment of the dreadful reviews by reminding people that it was meant to be entertainment. It was also a fact that the show was a sell-out and, therefore, would go down as one of the ENO's biggest box-office success.

He admitted in August that year to Fiona Maddocks, a writer for the *London Evening Standard*: 'It was shockingly, gloriously awful. It was like being in a cross between *Springtime For Hitler* and *Carry On Camel*. I'm sorry I just have to get this off my chest. It was truly unbelievable. *Kismet* had all the isms – racism, sexism, you name it. It's not funny. The book is old-fashioned and clunking but I think no one knew if one of the writers was still alive and we weren't allowed to change a word.'

The problems, for Michael, were down to the management of the project – and he held particular distain for the show's ultra-fashionable designer Ultz, whose real name is David Fisher, claiming: 'It was the worst designed production ever but it's got a fantastic score. It's not an awfully good book, though. You really have to work hard to eke out any laughs from that script. You had an award-winning director, designer, choreographer and musical director, a creative pot which should come up with something extraordinary, but did the exact reverse.'

Michael alleged that the rehearsals were a 'shambles'. He added in his interview with the *London Evening Standard*: 'People were standing around on stage saying, "I don't know what I'm supposed to do." Can you believe it? I've never had a dance lesson in my life but I suggested a few things, just because you have to come up with something with all those people looking at you. It was as if a member of the Stedham Village Players had won the Lottery and said (Michael adopted a strong northern accent to accentuate the point): "I'm putting on *Kismet* and I'll do it my way." It was like *Aladdin* at the Bradford Alhambra, circa 1978.

'I'm going to be in trouble but I don't care. It shouldn't put actors through such things. When it comes to doing musicals, ENO is amateur. Doing musicals is a different business, technically, musically, dramatically, and you can't do it the same way as opera. That's why musicals always have previews. *Kismet* only had one.'

Michael had realised very quickly that the production would be a disaster. But he said: 'When they asked me a year ago, on paper it all looked great. Award-winning creative team, beautiful music, huge resources, great orchestra and chorus. I was very excited. But the choreographer walked out. And the director buggered off on a plane straight after the first night, just when he was needed to boost morale. You would never have that in commercial theatre.'

Michael was also very critical of the design, indicating that it was wrong to 'stick it all in a bloody great Day-Glo pink blancmange with no room to move'. He alleged it was also wrong to have the male dancers dressed in the same colour as the set.

The Times newspaper put it to Michael that surely he could tell that this wasn't the time for a Baghdad-set American musical? He replied: 'I know what you're saying. Probably with hindsight, it was daft. But the thing is *Kismet* is such a good show. What's wrong is not to have taken advantage of that, and to be so crass as to say, "Bring on guns", right at the beginning. You don't need to do that. The audience isn't that stupid.'

Michael explained to Ms Maddocks why the dreadful reviews did not really affect him. 'This is where you see the difference between a place like ENO and the commercial West End,' he said. 'We knew we had sold out, and that it was a finite run. It didn't matter what the reviews said. The money was in the bank. The show wasn't suddenly going to close. I wanted to come to the front of the stage and say, "We know it's as bad as you think. We're not crazy."'

Michael believed the problems with ENO and this production was a matter of attitude, not least to rehearsal. He explained to the *London Evening Standard*: 'At ENO, because it's subsidised, there is a civil-servant mentality. Even if you are in the middle of a song, if the rehearsal reaches its scheduled end, you all down tools. I found that completely shocking. There was no collective sense of continuing to the end – just a matter of minutes – to make the whole enterprise better. One or two people might have done it but the others had already gone home. But in spite of all that, I loved every second. The people were great and I would be happy to work at The Coliseum again.'

Michael, despite the criticisms of the *Kismet* project, emerged with nothing but glowing praise, which is probably one of the reasons he could be so frank about the whole ENO production. But he was about to upset the musical arts purists again, within just six weeks of his *Kismet* debacle.

Such was the growing reputation of Michael, he was inundated with offers and next up was the prestigious *Proms*, recorded and aired by BBC television and BBC Radio 3, with him being asked to be the first musical theatre performer ever to have his talents showcased at the traditional festival on 28 August, Bank Holiday Monday.

Yet the knives were out. Not so much for Michael but for the BBC, which was accused of 'dumbing down' its classical event. But *Proms* controller Nicholas Kenyon, in explaining in April his decision to extend the invitation to Michael, jumped to the defence of the festival, which is an eight-week annual summer season of daily orchestral music – 'promenade concerts' held essentially at the Royal Albert Hall in London and whose roots date back to 1895.

He said: 'Our job is to cover the whole waterfront. The real test is the audience. We are responding to what they want to hear. Michael is one of the great, intelligent singing artists alive today. He deserves a place at the *Proms* just as much as performers in the great classical tradition.'

Michael, as the pre-concert criticism started to pour in, insisted defiantly to the *London Evening Standard*: 'Nicholas Kenyon's office rang me up. Would I like a *Prom*? I said, "What, as someone's guest?" He said, "No it's your own show." Then, there was all the controversy from the purists, people saying, "Lloyd Webber at the *Prom*? Over my dead body." Don't you love it? These people ought to get over themselves.'

And he added: 'I have never been more proud of anything. What I'm not going to do is take the mick. It's not just another Michael Ball gig, rather it's me being asked to do a *Prom* and no one has been given that privilege before. I suppose people are going to see it as a freak-show event, like Shirley Bassey doing Glastonbury, but I can assure any classical-music purists that it's not something I take lightly. It's a huge privilege to have access to a full 70-piece orchestra. And, not only is it a huge honour to play at a *Prom*, but there is a responsibility that comes with it.'

Michael did not like the snobbery that he had detected in classical music circles. He felt that Baron Lloyd Webber was treated the same even though he came from a classical background. Michael said he hoped 'that *Prom* aficionados will come because there are some glorious songs in musical theatre that, when you give them the full symphonic treatment, are hard to beat'. And he promised that his performance would not be 'Michael Ball sings Stockhausen'.

He added: ' I'm going to take advantage of the situation I find myself in. I have the BBC Concert Orchestra, who are phenomenal, and I'm back in the Albert Hall, where I've been before doing my own shows. I'm not an opera turn and I'm not going to do myself a disservice by doing things that I can't do. The fact is I love musicals because it's one big song after another. You can wait for hours in opera and nothing happens. In New York, I was taken to an opera. Bugger me, what was it? Cappuccino? No, *Capriccio*, Yeah, that's the one. I was sitting there thinking, "Jeez! Let's have a tune" and silently yelling, "Go on, snog her, snog her." It was driving me insane. Interminable.'

The night before the *Prom*, Michael took part in the annual Faenol Festival, which is held in Gwynedd, north Wales by Bryn Terfel, the Welsh base-baritone who is three years younger than Michael. The pair met when they shared the stage at the opening of the Millennium Centre in Cardiff, and Michael said: 'Bryn brought his kids to see me in *Chitty Chitty Bang Bang*. He is a great guy. What a voice.'

Michael explained that he cannot read music, but learns quickly by ear, saying: 'I work with a repetiteur and have it put down on tape so I can sing along. You learn in rehearsal, too. But the difference between my voice and a big operatic one like Bryn's is that I start and finish with natural ability. He has put in years of hard graft on top of that. I haven't done that and wouldn't want to or be able to.'

Against this background, Michael had to go out and prove to the stuffy world of classical music that he was worth his *Prom*, with the full title being *Prom 58: An Evening With Michael Ball*. But the venture did not cut the mustard with the critics.

Clive Davis, in *The Times* under the heading 'Vocal broadside against snobbish critics misfires', gave the concert only two stars and wrote: 'All fired up by the occasion, Michael Ball could not resist aiming a few barbs at snobbish critics who had been outraged at his inclusion in this year's *Proms* season. To some extent, he had a point. There is, after all, a long and honourable tradition of serenading Sir Henry Wood's ghost with musical theatre standards. Besides, Ball is a hugely personable actor-singer who gave a polished performance a few years ago when he played a slot in the much-missed cabaret season at the Donmar Warehouse in London. But is it really snobbishness to wonder what on earth John Miles' Music, that painful slice of Smashie and Nicey pop schlock, is doing in a *Proms* concert? Shouldn't the *Proms* be about more than playing to the lowest common denominator?'

It was clear that Davis did not really appreciate the talents of Michael, whatever stage he was performing on. Prior to claiming that it was 'all in all, a pointless evening', he wrote: 'Maybe Ball could have won over the sceptics if the crowd-pleasing anthems had been draped in some mildly adventurous arrangements. But the extracts from *The Phantom Of The Opera*, *Sunset Boulevard*, *Chess* and *Les Misérables* were all given the usual, drearily overblown arrangements, with the BBC Concert Orchestra (conducted by Callum McLeod) reduced to going through the motions as Ball – a portly figure nowadays – struck one matinee idol pose after another.'

That review was an improvement on some, who managed to give Michael's show only one star with comments such as: 'It was nothing short of cringe making.' But while the aficionados stayed away, the 'Ballettes' turned up and enjoyed the experience immensely. And Michael went full tilt into September to make sure that his latest solo album, his 15th, *Back To Bacharach* was ready to be released on schedule on 22 October.

Bacharach, the American pianist and composer who was born in 1928, wrote at least 70 Top 40 hit songs in the United States, 52 of which made the Top 40 in the UK. The songs on the album included: 'The Look Of Love', 'Make It Easy On Yourself', 'Alfie', 'Arthur's Theme (The Best That You Can Do)', 'One Less Bell To Answer', '(They Long To Be) Close To You', 'Anyone Who Had A Heart', 'This House Is Empty Now,' 'This Guy's In Love With You', 'You'll Never Get To Heaven', 'Reach Out For Me' and 'What The World Needs Now'.

Michael told the *Sunday Times*: 'I've recorded a few Burt Bacharach songs over the years and performed some in concert and always felt they suited me. I love the stories, and the lyrics (many by Hal David) have always struck a chord with me, especially on the more serious numbers. Bacharach has such a brilliant ear for melody and his music has a completely timeless feel to it that I thought it would be great to do a whole album of his music and to record with a full orchestra and big band, which is something I hadn't done before. I thought it was also time I made a sort of "late night" album with sophisticated arrangements – and he is definitely the king of all that.'

Kismet and *The Proms* were behind Michael now, his album was certain to turn Gold because his fanbase was growing ever larger. And he had learned to ride rough-shod through the barbed words of the critics. He was proving he was no shrinking violet, it was very much a case of: 'Bring on the next improbable task.'

And they, the producer-type people, duly supplied one. His next character was a vastly over-weight, agoraphobic American woman from the early 1960s who personified the pushy parent for her woefully nerdy daughter. Yes, enter Edna Turnblad for the stage version of the hit movie *Hairspray*.

Michael could not have been more delighted. 'It's a dream,'

he told the *Financial Times*. 'I saw the show on Broadway for my Radio 2 programme *Ball Over Broadway*, and I had one of the best nights I've ever had in the theatre. I laughed my arse off. It was clever, it was political, but it was also utterly escapist. I left the theatre thinking, "Damn, if this ever came over to London, they would never in a million years consider me for that Edna role."'

But they certainly did and Michael explained exactly how he would interpret his iconic role. 'You have to play it as a woman, not a drag queen,' he insisted. 'You have to believe in the family unit. It's intrinsically funny that it's a man dressed up, but nobody mentions it. It's like Dame Edna. There are no double-entendre jokes, no innuendo – we are all part of the conspiracy. And one of the most beautiful moments is the soft-shoe shuffle, where Edna and her husband Wilbur express their love for each other through dance. It's genuinely moving. I loved the original film but I wasn't too keen on the Travolta remake. It just didn't work for me. Travolta wasn't Edna.'

Hairspray has this quality of the underdog and this is very much a quality that Michael admired about the whole production. He told the *Financial Times*: 'It is about people who have been marginalised throughout history – fat people, black people, gay people, teenagers – who suddenly become central to the action. Suddenly everyone wants to be like them. The uncool outsiders are actually the coolest.

'I thought then, "This is what I would adore to do." We can't do juvenile leads for ever. This is the direction I'm going, as a grown-up character actor. To be entrusted with one of the most iconic roles in musical theatre is fantastic. I'll have wigs, make-up, dresses. How pretty is that?'

And the bonus for Michael was that he had to 'put on' weight for the role, which was just as well as his schoolboy figure was becoming fuller and fuller, not least down to his personal smoking ban, which by autumn 2007 was still in existence. He admitted: 'I've been eating for England, but now I can say I'm doing it for my art.'

Was Michael worried that the role had previously been associated with openly gay actors such as Divine, in the original movie, and Harvey Fierstein, when the show opened on Broadway? 'Actors of various flavours, shapes, sizes and proclivities have done it since,' said Michael. 'We're just being actors, playing a part. If people want to be prurient, that's up to them but it never occurred to me.'

He thought it amusing that he was singing 'Mama, I'm A Big Girl Now' and he signed up for a six-month run – for which he was allegedly being paid £25,000 a week – to play the lead in *Hairspray*, with previews starting on 11 October 2007 at the Shaftsbury Theatre in London's West End.

The show was at that point running so successfully on Broadway that it had collected eight Tony Awards. This adaptation – with music by Marc Shaiman and lyrics by Scott Wittman – was based on the 1988 John Waters movie, which told the story of plump teenager Tracy Turnblad's dream in 1962 to dance on a local TV programme, *The Corny Collins Show*, in Baltimore. The message, in reality, is about the injustices of parts of American society during those times.

Jack O'Brien, the veteran Broadway director who was backed up by choreographer Jerry Mitchell, was banking on Michael – in the role played by John Travolta in a 2007 remake of the movie – and co-star British comedian Mel

Smith, of *Alas Smith And Jones* television fame, who was to play Edna's understanding husband Wilbur, to put the bottoms on the seats.

Smith was making his musical debut at the age of 54 and was back in the West End for the first time since 1983. He said in an interview in the *Guardian*: 'I have attached myself, limpet-like, to Michael Ball. If getting through this smash-hit American musical is my Everest, then he's my guide and sherpa. No way can I plummet to theatrical death if he's on the other end of the nylon rope, even allowing for the fact that he is rehearsing in high heels.

'I'm relieved to see him calling everyone "gorgeous", "lovey" and "honeybun" – two West End wendys together.'

The singing experience of Smith was not legendary. He made it on to *Top Of The Pops* with his 1987 festive duet with Kim Wilde – and that was about it. But he explained: 'When you are singing with Michael Ball, it is a rather different class. The best I can do is to sing in tune and keep my end up, as it were.'

Another piece of inspired casting was giving the part of Tracy to Leanne Jones – a British newcomer who was just 22 at the time and who only a few months earlier had been working in telesales at the Moorgate branch of the Halifax bank in London. She was to go on to receive a Laurence Olivier Award for Best Actress in a Musical.

That fact that Leanne ended up anywhere near a West End stage was due in part, unwittingly, to Michael. She had graduated in 2006 from the Mountview Academy of Theatre Arts in Wood Green, north London, having been born in Stoke-on-Trent in 1985 before being brought up in St Ives in

Cambridgeshire. She had not even heard of *Hairspray* until friends told her to try out for it.

But Leanne had spent her teens dreaming about starring in a West End musical, explaining: 'When I was 11, I was given the 10th-anniversary video of *Les Mis*, where Michael was Marius. We sang those songs at school but I didn't know what a musical was. I watched the video and I thought, "Oh my gosh, what is this? It's singing but with a story and amazing costumes."'

From that moment, she was determined to become an actor and held strong to her self-belief – never worrying that her large frame could rob her of certain roles. Instead, she told the *Guardian*: 'It's difficult casting. Tracy has to be big, but at the same time she is never off stage, and she is running around like a lunatic doing all these dance routines. Since I got the part, I've been going to the gym six days a week, and I've been running – though not very fast. In rehearsal we've done aerobic warm-up and I've been dancing every day. So I can just about do it now without being out of breath.'

O'Brien, who was brought up in Michigan, claims the era of the setting for *Hairspray* was 'America's last gasp of innocence' before President John Kennedy was assassinated in 1963 and the historical and social comments were integrated in a 'sweetly subversive way' that means the audience is not lectured to. He added: 'I remember that sex wasn't seen as a natural inclination, that you had standards and had to behave yourself in a certain way.'

All the dressing up as a woman and make-up, the huge fake 46EEE breasts etc, did not worry Michael at all, except perhaps the bit about putting on the false eyelashes. 'You have to get your eyebrows right. You have to make sure the make-up blends in but you mustn't over do it. Yet I've never enjoyed the process of getting ready for a show so much in my life.'

Maddy Costa, of the *Guardian* newspaper, got more than she bargained for when interviewing Michael in his dressing room prior to *Hairspray* opening. 'Look at this,' he told her and thrust forward both hands cradling the floppy, rubbery skin of a single, outsize plastic breast. 'It's got a nipple. A real nipple. And look at the sequins, the feathers.'

He gestured to his wardrobe, crammed with huge, brightly coloured and extravagantly embellished frocks.

Strangely, perhaps, Michael had no problem at all getting used to walking in the four-inch stiletto heels. 'It came surprisingly easily but they can get painful,' he said to *The Times*. 'Yet when this job came along, they said, "The fatter you get, the better." Well, that is my kind of gig.'

But perhaps Michael was a little fortunate to get through the part, as he explained: 'I went for a proper audition but I had a beard at the time. The first thing I said when I walked in was, "I see her being a bearded lady."'

Yet more seriously, he told *icWales*: 'I wanted her to be really real. There is a tendency to make her a drag queen but that is exactly what she's not. I wanted her to look as feminine as possible. Because I don't have a very angular face, when make-up is put on skilfully, it does look quite pretty – I look like my granny from Mountain Ash.

'But *Hairspray* is actually quite subversive. You think you are having frothy fun, but there is a really serious, important message being sent out. There is a positive message and there are positive role models. There are characters in there for everybody to identify with. People want to succeed and they do. It's great music and a funny script. When I saw it on Broadway, it was just one of the greatest nights in the theatre. Everybody just came out feeling better than they did when they went in. And that's what it is all about. Whatever I do, I want people to come out feeling better.'

With the 'fat-suit' – Michael was by now well used to this following his experience in *The Woman In White* – and wigs to wear, he claimed that he was starting to empathise with women when it comes to getting all dressed up for a big occasion. He told *WalesOnline* website: 'I understand now why women take forever getting ready. The make-up has got to be right, you have to decide whether to wear your hair up or down and the shoes have to coordinate with the handbag. Cath will be going to a wedding or opening night and saying, "What the hell am I going to wear to this?" But I won't be shouting, "Hurry up, honey" any more.'

Michael relished the role. He said: 'I really feel like I'm married to Mel Smith – married without the perks. And if I was a mother, I would want Leanne to be my daughter. I would be that proud of her. She is fabulously talented and one of the most lovely girls that I've ever met. She deserves success.'

And success was exactly what she, Michael and the rest of the company got following some scintillating reviews when it opened officially on 30 October, having already taken £5million in advanced bookings.

Nicholas de Jongh, in the *London Evening Standard*, wrote: 'Here it is at last, the plump girls' feelgood, romantic comedy of a musical, whose dancing heels take a knockout kick at racist bigots in downtown Baltimore 45 years ago. Hairspray catches the heady, hopeful atmosphere of America teetering on the verge of Sixties cultural and political change. Rhythm and blues and Motown, then in their earlier stages, pump out the musical's seductive beat in the hectic dynamism of Jack O'Brien's production with Jerry Mitchell's quicksilver choreography.'

Mitchell has always produced dynamic routines and was the perfect choice for this production. What better partnership than a dynamic choreographer and rhythm and blues and Motown music set against the back drop of the civil rights movement? De Jongh's review claimed Hairspray, now in its fifth Broadway year, 'sent the rare, sweet smell of success wafting through the Shaftesbury last night' and that it 'paints a wicked picture of blue-collar Baltimore, where girls crave their 15 minutes of fame on TV and boys crave girls'.

Michael could not have received higher praise. 'Ball deliciously fattened up and dragged down in bland frocks and lurid gowns, majestically slips into the role of the fat, fog-horned laundress, Edna Turnblad, who responds to a large insult with a majestically contemptuous "Excuse me".'

And everyone hailed the performance of the newcomer Leanne as Tracy. De Jongh called it 'an astonishingly accomplished stage debut', adding that the youngster 'effortlessly commands the stage – she will hearten all actresses who imagine that only the pencil-thin can inherit the lead dressing room'.

The critics and the audiences adored Hairspray. Michael's layers of foundation, wigs, false eyelashes and huge bosom – all of which took him around 40 minutes prior to each performance to put on – had some diehard Ball fans complaining to the theatre management that they should have been informed prior to the performance that the lead actor, that is Michael Ball, had been changed.

The show's producer Adam Spiegel, the son of the late Sam Spiegel who produced films such as *The Bridge On The River Kwai* and *Lawrence Of Arabia*, admitted to the *Telegraph*: 'We had a dozen complaints to the box office staff at the intervals during the previews. We had to assure them that they were mistaken. Michael was extremely flattered that his disguise was so good. He does make an extremely impressive woman.'

And the secrets came out at the after-show party held at the Bloomsbury Ballroom in central London – to Michael's amusement and mild embarrassment. Cathy revealed to the *Observer*: 'He had a lot of fittings at home so it wasn't such a surprise to see him look so convincingly female. In fact, it's odd to see him in a suit now.'

Much was made of Michael's lingering stage kiss with co-star Smith. His old opera friend Lesley Garrett found it too convincing, saying: 'They seemed to enjoy it a bit too much.'

And that was all down to Smith, according to his partner in comedy Griff Rhys Jones. 'Mel coaxed Michael to go for the big smacker and the audience loved it.'

Michael's only comment was: 'Let's say, Mel is a slobberer.'

With Michael's album, *Back To Bacharach*, selling well, just as his previous 14 had done, the past 12 months had been a time of great achievements – packed with the controversy of the challenges that so inspired Michael.

Michael appeared in his fifth Royal Variety Performance at the Empire Theatre in Liverpool on 3 December 2007 singing

'You Can't Stop The Beat' with the rest of the cast from *Hairspray* and such were the plaudits for the show that it was announced that Michael would extend his initial six-month contract for a second six months, meaning he was scheduled to play Enda Turnblad right through until 15 October 2008.

Hairspray, which was to run until 28 March 2010 with more than 1,000 performances, was indeed a huge success and the show collected a record 11 Laurence Olivier Award nominations, beating the nine awards five years previously for a revival of Cole Porter's *Kiss Me, Kate*. *Hairspray* was put forward for Best New Musical and both its leading players received Olivier nominations – Leanne Jones as Best Actress and for Best Actor, Michael Ball.

CHAPTER 17

You Can't Stop The Beat

L ife was starting to taste particularly sweet for Michael as he ventured into 2008. He had transformed himself from the romantic lead to a genuine leading man in musical dramas, playing characters with real edges to them and wonderful eccentricities. His concert and album image of curly locks and swooning housewives had been subtly morphed into one of a seasoned performer who the audiences, if not always the critics, appreciated across a breadth of genres.

Award season was a time of terrific celebration for everyone connected with *Hairspray*. The cast was given the Critic's Choice Award and managed to secure 10 nominations for the Theatregoers' Choice Awards, including Best Actor In A Musical for Michael.

On 2 March, he appeared as the guest on the popular BBC Radio 4 offering *Desert Island Discs*, where he spoke in detail about his problems with stage fright and panic attacks, as well as revealing the songs he would wish to be marooned with. But the one item that he really would have wanted to be shipwrecked holding was a Laurence Olivier Award, the trophy for which he would attend the awards ceremony seven days later.

Dressed in his black suit and tie and with Cathy clutching his arm, Michael headed for The Great Room at the Grosvenor House Hotel on London's Park Lane for the evening hosted by actor Richard E Grant. As he arrived on the red carpet Michael said: 'It is my first nomination and I could not be more chuffed.'

Well, he could be more chuffed. And that was if he was to win the Olivier honour. Leanne had already been given the Best Actress award and the show was to collect the Best Musical. So it was down to Michael as the nominees were announced by *Carry On* legend Barbara Windsor: Michael Ball for *Hairspray*, Bertie Carvel for *Parade*, Henry Goodman for *Fiddler On The Roof* and Bob Martin for *The Drowsy Chaperone*. The gold envelope was opened and Ms Windsor announced Michael Ball.

A dream had been realised. At last, one of the iconic busts of Britain's greatest theatre actor – weighing 1.6kilos – was in Michael's possession.

He was bullish in his remarks to *Hello!* magazine. 'When I was cast, people said I wouldn't pull it off. When I did and I won the Olivier Award, I can't tell you the satisfaction. Everyone says, "Oh, awards don't matter." Rubbish. Acknowledgement by your peers as well as the audience is very heady and potent.'

And he added about the Olivier recognition: 'That one meant everything to me. It meant, "All right, you can be in our club." It was so satisfying. I took it into work the night after the ceremony and it appeared in every scene. When I burst out of the hairspray can at the end, I was dusting it.'

Michael was still dusting it down when he landed a plum radio assignment. Never mind the song from *Hairspray* entitled 'You Can't Stop The Beat', this was now 'You Can't Stop The Ball'. More than a few eyebrows were raised, because of his inexperience in this field, when he was offered the chance to take over the baton from veteran broadcaster Michael Parkinson on 6 April to present the chat show *Sunday Brunch*, a coveted job on BBC Radio 2. 'It's my dream slot,' he said. 'They took a real risk giving it to me because pretty much everyone would have been after it.'

His first radio guest was Dame Judi Dench, whom he met when being interviewed by Parkinson about taking over his seat. 'It was suggested she sing "Send In The Clowns",' said Michael – Ball that is, not Parkinson. 'But I told her that was too safe, too predictable. So I offered to write new lyrics to "Thanks For The Memory", mentioning everything and everyone from Emu to Barnsley to Meg Ryan. It went down a storm. So I called in the favour and she was a guest on my very first show.'

And Michael fitted in so well to radio. 'Because it is the easiest of everything – it is just me chatting away,' he told the *Scotsman*. 'I think I'm quite good at giving interviews because I'm not worried. I'll just waffle on and, hopefully, there is something in there that can be useful. It's handy because I've been on the receiving end so I know how it should be done.

'On radio, it is much easier. On TV, people are always worrying about performing and looking right and making the studio audience laugh. On radio, you just have two people having a chat. I never sit and plan. When we have a guest, I don't have a list of questions written out. You just have a conversation. The best interviews are the ones where the interviewer isn't working from a list of questions, doesn't have an agenda. And I think that people relax with me. I am not a journalist. I am not Jonathan Ross. I am just interested in people.'

Michael at one point was doing eight shows a week in *Hairspray* and then arriving first thing on the Sunday morning at the BBC to do his radio slot, which ran live from 11am for two hours. 'It was fine because I knew it wouldn't be for ever; I knew that eventually I'd be getting Monday nights off. You run on adrenaline and you run on joy.'

He did have a crammed diary but he was still determined to fit in a series of concerts, not least a trip back to Liverpool to take part in the 2008 Summer Pops festival, which was being staged for the first time at the city's new ECHO Arena.

In May, he told *What's On Stage*: 'I'm really looking forward to playing the [ECHO] Arena. It looks amazing, it's a new venue, which is always an exciting prospect, and I hear it's got state of the art acoustics. It's great that Liverpool has a place now to host bands and other artists on a regular basis that is really state-of-the-art; something I think may have been lacking in the past.'

He also managed to fit in a string of open air concerts – at Hampton Court in west London, Kenwood House in north London with Lesley Garrett, Audley End in Essex and Patchings in Calverton, Nottinghamshire. He added to interviewer Chris High: 'I usually go out and tour the UK regularly but with my theatre commitments over the last couple of years it has been difficult to organise. So this summer seemed like the perfect opportunity to get out there, put on a pair of trousers and a jacket and sing some of my favourite songs at some great venues. I love doing it and I think it's important to perform outside London. Not everyone is in the position to come to the West End, so this is a great way for me to keep in touch with fans.'

Everything was going Michael's way in the summer of 2008 and he told the *Scotsman*: 'I've really never been happier in my life – my personal life and my professional life. I touch all the wood in the world because you know it won't last because it's life, but it is really nice – and I'm old enough now to appreciate it. I don't take it for granted. It is a golden time. The stars have all aligned. Seeds that you plant, if you can get them to harvest at the same time, great – and you have to be prepared to do the work.

'I hate the physical thing of getting older. I don't like everything going south. That's a real drag. But there are definitely advantages. You learn to care less about other people's opinions, those that are negative. If people are down, you can say, "Oh whatever."'

The panic attacks that he had suffered all those years ago were very much under control. He explained to the *Sun*: 'I can deal with them now. You talk yourself down, distract yourself. You literally have a conversation in your head. They are awful. It is tunnel vision, heart thumping and you think you're going to die. It's all wrapped up in depression and you think you're going to die. It's a drag.

'When it happens, you can never make it un-happen – it is always going to be part of you. You are always going to be aware that you have had a vulnerability, that you are susceptible to those sorts of things. Everybody in show business gets nervous; everybody gets stage-fright to a lesser or a greater extent. Or at least I would hope so, otherwise they are in the wrong business. Ultimately, it makes you a better performer. It makes you a more understanding human being. If I'm run down or stressed out, I'm still susceptible to it, but I cope with it privately. I just don't go out for a few days, I don't inflict myself on people.'

Michael explained how you needed particular qualities to perform in musicals on a nightly basis, qualities that separate professionals from amateurs, not least because you have to be 'really disciplined and pretty tough'. He told the *California Chronicle*: 'You have to stay healthy, you have to stay focused, you have to learn how to deal with the repetition of something over and over again. The pacing of yourself, the understanding of what it is like to be in front of an audience every night, to acknowledge and realise that you are vulnerable. It all comes with practice – you learn how to deal with that, how to respond to it and how to actually enjoy it.'

In September, it was announced that Michael would extend his *Hairspray* contract, due to be concluded in October 2008, for a further six months, keeping him tied to the show until 25 April 2009, meaning this would be the longest continuing stage contract of his career.

The show had become an amazing success story, recouping its entire £3.5million capitalisation in a record-breaking 29 weeks – and very quickly in 2008 it had burst through the 500,000-ticket purchases mark, rejuvenating the fortunes of the Shaftsbury Theatre in the process.

Adam Spiegel, from the show's UK producers Stage Entertainment, said in a press release: 'I am absolutely delighted that Michael and many others in the cast have decided to stay with the production. *Hairspray* is the happiest show in London, both on stage and behind the scenes, and knowing we have Michael leading us into our second year is a dream come true. That he is doing so in a dress is simply a bonus.'

Michael told *Broadwayworld.com*: '*Hairspray* has without doubt been one of the happiest and most fulfilling experiences of my professional life. And I am delighted to carry on being part of this phenomenon. I'm proud of what has happened in the last two years. To rejuvenate this theatre, to have won the Olivier Award and still to be making records.'

So Michael was particularly content as he headed into 2009, the year that would herald his landmark 25 years in show business, all the way from his debut in *Godspell* on 14 July 1984. He would mark the celebrations with a new album and a UK tour.

His *Past And Present* album, his 16th solo offering, was released on 9 March 2009. The 20-track offering featured the songs: 'The Impossible Dream', 'You Can't Stop The Beat', 'Being Alive', 'The Prayer', 'This Is My Beloved/Stranger In Paradise', 'Gethsemane', 'Love Changes Everything', 'Empty Chairs, Empty Tables', 'All I Ask Of You', 'The Boy From Nowhere', 'Loving You', 'Sunset Boulevard', 'This Is The Moment', 'Tell Me It's Not True', 'If Tomorrow Never

Comes', 'Not While I'm Around', 'The Winner Takes It All', 'Just When', 'One Step Out Of Time' and 'The Show Must Go On'.

For his album dedication, he remarked: 'How wonderful that I'm able to celebrate 25 years in this business with this special album – and I have to thank everybody at Universal for getting behind it, and enabling me to do it properly. Not many artists are given a 75-piece orchestra and the run of Abbey Road Studios to record these new songs the way they should be. In the last 25 years, I've worked with some of the most creative and talented people in this business. Many of them have remained great friends for me, listening to this album reminds me of all those wonderful times we've had together, both on and off stage.'

But Michael added that the most important aspect for him was the audience. 'That is who we do it for,' he said. 'That is who we want to please. I'm blessed with having an extraordinary family of fans who have helped to give me freedom to express myself in so many different mediums and continue to do so. Thank you and see you in the next 25 years.'

Even Michael's weight was coming down as his contract with *Hairspray* was drawing to a close. He told the *Sun*: 'Now we're coming to an end, I'm taking it off and I've lost about a stone. I'm doing it slowly. I'm not going to do a fad diet but I'm eating better and the show helps me keep fit. I should be back to my fighting weight soon. I don't find it difficult to lose weight. I love my food and drink but you only need a little more discipline.'

Yet, shortly after saying this, he was to announce that he

would extend his run in *Hairspray* even further, this time, and finally, to 25 July 2009. He stepped down in an emotional farewell and handed over his frocks and wigs to comedian Brian Conley after more than 600 performances. For sentimental reasons, he kept hold of his 46EEE falsies, saying: 'Mel Smith wanted them as a memento – but I wouldn't part with them.'

However, would Michael not miss his drag role? 'Well Edna hasn't made me a cross dresser, in public anyway,' he joked to the *Daily Record*. 'But what I do on the coach between shows is my own business.'

Then in August 2009, his career went off at yet another positive tangent with the announcement that, though he had finished in the West End production of *Hairspray*, he would be taking the show on a UK tour in 2010. In addition, it was revealed that Michael's close working relationship with the show's UK production company, Stage Entertainment, meant that he had been appointed associate producer to work developing new projects and roles, including ones specifically tailored to the actor. He added: 'This is an honour, and something I can't wait to get stuck in to.'

Producer Adam Spiegel added in a press release: 'We are over the moon that Michael has agreed to launch the *Hairspray* tour for us. The show has been a huge success in London, not to mention around the world, and Michael has been a big, big part of the *Hairspray* story. It's doubly exciting that not only do more people around the UK now get to see his gorgeous Edna Turnblad, but we as a company get to work with Michael more closely than ever behind the scenes as we develop new work together.'

The *Hairspray* tour would open at the Cardiff Millennium Centre, where it was due to run from 30 March to 24 April 2010, before continuing through to 4 September in Glasgow, Southampton, Wolverhampton, Leeds, Manchester and Liverpool – with possible further dates to be announced. 'I didn't tell the show's other producers they had to open it in Cardiff, but I did suggest they think about it,' he said.

Yet Michael had to concentrate on his UK solo singing tour in September and October. It would start in Oxford and end in Plymouth and would be filmed for DVD release at the end of 2009. Dates at Birmingham, Cardiff and Brighton were also included. He was also further developing his concert routine and by 24 September 2009 when he played the ECHO arena in Liverpool – all part of his 25th anniversary celebrations – he had added to his normal 12-piece band and three backing singers by including a string section and he also promised various guest artists. The North Wales *Daily Post* reported Michael as saying: 'It's a more theatrical show that I'm putting together. It's the first time I'll have done the whole evening too, rather than having a support act, and I can choreograph the whole event.'

Michael caused a bit of a stir in the autumn of 2009 when he was questioned by Rick Fulton on the *Daily Record* as to whether he thought Susan Boyle, the Scots lass who came second on the popular ITV show *Britain's Got Talent*, could make it as a stage performer. She was at that point recording her debut album and said she wanted to follow her heroine Elaine Paige into London's West End.

But after a very public meltdown and some no-shows on the *Britain's Got Talent* tour, many felt that psychologically Susan could not cope with the pressure – and Michael agreed. 'Could she cut the stage life? I really don't think so,' he said. 'It takes professionalism and strict control of yourself and dedication to it. It's not an easy gig. You have to really want it. I watched that programme. It was wonderful to watch when she first came out. Good luck to her, whatever happens she is going to do well. But it's sustaining it. It's having the people around you who aren't just there to exploit you.'

Reflecting on Michael's years in the business, Universal Music TV managing director Brian Berg said: 'Ball is a multi-talented entertainer, from musicals to TV and radio to making records, and he has an amazing voice.'

More than 20 years since Michael first signed for Polydor on the back of his *Aspects Of Love* success – he has also spent time with both Sony and EMI, returning to Universal both times – Berg suspects that he may still have a gear or two left in him as far as record sales are concerned.

'He did well over 400,000 with the *Movies* album,' Berg told *Music Week*. 'He is normally good for at least 100,000 sales, and sometimes a quarter of a million or more. It is frustrating for us sometimes, when he is locked into a musical and he can't promote anything, but I think he has got a chance now to move it up another level.'

Michael's albums, much to Berg's frustration, did seem to have a strange habit of peaking at Number 11 on average in the UK charts, which is the sort of bogey that many people would not mind having. Even so, it is in his recording career that Michael possibly comes closest to underachieving. There has always been this feeling, perhaps unfairly, that he could have stretched himself much further.

'I got into this path of doing nice albums with a lot of covers on them and that sort of thing,' he told *Music Week* magazine. 'I enjoyed making those, but I think I could have spent more time exploring other avenues. I did record a few songs I wrote myself. I would never be a great singer-songwriter but I could have done more of that. I could have looked for better original material. But then those albums might have died a death and I wouldn't have had a contract.'

When asked about his longevity, Michael said: 'It should appear effortless, even if the reality is different from that. I'm quite lucky because quite a lot of people haven't lasted as long. I have never sold records in their multi-millions but I have always had a market, always had a bit of a following and always found new things to do. I haven't controlled it. I have had ideas. I hope I have got an instinct of the things I'm better at, but I have never had a game plan. I am an eternal pessimist – I think every gig is going to be the last, I think I'm always about to get found out. But I haven't been.'

A nice touch came in October when Michael broke off from his concert tour to officially open the Emma Dodd School of Performing Arts at the Kesgrave Community Centre in Suffolk. He was on a break from *Hairspray* and was more than happy to help Ipswich actress Emma, who was performing with him in the show at the Shaftsbury Theatre.

After watching the youngsters perform, he told the *Evening Star*: 'I didn't know what to expect today and I must say I have been bowled over by the talent in Suffolk. It is a testament to the drive and determination of these children that they have reached such a standard in such little time. They were fantastic. I am overwhelmed. It is so nice to watch talented kids on the stage.'

Emma, who had also appeared in the West End productions of *Evita*, *Chitty Chitty Bang Bang* and *Starlight Express*, said: 'It has been the biggest dream of mine for years and years to run my own theatre school and I can hardly believe it is coming true.'

Michael made a trip to Nashville to meet Dolly Parton in autumn of 2009 for a two-hour BBC Radio 2 special, which was also filmed. He had been on Broadway performing in *The Woman In White* when he bought tickets to see the country singer at Radio City Music Hall. He said to *Irish World*: 'She puts a show together the way I would. It's a journey, with lots of talking. And she is so versatile. She will crack you up, but then she will sing "Little Sparrow" and make you cry. I thought God, "I'd love to meet her". And the opportunity arose.'

Dolly greeted Michael at the pink gates of Dolly Central. He said: 'It was two hours of pure hero worship. I have a Dolly T-shirt, which I sometimes sleep in, and I got her to sign it for me. I gave her one of mine and she has promised she will sleep with me.'

On 16 October, it was revealed that from January 2010 Michael's workload with *Sunday Brunch* would be lessened – with Terry Wogan and him sharing the two-hour show. Michael would do four shows in a row and then Terry would do 12, and so on.

Also towards the end of 2009, Michael was only too pleased to pledge his support to the Shooting Star Children's Hospice, based in Hampton, west London. He told the charity magazine *Shine*: 'We are careful what we involve ourselves with, it has to be something we feel personally motivated by something where we see a difference happening. When we were introduced to Shooting Star and saw the work, we simply had to get involved. This place is absolutely incredible.'

Michael revealed that the first time he went there he did not really know what to expect. And he was devastated to learn that on that very day one of the children had died, producing as you would expect a tremendously sad atmosphere. So when he returned there was a lot more going on and he spent part of his time in the Sensory Room up to his neck in the ball pool.

He said: 'It does not feel like a sad place, a place of sickness. It feels like a place of life, a place of positivity. There are a lot of care professionals around, people who know what their job is and focus on putting the kids first.'

And he added: 'Everybody needs music therapy. I don't care if you're a one-day-old baby or a hundred-year-old great grandparent, we all respond to music, it is within us all. Whatever problems the kids are facing, the sounds are getting through and it has such a positive benefit. It's a way of bringing people together, it's a way of lifting spirits, of keeping the mind involved and interested. It is fantastic'

What Michael did for the charity was to organise a concert on 12 December to raise funds. He explained: 'We know a lovely school called Feltonfleet in Surrey and I went down to the school and talked to the Headmaster and persuaded him – I didn't give him much choice – to let us hold a concert in the grounds in aid of Shooting Star. Now it would have been much easier to go to a West End theatre or one of the concert halls, but I really wanted to make this different, to make it personal, so we are going to give a big "Michael Ball concert" with all the musicians, choirs and who knows what else for an intimate number, about 650 people. It's going to be great fun.'

CHAPTER 18

The Tide Has Turned

The profile and exposure Michael garnished following his success in *Hairspray* started opening all kind of doors, and normally nice ones at that.

He was asked, rather controversially, by ITV to stand in on the popular prime-time television offering *Dancing On Ice*. Head judge Robin Cousins was off to cover the Winter Olympics for the BBC in Vancouver, Canada, so Michael took the reins on 12 February 2010 with television 'sources' to counter the criticism insisting: 'Even though Michael isn't an ice dancer, he has had loads of theatre experience and will be judging the contestants on performance skills.'

But his main theatre focus was still *Hairspray*. He was refining his new role as associate producer while the finishing touches were put to the much-heralded UK theatre tour. The West End production, with comedian

Brian Conley having stepped in for Michael the previous summer, was to close on 28 March after more than 1,000 performances – becoming one of the most successful shows at the Shaftsbury Theatre in nearly 40 years. Just two days later at the Millennium Centre in Cardiff, the tour was to start.

Michael, Brian Conley and Michael Starke, best known for playing the role of Thomas 'Sinbad' Sweeney in the popular Channel 4 soap *Brookside*, were to share the role of Edna Turnblad as the show, with his schedule now finalised, hit the road – following its Welsh run from 30 March to 24 April to Glasgow, Southampton, Wolverhampton, Leeds, Manchester, Plymouth, Liverpool, Sunderland, Milton Keynes, Oxford, Birmingham, Dublin, Bradford and Edinburgh, which would mean that Michael and Cathy would see in the New Year north of the border.

Comedian Les Dennis, better known for hosting ITV's *Family Fortunes* game show, would take over as Wilbur Turnblad during the tour. He said: 'Michael and I have really hit it off. I think he is just the most brilliant performer. He has got a fantastic voice, a great sense of comic timing and he is a really good actor. He is just great to work with. And I get to snog him eight times a week.'

Michael was more interested in the production itself, saying: 'I am so excited to be bringing this show to Welsh audiences.'

His associate producer role presented him with an enormous challenge, with him working as much behind the scenes as at the front of house. He said: 'I will be producing a show for the first time and am really excited about that. I feel like I have learned so much in my career, and as you get older you want to pass it on. I am hoping it will be a new and on-going venture for me as producer and leading man. There are other shows I would like to be involved with, but I have really enjoyed working with the younger cast from *Hairspray* and helping them to grow a bit.'

Each new venue on tour brought another interview from Michael and he was always good value when talking to the regional press, newspapers such as the *Bristol Evening Post*, about Edna with comments along the lines of: 'I've had several husbands and I love them all. I'm looking forward to working with Micky Dolenz who'll be my husband in Bristol. I was a huge fan of The Monkees – wasn't everyone? And having met him, I know he is a genuine talent and a really funny guy. He looks like a great kisser, too.

'Quite often with a musical, the music is terrific but the story in between the songs is a bit of a let-down, yet this one is terrific in both respects. It's a lovely look at people who are forced to be excluded from society and how they are brought in through the dancing of a chubby girl. Women have been asking whether they could play the role of Edna, but if it were played by a woman it would be rather cruel. There are a lot of body-image jokes and it would be a bit uncomfortable if it were played by a woman.

'*Hairspray* is truly one of the greatest experiences of my career and the chance to have just a few more nights in those frocks was an opportunity I couldn't miss. I love everything about Edna. She would be great as my mum – I mean, I love my mum, but I do adore Edna Turnblad. Being Edna for a couple of hours each night is fine by me. Although, I think if I had to be a woman permanently, I'd rather be Carla Bruni.'

While Michael was tidying up those last-minute *Hairspray* tour jobs, which would keep him on his toes into the early part of 2011, he was also furthering the other areas of his career. There was no new solo album planned for 2010 – that would come with *Heroes* the following March – but his radio and upcoming television work would prove absorbing.

He said to *Wales Online*: 'The thing that is so good about the radio is people are not self-conscious. There is no live audience there, there aren't cameras and lighting breathing down your neck and you are not worried about how you look. It's just a chat, a conversation, and I want as much as possible to make it that relaxed.'

His *Sunday Brunch* programme had an audience of almost three million listeners and Michael had scored some notable hits. 'I was humbled that Melvyn Bragg talked for the first time in public about the suicide of his first wife when he came on the show. I was quite nervous, but he was very relaxed and revealing.'

And he negotiated some tricky situations as well. He added: 'There was an edgy moment with Bette Midler, who arrived at the studio jet-lagged and cold. She had some sort of a wrap folded round her hunched body, and it was clear she wasn't going to join in. But then I think she gradually realised what the show was all about. Off came the wrap, and she turned into the wittiest company you could imagine.'

With the *Hairspray* tour progressing nicely, Michael had a new breakthrough when on 24 June 2010 ITV1 Daytime announced that he was to host his own show for six weeks from 16 August to 24 September at 3pm daily. The programme was to be 'a topical mix of entertainment, discussion and showbiz glamour with the occasional musical treat thrown in from the man himself'.

It was a brave step forward. His chat shows in 1993 and 1994 had not been appreciated but his maturity now, he believed, could see him home this time. Michael said: 'This show is a great challenge, which I hope will be lots of fun and feature lots of old friends as well as some new ones. I'm really looking forward to getting started.'

David Hall, who was to be the series editor, said in a press statement: 'Michael is a showbiz legend – it's in his blood. He is an absolute natural in front of the camera, has incredible warmth, and this show promises to bring a smile to everyone's faces. It's the perfect afternoon treat.'

Michael, booked to follow antiques expert David Dickinson who was given by ITV just one series in this slot, added: 'I don't want people to be uptight during it, and I want to have fun elements in there that bring out the best in people. It is what the job is. To bring out the best in the guests that you have, whatever they are doing in whatever capacity, so that people at home want to share time with you.

'I've been a guest presenter on *This Morning* and other shows, and that gave me the confidence to try this. It will be an afternoon treat with celebrities, music, cooking and topical chat; and we will also be meeting some of Britain's unsung heroes – real people with real stories to tell. The show is a huge challenge, but I hope it will be lots of fun.'

Michael cited his ideal guest, rather surprisingly, as Camilla, the Duchess of Cornwall. 'She has had a fascinating life and I think she would be really funny, too. Everyone always gasps when I say this, and then they think about it. With A-list celebrities from a movie that is coming out, they are on a junket. They don't talk well. We know everything that they are prepared to share. It is kind of, "Whatever".'

But what new dimension would Camilla bring to an interview? Michael told *Wales Online*: 'You wouldn't expect it. I have no agenda when I'm interviewing. I'm not trying to stitch anybody up. I just want them to be comfortable and to be interesting.'

And he revealed to the *Daily Telegraph*: 'The night that Prince Charles and Camilla came to see *Chitty Chitty Bang Bang* was a memorable one. The car went into reverse instead of forward, and this huge piece of scenery, a huge boat, fell backwards and nearly flattened a stage-hand, smashing up the stage. We had to cancel the show. Afterwards we went to the royal retiring room and had a drink with Charles and Camilla instead of doing the rest of the show.'

Michael added about the task in front of him. 'I'm under no illusions. It may fall flat on its face. These things often do. But we might find something there,' he told the *Daily Record*. 'If I enjoy it, if ITV like it and there is an audience, we might even come back for more. I'm old enough and wise enough to know the first show isn't going to be the best one we ever do. It will get there, however. The trouble with this is there is no training. You are kind of winging it. But you surround yourself with good people, hold your nerve and hope it will be fine.'

And fine he was. This daytime slot had not long been vacated by Alan Titchmarsh, once billed as 'the thinking women's crumpet', who had worked hard to build an audience above the one million mark. Michael strode in and attracted 1.3 million viewers from day one and was powering towards 1.5 million during his second week.

Insiders could not really explain why Michael – who had taken a six-week break from his *Hairspray* tour commitments – had been so popular but his fanbase had obviously served him well with one colleague reporting: 'His fans love everything about Michael. On one occasion, he happened to mention he liked New Zealand wine. Now he has been given hundreds of bottles.'

Just prior to his venture back into daytime television, Michael appeared amongst a star-studded line-up at Syon Park, west London – joining the likes of Tony Hadley, comedian Bobby Davro and TV presenter Laurence Llewelyn-Bowen – for a party to celebrate the fifth birthday of the Shooting Star Hospice in Hampton, west London. Around £50,000 was raised from the event towards a charity that needs £3.5million a year to survive.

But Michael, since June, had been working on another project very dear to his heart. It had been on a break to his and Cathy's retreat in West Wittering that he took his mum Ruth to their local Chichester Festival Theatre to see the show *Love Story* – a musical adaptation of Erich Segal's 1970 award-winning movie starring Ali MacGraw and Ryan O'Neal. The film, directed by Arthur Hiller, was considered to be one of the most romantic of all time by the American Film Institute, not least because the leading lady Jenny falls in love but then is stricken down with leukaemia.

Michael thought the visit was 'a bit of a busman's holiday' but was immediately smitten by the production, saying: 'I loved it. It was on telly over Christmas when I was 12 and I sat there with my family and cried my eyes out. We were blown away by the show. The performances were outstanding, the music was great, and the story was handled with dignity.

Speaking to *The Times*, Michael said: 'It affected us deeply because Cathy's sister, Angela, died of ovarian cancer. When you have witnessed how cancer invades and destroys families, this musical is so moving. It was cathartic for us to watch this together. There wasn't this overhanging air of sadness throughout the piece, it was just a beautiful, life-affirming love story. It was very funny, too.'

This experience inspired Michael to phone Adam Spiegel, his friend and colleague at Stage Entertainment, who was the show's producer. Spiegel told him that he was thinking about taking it to the West End in London. Michael said: 'I told him he must.'

Spiegel asked him to come on board as a co-producer – along with him and Stephen Waley-Cohen – and Michael agreed immediately as 'this would give me more creative responsibility – and it will be my first time as a full producer, bring it on.'

So he moved into top gear to try to ensure *Love Story* – with the book and lyrics being written by Stephen Clark – was taken to the West End before the end of the year. 'It's like doing a huge jigsaw puzzle – booking the right theatre at the right time, making sure the actors we want are available, getting the director on board and opening before Christmas so we can cash in on the buzz of the Chichester run,' said Michael. 'It's up to us as producers to work on budgets, get investors and pay the bills.'

He invested his own money in the project – an amount

guestimated by Baz Bamigboye in the *Daily Mail* to be around £250,000. 'I feel passionate about this, it's hard when there isn't a lot of money around,' said Michael, who set up everything for the rehearsals and met with Howard Goodall, the composer, and Rachel Kavanaugh, the director, before the cast was chosen. This was all new territory for Michael, who admitted: 'We have had the odd shouting match but we all have the same goal.'

Peter Polycarpou, Emma Williams – who Michael had appeared with in *Chitty Chitty Bang Bang* – and Michael Xavier were signed up from the cast at Chichester, which had been a sell-out, and in November rehearsals started in 'a dodgy church hall' in Kennington, south London. Michael was battling to juggle his commitments to *Hairspray* with those of the *Love Story* project, not least making sure he was there when the previews got under way on 27 November.

The opening night went ahead at The Duchess Theatre in Catherine Street in London's West End on 6 December – and Michael said to *The Times*: 'I was thrilled by the audience reaction. At the end of the show, I heard all these snivels. It's a terrific sign. I'm really proud of my debut as a West End producer and I definitely want to do another. But nothing could ever stop me from performing.'

The show was booked through to 30 April and the reviews were not too damaging.

Zoe Craig, in the *London List*, wrote: 'What makes this little, domestic musical satisfying are the performances, and the melodies. Emma Williams gives Jenny Cavilleri just the right amount of bold spirit and humour; her singing voice is a complete pleasure; that she can act through these pretty songs is the icing on the cake. As Oliver, Xavier has less character to play with, but possesses another gorgeous voice, and can certainly do grief when he needs to. Yes, it's slushy. Yes, it's sentimental. Yes, the plot's stick-thin. But the talent on stage carries this love story for us. And if you like that kind of thing, we reckon it will for you, too. Bring tissues.'

Charles Spencer was qualified when he wrote in the *Daily Telegraph*: 'One show that has transferred, despite my giving it a pretty good drubbing when it opened in Chichester, is the stage musical version of *Love Story*. Even I am prepared to admit that Rachel Kavanaugh's stylish production is superior to the soppy film, and Howard Goodall's music is both haunting and tuneful. Meanwhile Stephen Clark's book and lyrics boast moments of wit amid the maudlin slush, and Emma Williams has great charm as the doomed Jenny. If you like the movie, then you will probably love this. But art, even popular entertainment, should aspire to something more than getting audiences to sob into their Kleenexes.'

The reality was that *Love Story* did prove popular and received three nominations in the 2011 Laurence Olivier awards – for Best New Musical, Best Actor for Michael Xavier and Best Actress for Emma Williams. As one of the songs from *Love Story* said 'The Tide Has Turned'. It certainly had for Michael, who was running up a most impressive list of all-round achievements.

With his responsibilities towards television, radio, *Hairspray* and *Love Story*, Michael had to shelve plans to do a concert tour in Australia in the autumn and he spent what little spare time he had in October and November working on his *Heroes* album, which was due out in March 2011. He also made two concert appearances – on 12 September in the *Elvis Forever* spectacular in London's Hyde Park, at which he sung 'You Don't Have To Say You Love Me', and on 3 October at the 25th Anniversary gala for *Les Misérables* at the O2 Arena in south London.

Once again, he had learned valuable lessons in the past 12 months, not least the intricacies of being a producer. 'To deal with actors, you understand what a pain in the arse they can be, and how fragile, and naughty, and frustrating and fabulous and exciting they are,' he said. 'I understand the management point of view and the actors' points of view. They can both come to me and I will treat every problem fairly.'

Michael dropped in to Shooting Star House for a special Christmas tea party, having performed a special concert, *Michael Ball and Friends*, at the Prince of Wales Theatre on 10 October which raised more than £105,000. Several Shooting Star families were invited to watch as Michael was joined on stage by Jason Donovan, Shooting Star patron Tony Hadley and Tony Christie.

On 8 December, BBC One Wales featured Michael on their *Coming Home* programme, which researched his family tree and uncovered his mum Ruth's family roots in Wales back to the mid-19th century, a real labour of love for Michael.

CHAPTER 19

The Worst Pies In London

Michael, by 2011, had now achieved a certain respectability about his whole show-business persona, a maturity that had moved him from being the curly-top juvenile lead heart-throb to having a huge legion of respectable fans and then on to a position within theatre circles of authority and grandeur. His movement into producing, and the qualified success of *Love Story*, plus his powers of organisation when it came to sorting out the *Hairspray* tour, had earned him a new status.

This was reflected when he was asked to co-host, with Imelda Staunton, his soon to be partner in *Sweeney Todd*, the 2011 Olivier Awards at the Theatre Royal, Drury Lane, in London's West End on 13 March.

Television was becoming more and more focused on Michael, following his successful ITV Daytime production the previous summer. And now he was wanted to step in for

Lorraine Kelly to guest host her early morning show *Lorraine* while she was off to Africa for *Comic Relief*. Michael said: 'I have to get up at 5am and be in the studio by 6am. I don't know how she does it.'

But the hours were not so bad that they could drive Michael back to smoking. He had now stayed away from the weed for almost five years and he was proud of the fact. 'When you've been a smoker for more than 30 years, you have to be philosophical about whether all the damage you've done will catch up with you one day,' he said.

'Even so, there is nothing that could ever make me wake up one day and think, "Oh, I do wish I hadn't given up smoking." It's like being released from prison. But I'm not one of those ex-smokers who hates being around smokers now. All I ever say, if the opportunity arises, is no matter how many times you've tried to stop before it's always worth one more try to see whether this is the one that works for you. For every cigarette you manage not to smoke your health will thank you. Without question, giving up smoking is the biggest thing I've done for my career and my life. I've never sung better in my life in a studio and it has never been easier.'

The spring was a strong time for Michael. Not only was he still chugging along with his BBC Radio 2 *Sunday Brunch* programme – he did 11 shows straight from January through to late March even though he was still sharing the role with Terry Wogan – but he was also able to release, on 14 March, his first solo album for two years and his 17th to date.

Heroes included the tracks: 'Let The Heartaches Begin', 'I'll Never Fall In Love Again', 'Play Me', 'Summer Wind', 'For The Good Times', 'Misty', 'When I Fall In Love', 'You Don't Know

Me', 'Weekend In New England', 'New York State Of Mind', 'Joanna', 'I Can't Help Falling In Love With You', 'He'll Have To Go, For Once In My Life' plus 'Avenues And Alleyways'.

His album dedication said: '*Heroes* is the album I've wanted to make for some time. It salutes/honours some of my all-time musical heroes – legendary performers who have influenced me and entertained millions of people over the years. I've chosen unashamedly old-fashioned, romantic songs that have stood the test of time, songs that touch on emotions and relationships, which are as relevant to listeners today as when they were written.

'I grew up hearing Sinatra, Mathis, Jim Reeves, Tony Bennett, Perry Como at home. I bought Manilow, Neil Diamond, Tom Jones, Billy Joel records in my teens and practised their vocal styles and their phrasing. I've learned to sing by listening to them and singing along with them. They have taught me how to perform, what makes good song and how studio singing is so entirely different from singing onstage.'

Michael also insisted that, after recording for 20 years, his voice 'is in the best shape it has ever been'. Speaking to the *Express* he added: 'The industry has dramatically changed and it's affecting all artists not just me. I have a loyal fanbase. I don't sell millions upon millions but what I do sell is constant. New artists that are produced on shows like the *X Factor* will sell millions on their first album, they make a second and then they are gone.'

He was not having a dig at the contestants on British TV talent shows, he was almost sympathising with them, explaining: 'I love *X Factor* and shows like it, but it is a cruel show. These artists have got a contract before they have even made a record. It's a harsh industry.'

Heroes was an immediate success for Michael, jumping straight into the album charts at a more than respectable number 10. 'I am happy with that,' he acknowledged.

Hairspray added more dates to its UK tour – at the New Wimbledon Theatre, south-west London, and at Bristol's Hippodrome – taking it through to 30 April – while *Love Story* rounded off its limited 10-week run on 26 February 2011. Michael could now focus fully on his 22 concerts, between 24 May and 26 June.

Though illness forced him to cancel the Nottingham gig on 8 June, he especially enjoyed his appearance in Liverpool on 4 June. The *Liverpool Echo* ran an article in which Michael expressed: 'The Empire is one of the first places I ever did a concert. It was my first tour, I think it was the first night or the second night, and that was the first time I experienced pandemonium at the stage door. And I've been coming back ever since. I love the Empire, it's a proper old theatre. It's got the atmosphere, it's a good size – it's one of my faves.'

Not that it mattered for his continuing BBC Radio 2 *Sunday Brunch* show but Michael was looking a lot slimmer these days – but this was important for his next stage challenge playing the demon barber in *Sweeney Todd*. Even if this character did have a lot to do with pies, he did not have the *Hairspray* excuse that he could put on weight 'for his art'.

Sweeney Todd, The Demon Barber Of Fleet Street – based on the 1973 play by Christopher Bond – had music and lyrics by Stephen Sondheim with the libretto by Hugh Wheeler. It had opened on Broadway at the Uris Theatre on

1 March, 1979 and ran for 557 performances. The musical tells the story of razor-wielding Benjamin Barker, alias Sweeney Todd, who returns to 19th-century London having spent 15 years imprisoned falsely abroad. He vows revenge after finding out from his former landlady, Mrs Lovett, that his wife poisoned herself after being raped by the judge who wrongly had him transported.

The casting seemed to be perfect. Mrs Lovett would be played by Imelda Staunton, an Oscar nominee for *Vera Drake* and known widely to film audiences for playing headmistress Dolores Umbridge in two *Harry Potter* movies. She would be making her long-awaited comeback to musicals that had earned her a Laurence Olivier Award 20 years previously in another Sondheim production, *Into The Woods*. Michael was fresh from his own Laurence Olivier success in *Hairspray*.

He had first put forward the concept of *Sweeney Todd* in February 2009. 'Doing the show was my idea and I got it going – it happened on my radio show,' he told the *Sunday Express*. 'Imelda came on and in between records I asked her if she fancied playing Mrs Lovett and she said, "All right then." But it has taken all of this time for us to get together. There was never anybody else considered or wanted.'

Michael explained to the *Chichester Observer* how he was first gripped by the production. 'I knew of the show and I knew the music, but I had never seen it until I was in New York. I was doing *The Woman in White* on Broadway and they were just starting the John Doyle scaled-down version of *Sweeney Todd*. Stephen Sondheim invited us to the dress rehearsal of the show. The show knocked the socks off me.

'First of all, it is the music. I think it is Sondheim's greatest work. I loved the production, but it made me wonder what it would feel like with a full orchestra and 26 voices and done on the big scale, which hasn't really been done since the original. It wasn't even a big success when it first ran in London. It's the *King Lear* of musical theatre, which is why I wanted to do it. On the back of *Hairspray*, it has taken me to both ends of the extreme, having to change myself in every way.'

Indeed, once the play had opened in Chichester, just as happened with his role as Edna Turnblad, there were complaints that Michael was not in the production; such was his transformation in appearance. He had lost almost two stone in weight and had grown a goatee beard as well as wearing a hair-piece so that he had straight black hair 'which I can flick to hide my face'. This gave him a psychotic, almost Hilter-esque appearance to accentuate the character's murderous madness.

The show was also a vocal challenge for Michael. 'I have a high baritone voice but I've awakened this bass baritone and can flip into the higher one when I need to,' he explained to the *Express*. 'This score requires the biggest vocal range I have ever had to use.'

The character Sweeney Todd is the archetypal anti-hero but Michael claims there is a noble quality about him, explaining to the *Chichester Observer*: 'He is not just a mental serial killer. He has been so abused by the system he suffers a kind of madness. Sweeney is this brooding menace. Imelda is deeply funny in this, edgy and very dark.'

Michael, who was appearing for the first time at The Chichester Festival Theatre despite having a home in the area since 1994, went to famous London barbers Trumpers to learn how to use a cut-throat razor. His mother Ruth told him that she really was not very keen on the beard he grew for the role. 'She said it made me look shifty. I said, "But I am playing Sweeney bloody Todd."'

The show opened to strong reviews on 24 September for its limited run through to 5 November. Michael said to the *Daily Express*: 'I couldn't be more proud and thrilled. It has just been a joy to do from beginning to end.'

Paul Callan in the *Daily Express* wrote: 'There can be no doubt that this is one of the best productions to come out of Chichester in recent years. Director Jonathan Kent is to be congratulated on giving us a memorable version of Sondheim's masterpiece. The circular stage throbs with movement, high emotion and humour. The performance last night seemed so overwhelming the audience just leapt to their feet and cheered. It was the triumphant pairing and performances of Michael Ball as the crazed Sweeney, and Imelda Staunton as the eccentric murderess Mrs Lovett. Together, they brought a new power to the show perfect for each other's exceptional artistry. Ball was immensely strong. He had to express not merely brutality, but also tenderness at the loss of the woman he loved. These he did perfectly. But it was Imelda who stole the evening. Her comic timing, sweetness of voice and ability to project humour into one of the stage's darkest roles was remarkable. A meaty show, indeed.'

And Baz Bamigboye wrote in the *Daily Mail*: 'The production is a huge hit, featuring two of the best performances in a musical this year.'

Big Baz revealed that the on-stage pies, so pivotal to the

plot, had caused quite a stir with the cast. Michael claimed they were 'horrible and greasy' and that he never touched them – which all seems in contrast to Mrs Lovett's boast that they are 'the best pies in London'. The cast sing a number 'God, That's Good' during which customers have to consume three pies. 'They actually eat them,' revealed Michael. After numerous cast complaints, the original filling was replaced with sweetcorn and spicy tomato, to give the filling a realistically grisly appearance. Michael was still unimpressed.

But all this did not stop the production transferring on 10 March 2012 to the Adelphi Theatre in London's West End for a 26-week pre-set run, scheduled to end on 22 September. The producers behind *Sweeney Todd* worked closely with director Jonathan Kent and Chichester producer Alan Finch to create a model that would have the ability to move easily to London. And the £2million budget was impressively low for the West End.

Michael was delighted as he had always wanted to worked with Imelda, saying in an interview with the *Daily Mail*: 'She's the consummate actress and I wanted to be in her league. We've developed this telepathic connection, working together.'

He had come to the end of 2011 and the conclusion to yet another higher successful year. Such was the accolades for *Sweeney Todd* that Chichester Festival Theatre in January 2012 got voted Britain's top regional theatre.

The production transferred successfully to the Adelphi Theatre, opening on schedule on 10 March with Henry Hitchings writing in the *London Evening Standard*: 'If you think you know Michael Ball, think again. The popular lyric baritone is almost unrecognisable as the demon barber of Fleet

Street, the pale-skinned psychopath whose murderous passions are the dark heart of Stephen Sondheim's classic musical.

'It's a chilling performance, sinister and saturnine. Ball is usually associated with warmth and a dimpled, chummy charm. Here, bearded and with an unfamiliar side parting, he is a revelation as the gory slasher whose desire to avenge a wrongful conviction turns into a crusade. And he conveys with a lovely, sonorous strength the malign urges that define Sweeney as he turns customer service into a contact sport. This is an atmospheric Sweeney Todd, an unsettling musical thriller made razor-sharp by its two superb leads. When Ball and Staunton aren't on stage we are impatient for their return.'

As Michael celebrated his 50th birthday on 27 June 2012, some of his fans had been a bit freaked out by his sudden weight loss, but he insisted to *whatsonstage*: 'They have been shocked and surprised but the response has been good because I wanted to shake up what I do.'

The fans have always meant so much to him. He has shown them great respect, supporting not only the official fan club but also other related organisations as well as having his own *michaelball.co.uk* site. There was even a fanzine at one stage that came out three times a year and lasted for more than 12 years.

Michael told *Yours* magazine in February 2011: 'My fans mean everything to me. I always make a point of signing autographs at the end of each show. I chat to them like friends, which many of them have become. It is why I don't surround myself with an entourage. I like direct access to the people who made me what I am. I know how important they are and

I like to repay that loyalty. I do have the most loyal fans – they have been absolutely great.'

The Colchester, Essex-based Michael Ball Fan Club is endorsed by him officially. It boasts more than 4,500 members and has been run by Gill Oakley and Maureen Wilkinson-Rouse since it was founded in April 1992. With members in Europe, USA, Australia, New Zealand, Canada, Hong Kong and South Africa, they aim 'to keep members up to date with information concerning Michael's activities as well as providing a means for fans to keep in contact with each other'.

Kerstin Wohlgemuth and Julia Sedat have been mad on Michael since 1999 and run an extremely detailed *JustBall.net* site, having seen him perform over 200 times between them. This *JustBall* site provides a wealth of detail on Michael's career, detailing the theatre performances, concerts, albums and newspaper clippings – as well as upcoming dates. The pair, who call themselves Ball's Bunnies, met on the Michael Ball Fan Club forum. They write: 'Only weeks later we came up with the mad idea, "Let's do a website." You should have seen the looks we got by the people around us. A website? You could tell most people thought, well they won't last long.

'Was it worth the work, the trouble? Yes it was. We made many friends through *JustBall.net*, which initially started off as *Balliosi.co.uk*. We've matured and so has the website.'

Michael does appear rather fed up with the 'housewives' favourite' put-down, saying to *The Times* newspaper in an interview: 'You will always get lazy journalists and if they want to be really disparaging, it's "Darling of the blue-rinse brigade." I don't know if anyone has blue rinses any more but it's a little tag you can stick on.'

Yet he is realistic about his fans, admitting: 'A lot of people who follow what I do are certainly women of a varying age range.'

And he accepts that people react in many different ways. 'Well, I don't like the letters where people go a bit mad,' he told *Best* magazine. 'The ones who tell me they have contacted my granny from beyond and she has told them I need to leave Cath and go and live with them. And while it's flattering, I'm not over keen on the knickers.'

There is also all manner of Michael Ball merchandise on sale, from branded T-shirts and bags to mugs and key rings as well as calendars, programmes and brochures at each of his shows and concerts.

Michael has, in the main, been stalker-free, though there was the incident with the woman who insisted on seeing him at the Prince of Wales Theatre in London's West End in 1989 only to drop a large carving knife from her bag. This prompted police to rush to the scene, but fortunately the situation ended peacefully.

However, he did have one rather worryingly 'freaky' experience just before he went to New York to make his Broadway debut in 1990. He is quoted on the fansite *JustBall.com* saying: 'I was talking to my girlfriend on the phone. I just got back to the flat after doing the show at night and, as I'm talking, I'm closing all the curtains in the house, listening and talking for about 20 minutes. I put the phone down, it rang again and this girl's voice went: "Why have you closed all the curtains in your flat? I can't see you now."'

To illustrate Michael's loyalty to his fans, he tells the story – reported on the *Justball.net* site – of the night before an album of his was due to be released in a central London record store. He said: 'Cathy and I wanted to see the pictures in the window. All excited, we drove past, and we saw these two lovely girls, sitting outside in Michael Ball T-shirts at one o'clock in the morning with their sleeping bags, and all their things around them, surrounded by some very dodgy characters in London's Piccadilly and they were obviously terrified. So we just snuck in and put them in a hotel around the corner. Bless them, they were back outside the shop again at six o'clock in the morning.'

So do all his female fans, given that he is in a relationship with Cathy, simply want to mother him? 'I'm not sure it's mothering they want to do,' he told *The Times*. 'At least, that's not how my mother mothered me – I'm not doing Oedipus. People say, "Don't you think it is sad that you see the same people coming to every night of every show?" And I say, "No, why the hell not? There is a camaraderie." It's two-way traffic. I'm just very open. I'm not afraid to show emotion and I like people to show me their emotion.'

CHAPTER 20

I Don't Want To Miss A Thing

When you look back at footage of the fresh-faced 26 year-old Michael Ball bounding up to collect his first award – for Most Promising Artiste from the Varity Club in 1989 – you realise what a very different man he is today and exactly how much has happened for him in those intervening years. 'A Boy From Nowhere', a number from the musical *Matador* that he sung on his 2001 *Centre Stage* album, grew into a most talented performer who reached the pinnacle of his profession.

In 2009, Michael celebrated 25 years in show business. And in 2012 as he reached the ripe old age of 50, success on stage, with albums, in concerts, on television and radio had become every day occurrences for him.

With that landmark birthday on the horizon, he told *Yours* magazine: 'Although I tasted success almost fresh out of drama

257

school, I was prone to bouts of depression in my 20s. I'm now convinced that a boy doesn't become a man, doesn't truly find himself, until he is heading for his 30s. I'm confident enough now not only to stop and smell the roses but to appreciate them. I'm happy at home, happy at work, I never stop pinching myself, because it will change. Things do. So my mantra now couldn't be more simple: Relish the day.'

Michael added: 'My mum said to me that I had changed since winning the Laurence Olivier Award for *Hairspray*. And she is right. I've acquired an inner strength. There's no need for bravado anymore. I take nothing for granted and it could all end tomorrow, but, in truth, that doesn't seem very likely. I am a workaholic, I love performing and trying new stuff.'

So what is 'Michael the man' really like? Behind the stage paint and without the fat suits? When there is no song to be sung?

Once the show is over and Michael can squirrel himself away in the haven of either his home in Barnes, south-west London, or his retreat at West Wittering, West Sussex, his tastes are simple, with him insisting through his forties that he preferred the company of Cathy to wild partying and claiming he found himself happier with a glass of single malt whisky than a barrel load of beers.

In his younger days, he had admitted to *Saga* magazine: 'When I drink too much, I get a bit giggly. I get too loud, dance and then fall asleep.'

But as he moved into his late 30s and 40s, Michael acquired a love of wines and stocked up his own wine cellar, saying to the *Sunday Telegraph*: 'I like New World wines from New Zealand and the Marlborough region. I love the whole social thing around it too, sharing bottles and discovering new tastes together.'

Yes, he rated 'sleep' as one of his 'likes' but during the waking hours cooking is a particular favourite of his. 'I love it,' he told entertainment guide *Ents24.com*. 'Before I started the radio show, I used to cook Sunday lunch for family and friends. Now I do it in the evening. There is nothing more satisfying than producing a huge roast with all the trimmings; I'm a big fan of organic food and I like to buy all my meat and vegetables from the local shops. I also love walking the dogs. We go to the nearby park where they have been known to chase deer and end up in the pond.'

When Michael and Cathy decided to move in together, he was living in West Hampstead and she was living with daughter Emma in Barnes, which is about seven miles from the West End of London. Having lived previously in the capital at Cricklewood, Kilburn and Finsbury Park, Michael was rather 'against moving to south London', but he swallowed his pride, gave up his flat and headed the eight miles to the other side of the Thames at the behest of his good lady. After that, he admitted that he 'fell in love with the area'.

In October 2007, he told *The Times on Sunday*: 'Barnes is a proper old village with everything you might need. I know all the shopkeepers. We have a fabulous family butcher, a greengrocer, fishmonger and cheese shop. We also have White Hart Lane, a row of gorgeous shops in Mortlake. I love looking in The Dining Room Shop and Tobias And The Angel.'

Michael loves the open spaces of Barnes, where he and Cathy could walk their beloved Tibetan terriers. He added:

'Nice areas of London are often surrounded by dodgy places, but Barnes isn't like that. I walk the dogs at night and never see any trouble. It's quite an arty area. We live next door to Andy Bown, from Status Quo, and there are quite a few business types. There is a brilliant studio Olympic, where I've recorded nearly all my stuff. It's so close I could run a microphone lead to it from my bedroom.'

Michael simply feels at home in this part of the world, admitting to a sense of belonging having lived there so long now. He told local magazine *The Green*:'I love being by the river. You cross Hammersmith Bridge and your shoulders go down. I'm a home boy. Barnes has a real sense of community. People leave you alone, they are not nosy. I like having people round, then going to Riva and walking back for coffee and a late night. It's our local Italian but happens to be one of the best restaurants in London.

'The downside is that Barnes does not have a Tube, but I normally drive or take the bus. If the traffic is not too bad, I can be in the West End in 20 minutes. The only other drawback is that it's on the Heathrow flight-path. But in north London we had knife crime, so I'll stick with the planes.'

His Barnes home is more often than not plastered with *Post-it* notes. 'They are the usual, everyday messages, filled with the stuff of two busy people's lives,' he said.

One note he clearly forgot to read led to an amusing encounter with a plumber. The story goes that a tradesman called Wally, who was nearly 70 and semi-retired, was asked by one customer to help out a friend. Wally, and his even older assistant Bert, turned up at the designated house to be greeted by Cathy. She directed them to the upstairs en suite but told them to be quiet as they worked because her partner was asleep. But as the two plumbers tried to locate the fault, making considerable noise in the process, a furious Michael appeared in his dressing gown and ordered the two men to get out. 'Well sir,' said an indignant Wally, 'Love changes everything but it ain't going to change that bleeding shower valve. Come on Bert, we're leaving.'

The place where Michael knows he won't be disturbed – and where perhaps he feels completely at ease – is at the home that he and Cathy share in West Wittering, West Sussex, eight miles south of Chichester.

He told *The Times*: 'It takes only an hour and a half to get there on the A3 yet it is worlds away from the bright lights of the capital. All the best decisions I've made have been made there.'

When Michael first got together with Cathy, they were desperate for a bolthole. They lived first in Bosham and then Itchenor before finding their ideal home in West Wittering, just 14 miles south from Singleton, where his mother Ruth lived until 2010 when she moved to the centre of Chichester, and 22 miles from sister Katherine, who lives in Stedham.

The draw to this part of the world for Michael – who after all grew up in the West Midlands, Dartmoor in Devon, South Africa, Plymouth and Farnham – is enormous. He said in *The Times* interview: 'The attraction is that it is "proper England". I love it. Family is here, which is great. I suppose it just feels like home to me. I've loved West Wittering since going there first as a child and then when I was at drama school, when a gang of us used to pile down there in a car for the weekend.

'It's a real sense of getting away. And when people do

recognise me, they are very nice. I think people have just got used to me being there. They are very happy to let us get on with our lives. People are very affectionate. They will ask for a picture or an autograph, which is great by me, but they just let us get on with it. In Chichester, which is a lovely city, they are used to people from television or the theatre walking around.'

West Wittering provides Michael with the perfect place to get in touch with 'normality'. The beach is popular with surfers and swimmers. So does he swim in the sea? 'You bet,' he replied. 'Whenever possible, though admittedly not in January. Outside the peak season it's so quiet and peaceful. Our dogs can go mad on the beach. You're also close to the South Downs. A visit to West Wittering just puts my brain into gear somehow.'

Normality for Michael, who even kept a boat down in that part of the world for a while, is having fish and chips from the local Boathouse restaurant after a stroll with Cathy. 'When you are walking along the quiet beach with the sun breaking through, you can't beat it,' he added. 'It feels safe here, too. It's a healthy environment. I listen to the waves crashing onto the beach, breathe in the clean sea air and just get in touch with nature.'

The fact that the nature is close to his loved ones adds to the lure. Michael has a great sense of family, an aspect of life nurtured by the care of his parents – even if he did feel rather isolated as a teenager – and a strong bond with his brother Kevin and sister Katherine.

His father Tony, who was made a Member of the British Empire in 1986 for his outstanding services to industry, is a most accomplished orator, with the *Daily Mail* newspaper calling him 'the top after-dinner speaker in the country'. He describes himself as a motivator and broadcaster.

Tony started his four-year apprenticeship on the shop floor with the Austin Motor Company in 1951 and rose through the ranks to become UK car sales manager within 11 years. A Freeman of the City of London and a Lord's Taverner, he was awarded the Prince Philip Medal for his life achievements. He has acted as marketing adviser to the Secretary of State for Energy and his numerous broadcasts include guest appearances on radio and television celebrity chat shows, documentaries and as a panellist on BBC's *Any Questions*.

His website claimed that he is 'noted for his irrepressible humour as well as his profound practical experience of marketing and management at the highest levels. Tony's speeches are always forward thinking and tailor-made individually to suit each different occasion. He always leaves his audience highly entertained as well as enlightened and motivated.'

Victor Kiam, the late American entrepreneur who was famous for promoting his own Remington products in the UK, once said: 'Tony gave the greatest, most entertaining speech I have ever heard.'

And Thames Television, in one introduction, paid him this accolade: 'Tony is acknowledged internationally as one of Britain's top marketeers and most popular public speakers – a brilliant motivator, humorist and raconteur.'

His accomplishments include devising and staging the opening and closing ceremonies of the Rugby World Cup at the new Millennium Stadium in Cardiff as well as the

Cricket World Cup and the European Cup ceremonies at Wembley Stadium for the Football Association. He also staged the British International Motor Show for the Scottish Motor Show, the centenary celebrations for the world's Motor Industry in Britain, the Lloyds Bank Playwright of the Year Awards, the ceremonies for numerous FA Cup finals, the 125th Anniversary Celebrations of the RFU, the Five Nations Championships and major internationals at Twickenham, as well as the Ceremony for the opening game at the new Stade de France in Paris for the FFR, the French rugby union federation.

Michael told *Woman's Weekly* in December 1994: 'My Dad and my brother Kevin own a marketing consultancy and my little sister Katherine works there as a secretary. I have a very special relationship with them all. They make the point that I'm much the same as I've always been. I don't know if I've changed or not, but then it's not for me to say.

'My dad wanted to be an actor, but his parents wouldn't let him – he had to get a trade. So when I told my parents I wanted to go to drama school and be an actor, they were thrilled. I guess I'm lucky enough to have the career he wanted. In the beginning, I was hopeless at business and my family advised me until I got savvy enough. I'm a lot more canny now – I am not the wide-eyed innocent who got the lucky break.'

Michael and Tony's careers have crossed on occasions. Tony was part of the organising team for the opening ceremony at the 1999 Rugby World Cup, at which Michael sang, and there was also a rather embarrassing escapade in October 2000 when both were invited to the ceremony to witness the final Mini motor car rolling off the production line at the Longbridge plant in the Midlands, where Tony first worked.

Michael has often joked about his first car being a red Mini called Poppy, adding in an interview with the *Birmingham Post*: 'Rumour has it that I was conceived in the back of one just ask my father about his bad back.'

When asked to attend together for the historic send-off, Michael said: 'I am thrilled to be involved with this monumental and historic day. The Mini has featured throughout my life.'

But matters did not go to plan. Michael and Tony claimed they had been promised they could drive the final model off the Birmingham production line but, at the 11th hour, they were told they should publicise the new Rover 75 while the honour of taking the Mini driving-seat would go to pop singer Lulu. Tony fumed: 'We have no connections with the 75. This totally undermined the whole purpose of our being there. It is just so very sad that moving the goalposts at the very last minute ruined what would have been a happy, historic day.'

Michael more diplomatically said: 'I had no problem with Lulu driving the Mini, in fact she is a very good friend of mine.'

All Rover would say was: 'It was a misunderstanding and a degree of not enough compromise.'

Michael is very close to his mother, Ruth, too. In 1991, He did his first-ever solo concert in Bedford Park in North Devon, near to where the family used to live, to support their local parish church that needed a renovation.

His siblings keep clear of the spotlight. Kevin was married for many years but divorced in 1990. With his ex-wife, he has two girls who were born in the early Eighties. Katherine is married for the second time and gave birth to James in December 2001.

Ruth and Tony divorced in 1997 and Tony married a lady called Jan Kennedy in 2000. Michael told *Woman's Weekly* in 2004: 'I think we had seen the divorce coming for some time but it was tough. A part of me thought they would soldier on. It's their lives, though, and they are both now terrifically happy. From my point of view, if this was the way it was going to happen, let it do so as peacefully and as maturely as possible. I was at pains not to take sides. It's an obvious thing to say, but your parents parting does not stop them being your mum and dad. I was already a grown man, so it didn't affect my own attitude towards relationships.

'The best thing they taught me was how I should accept everyone on an equal footing, without social, class or cultural barriers, and to treat everyone the same.'

Despite the love for his close family, having them at his shows does cause him concern. He explained to the North Wales *Daily Post*: 'I never allow them to sit near the front in case I see them. It's a horrible feeling seeing them, it really is. It makes me feel they would say, "Mike, we know it's you, stop showing off." You know they would never do it but your mind is kind of going for it – it is a tricky situation. It's like when you're a kid and you go over the top and they say, "Stop showing off, or there will be slapped legs, let the others have a go, why does it always have to be you?" If you are running around on stage and playing up to the audience, you just need to catch someone's eye and it will destroy the magic.'

But Michael overcomes any fear of chiding because of his

love of performing, especially in stage musicals. He can't decide which he likes the most; the first day of rehearsals, the first night of the show or the last night? 'They are fabulous and awful in equal measure,' he told *Westendtheatre.com*.

'The first day of rehearsals is exciting because you're like the new boy at school, everyone's getting together for the first time and there's great expectation in the air because you don't know what to expect. The first night is really exciting and supremely nerve-racking at the same time. Then on the last night of a show, you experience a mixture of emotions from elation to sadness.'

Michael is serious about his theatre, especially when it comes to musicals. He derides what he calls 'jukebox musicals', and said in an interview with the *Sunday Telegraph*: 'Some of them have been great. *Mamma Mia* was lovely but do we really want one based on the hits of Kylie? No, of course we don't. Those really bad jukebox musicals demean the whole thing.'

And the whole thing is that he relishes the depth to genuine musicals. 'So many people dismiss the entire art form through highbrow snobbery, but I think a lot of those people would be surprised if they actually saw some,' he said. 'Musicals are not two-dimensional froth. Take Stephen Sondheim, his work is as cleverly written, structured and profound as you will find in any writer.'

Michael is one of the few musical actors to have distinguished himself equally performing the works of both Baron Lloyd Webber and Stephen Sondheim, who many might contest are 'polar opposites' as songwriters.

'I'm very lucky that I've got to work with both,' Michael

said in his 2005 interview with *Playbill*. 'I was in Andrew's 50th party concert at the Albert Hall in 1998. That same year I was in a special show called *Hey, Mr. Producer*, a celebration of Cameron Mackintosh's work. There was a Sondheim section, and Cameron asked if I'd be part of it. I had already recorded "Losing My Mind" from *Follies*, which is one of my favourite songs of Steve's. But I hadn't yet done a particularly traditional treatment of it. Steve said he wanted me to do it absolutely straight, the way it was heard in the original show, which I was delighted about.'

Michael was honoured to work directly with Sondheim on the number, just the two of them and a pianist in a tiny room. He described it as 'an hour-and-a-half masterclass on this song'. And he added: 'I came away knowing every nuance – why he wrote everything that he did, why every note was in its place, why the phrasing was like this. Can you imagine how thrilling that was? And he is so articulate in explaining his work. You can be under no illusion why something is there. When you have that understanding, that is when his work opens up to you.'

Michael, writing in the *Guardian* in March 2010, expanded on his admiration for Sondheim, explaining: 'The first time I encountered Stephen was like everyone else, through snatches of old songs people performed in drama school, through "Send In The Clowns", which everyone knew.

'I wasn't aware at the time that he was the writing force behind *West Side Story* and *Gypsy*. It often gets forgotten, because people think of Sondheim purely in terms of making difficult, highbrow music, which he did. But as a lyricist, he also worked on some of the most popular musicals ever.'

Michael seems to have a very strong understanding of Stephen as a person, adding: 'I think he himself would agree, somewhat, that he has been a tortured soul throughout much of his life, and has found it hard to be on a search for happiness. A lot of brilliant artists are conflicted in the same way and it informs their work. It's not an irony that he works in musicals, it's ignorant to believe the form only works on a cheery, superficial level.

'Sondheim has never written typical musicals – the kind made famous in the US in the 1940s and 1950s – he writes about the human condition, with layer upon layer of depth. His is musical theatre – like plays with music – not musical comedy, and there's a big difference. It is also why his legacy is so important: Stephen Sondheim changed the face of the medium.'

Michael revealed that Sondheim is a 'very funny, very dry and very shy man' and that he never witnessed any 'diva-ish moments'. He said that, being a modest man, he always seemed so thrilled that people were doing his work.

Baron Lloyd Webber and Sondheim were born on the same day, almost two decades apart – and Michael put into perspective the well-documented rivalry between the pair by claiming: 'It is said that Sondheim would have loved Lloyd Webber's commercial success and, likewise, Lloyd Webber would give his left leg for a share of Sondheim's critical acclaim.'

When it comes to West End producers, Michael is surprised that they do not try to build more names, to create their own fount of publicity and showmanship.

He told the *California Chronicle* in 2009: 'Producers should invest time in creating stars but they tend to shy away from it and I think it's foolish, because if you get the right title with the right star name in the right theatre and it is a good production, you have always got a really good chance of succeeding. There is no guarantee that you will, but the odds are there. In order to become a name that could go above the title, I had to go away from the theatre and do other things. I had to make the records and do the concerts.'

Michael has never denied being in touch with his feminine side. He constantly made jibes about his good fortune to be wearing women's clothes while playing in *Hairspray*, but this was always done in a way to poke fun at the practice of men dressed as women, with him saying that it was just part of the theatre.

When Gloria asked him in 2000 if he would like to be in a Hollywood musical, he laughed and replied: 'I would even play Gipsy Rose Lee and pretty well actually.'

When he appeared in a Sondheim gala, he revealed to *German Musicals* magazine: 'I was allowed to open and end with "Beautiful Girls", "Loving You" and "Broadway Baby". I once more noticed that the best songs are always written for the female parts of the shows. Songs like "With One Look" from *Sunset Boulevard* and "Don't Rain On My Parade" from *Hello, Dolly!* are simply gorgeous but are originally written for women.'

Michael, like a lot of actors, is extremely superstitious and, when a show is successful, he tries to follow the same routines every time he gives a performance. 'None of us quite knows why something works, but you try to do everything you can to replicate that success,' he said. 'I really am a bit odd. I do lots of finger-tapping before I go on. I have to suck a sweet at a certain time, have a drink at a certain time, and nobody is allowed to whistle backstage. The last thing my dresser has to say to me is, "Are we smelling nice for the ladies and gentlemen?" I always get dressed in a certain order and I have to do "high-fives" with various members of the stage crew.'

Michael has always got nervous before performing, though he learned how to control this. He told *Radio Gloucestershire* in 2001: 'I get really strung out, I become really tired, and I can't stop yawning. So I go to bed for an hour. There is a little sort of cot thing in the dressing room. I go to sleep for an hour. And I just keep really, really quiet. I try to keep it focused. And then about 10 minutes before I go on stage, I do a bit of a vocal warm-up. I get all the company and the cast around and we have a "Madonna moment." We all hug each other and say a prayer and then we all shout "Madonna". It's taking the mickey. You see in the *In Bed With Madonna* video, they all get round and cuddle and pray together.'

Michael loves being mischievous during interviews, which endears him to presenters and journalists. He will joke that the best things to calm nerves before a show is 'a bottle of vodka' and claims that he 'throws three valium' down his throat. He also remarked once: 'I'm terrible. I don't have singing lessons. I don't do the best things for my voice. But it is kind of like any muscle – the more you use it, the stronger it gets. Actually, I shouldn't have said that, should I?'

Michael revealed in 2004 that he gets more nervous if he has to sing at a friend's wedding or a family party. He explained to the North Wales *Daily Post*: 'They say, "Oh, Mike, will you go up and give us a song." Then that's the worst kind of fear. Especially if it's in a church and everyone is there in their hats smiling nicely. That is when I

CHAPTER 21

From Here to Eternity

So what does Michael prefer – the stage and the musical theatre or the solo concerts that have become so much a part of his life in recent years? 'They both have their merits,' he told the *Daily Record*. 'Being part of a company in a West End musical is a totally different vibe to singing with a band. With a concert, it is just you that the crowd are focused on, so what you present to the audience is down to you. It's magical, the best kick in the world. It's why so many artists get into trouble with drugs, because they try to recreate that buzz. You don't know what to do with yourself after a high like that and that is what can get you into trouble.'

Millions like to listen to Michael's music but what music does Michael like to listen to? He told the *Daily Express* his favourite albums are: Barbra Streisand's *Guilty*, Joni Mitchell's *Court And Spark*, John Martyn's *Solid Air*, Pink

Floyd's *Dark Side Of The Moon*, Abba's *The Album* and The Carpenters' *Close To You*.

He explained: '*Guilty* captures Barbra at her very best vocally and the teaming of her with the Bee Gees was just inspired. All of the songs work like a dream. Joni is the greatest female singer-songwriter in my book. I love pretty much everything she has ever done. This album features some of her finest songs, simple but magical.'

Michael went on to explain what a big John Martyn fan he is and explained that *Dark Side Of The Moon* is his favourite Pink Floyd album. Abba are also one of his favourites, while he said of Karen Carpenter that 'no one has ever sung quite so beautifully'.

But when it comes to his iPod, the song Michael plays the most is the Supertramp number "If Everyone Was Listening". He said to *Playbill* in an interview: 'The lyrics have always meant a lot to me.'

His favourite song is the Baron Lloyd Webber composition '*Gethsemane*' from the musical *Jesus Christ Superstar*, which he first saw as a youngster. 'It is an incredibly powerful song and I absolutely love singing it onstage when I'm on tour,' he said.

When it comes to performers, Michael is a huge Joni Mitchell fan but it is Frank Sinatra who for him is 'the quintessential singer'. He added: 'With that voice and his unique delivery, I think his standard remains untouched.'

Michael names Woody Allen's 1994 offering *Bullets Over Broadway* as his favourite movie of all time, saying to *Playbill*: 'I just love it. It's funny, witty and it boasts superb performances by a great cast including John Cusack and

Dianne Wiest. I love that it cocks a snook at actors and the pretentiousness about putting on a new play.'

He is also a huge fan of vampire movies but is not over-struck on the *Twilight* series of films, claiming to the *Daily Record* that they are really 'a bit dull'. He adds: 'This is kind of "vampire light". Nothing happens. They just look at each other. Another long, lingering look and I think, "Just bite her."'

In life, Michael has his own private traits and nuances. He regrets not learning to play the piano and not being able to tap dance, and he seems to feel rather guilty about splashing out on a Cartier watch. He jokes that Johnny Depp should play him in a movie about his life – and claims the three things he can't live without are his iPad – 'I love it' – his passport – 'it never leaves my side because you never know' – and moisturiser – 'I've worn so much stage make-up in my time, if I didn't cleanse and moisturise I would have the skin of a rhino'.

He added: 'I always take off my stage make-up because I'd frighten people if I didn't, and I cleanse, tone and moisturise when I can be bothered. Also, a visit to the steam-room is a brilliant way of getting rid of any last traces of stale stage make-up.'

Michael, at points in his life, admits to having been obsessed with watching television, and would sit in front of everything from the soaps, such as the BBC's *EastEnders* and ITV's *Coronation Street*, to the reality shows, though he did promise in 2009: 'I have made a conscious decision to stop watching *Big Brother*. I was an avid fan but I felt it was time to move on.'

When it comes to motoring – and he admits to driving too fast – a satnav is very important to him. When fame came, he bought himself a top of the range £40,000 Porsche convertible but guilt about the state of the planet saw him down-size to a Mini Cooper, saying: 'I love it. It's big enough for my two dogs. It's so economical and looks beautiful.'

Such has been Michael's dedication to his work, and perhaps also his great sense of family, that it was 2007 before he managed to escape Britain for his first ever festive-season holiday. He got away to the Bahamas with Cathy for two weeks, leaving behind him the rigours of his role on stage as Edna Turnblad in *Hairspray*.

Prior to travelling, he said to *The Times*: 'I've booked what is my idea of the perfect holiday – a stay on the island of Eleuthera in a private villa with friends and family. I can't wait to get on that sun-lounger with a good book and give my back a rest from the high heels and fake boobs. We'll have our own beachfront and be quite isolated. You can drive to some restaurants nearby, and there's a bar owned by Lenny Kravitz, which is where we'll probably end up for New Year.'

Michael was certainly looking forward to that vacation but he has always given the impression of not being a big holiday person. And, indeed, he admitted earlier in that year that he had hated a previous trip to the Caribbean. He said: 'I went to St Barts on the most expensive holiday in the history of mankind a couple of years ago.

'St Barts is a playground for the rich and idle, and I didn't fit in because I'm neither rich nor idle. It is a beautiful place, but even the local shops sell Gucci and Yves Saint Laurent, which isn't my cup of tea. It was the kind of holiday where you can get away from it all, but only if you've got your own yacht. Cathy and I couldn't find a meal for less than £70 a head. We had been eating in posh restaurants, night after night, and they would bring out the *amuse-bouches* as a pre-pre-starter. We felt like saying, "Oh, don't bother about the rest of the meal, we'll just have that."

'Our hotel was very swanky but I wouldn't go back there – I like my holidays to be less Gucci. I can get all the glitzy shops and restaurants I need in London. When I'm on holiday, I like things to be simple and unostentatious.'

St Barts was not the only nightmare for Michael – Barbados in 2001 did not seem much better. He told *The Times*: 'I'd never return there. The last time we visited there were so many people I recognised and knew from my working life that the holiday was more like being on a works outing. If someone had dropped a bomb on the place, the British light-entertainment industry would have been wiped out. There was a well-known comedian shouting because he couldn't get a wet-bike, there were agents handing out cards over breakfast, there were people at Sandy Lane and the Lone Star dressed up for dinner in Chanel outfits and wigs in the sweltering heat. It was the sort of holiday where I had to swim out to a pontoon to avoid everyone, and I would end up lying there all day and getting sunburnt.'

But Michael insists he is easily pleased when it comes to holidays, so long as he can avoid crowds. 'I just need to be at an airport to catch an aeroplane that turns left at the end of the runway to take me away,' he said. 'It doesn't really matter where I am going but holiday sunshine is vital. I love lying around sunning myself with the family, and I like a bit of peace and quiet. I also appreciate one day's rain on holiday – that is important because it allows me to stay indoors and do nothing at all.'

Holidays when he was younger were obviously not so lavish. In 1983, when he was at drama school, a friend and he decided to drive to Greece. Michael added in *The Times* interview: 'It was going to take two weeks through France and Italy, and then we would get a ferry from Brindisi to the Greek islands, where we would meet more friends.

'But we were in an MG Midget held together with Sellotape. And we didn't get far because on the first night we had a crash that wrote off the car. It was 3am and we had pulled over to the side of the road to look at the map. A car came hurtling down the motorway and smashed straight into the back of us. Luckily, we weren't hurt – and, in fact, the accident turned out to be a blessing in disguise because I quickly realised that I would have gone mad if I'd had to spend two weeks with that friend. We didn't know each other well – it was just that he had the car. We hired another car to get back to the UK, and I caught a flight down to Greece instead.

'I met 10 friends and we had a brilliant time because, apart from the fact that I had survived a car crash, it cost nothing – and if you ran out of money, you could always sleep on the beach. We had split into smaller groups and arranged to meet in two weeks on Paxos. It was such an adventure. To us, each new island was like another country.'

Michael does have other cherished holiday memories. He says his best-ever holiday was during the Millennium year when he managed to take a break to Kuala Lumpur, Malaysia, albeit wrapped around a concert date. He explained to the

Daily Telegraph: 'After the concert, I travelled with my family to the idyllic island of Pangkor Laut, for a three-week holiday and the wedding of my step-daughter. Pangkor Laut lies off the Malaysian coast and is the most magical place I have ever visited. I was thrilled to be in this wonderfully sunny location, with palm-fringed beaches, a beautiful blue sea, and a lovely cocktail bar close to hand. Also, unlike many other islands in that area, Pangkor Laut is not too touristy.'

When it comes to the best hotel he has stayed in, Michael chooses somewhere that is a lot closer to home than Malaysia, saying: 'The hotel that impresses me most is the Merrion in Dublin. The food and service are wonderful, and the building itself is steeped in history. It's a lovely oasis.'

One reason, perhaps, why Michael is lukewarm about holidays abroad is that he hates the travel to and from the destination. He said: 'Everything is such a hassle – the crowds, the queues and the security checks. I'd like to just press a button and arrive at the end of my journey. If I had plenty of money, I'd probably consider hiring a private jet for travel. I'm always quite glad to return from holiday because my home in Britain is really where my heart is, which makes the going home so much better.'

He rates the worst hotel he has stayed in as a chain hotel on the South Coast, saying: 'It proved to be dirty, the food and service were awful, and the bar was full of undesirables. I stayed there for just 18 hours, then packed my bags and moved to the Grand Hotel on the seafront at Brighton.'

But bad planning is where his holidays have gone wrong. He explained: 'I realised that you should always thoroughly check out your destination and hotel prior to departure. When

I was going on holiday to Antigua in the West Indies with Cathy and stepdaughter Emma, Timothy Dalton, who had just finished filming one of the *James Bond* movies, recommended a hotel on the island. But it was horrible, more like a hostel, and it smelt of gutted fish.'

When Michael does get away, he will relax by reading – especially Wilbur Smith's novels. He also describes Ken Follett's *The Pillars Of The Earth* as 'a genius book', adding: 'This is about the building of a cathedral in 12th-century England and all the power struggles, religion and politics that went with it. It's meticulously researched and features richly detailed characters living in a world that is not dissimilar to ours. I love historical novels and this is one of the best.'

When asked once what his favourite job would be, Michael told the *Daily Telegraph*: 'Quality control manager at Cadbury. I absolutely love chocolate in all its forms – it is my downfall. I eat loads of it, in really big chunks.'

That, plus his passion for blueberry muffins, have obviously not helped the battle, since his teenage years, with his weight. Nor his passion for cooking. He was asked once for his best money-saving tip and he replied: 'Learn to cook. It is so much cheaper than buying ready-meals. I love making comfort food, such as shepherd's pie and an English roast. Having gone to drama school in my late teens, I had to fend for myself and cook, and I really enjoyed it.'

Michael, who likes Japanese and Italian cuisine, insists on making the Christmas dinner or the Sunday roast with all the trimmings. 'Cooking is my therapy. I do all the cooking at home and I cook just about every day. I love all food and I love making food for friends. It's another form of entertaining.

There is that same satisfaction of producing something that people can relish. I very much believe in the family meal where we lay a nice table, switch off the TV, sit down together and catch up.

'I used to be just a basic cook, and then one year Cathy gave up buying ready-made meals from Marks & Spencer for Lent and I took over all the cooking. I started by following Delia Smith. She gets slagged off but her recipes always, always work. Now there is no holding me. My roast potatoes cannot be beaten, I do a triumphant crispy duck and watercress salad, and my banoffee pie is an art form.'

Michael makes his own breakfast muffins. 'They take only 20 minutes in the Aga, and this delicious smell fills the house. The truth is they are brilliant. At our house in the country, I chose the Aga first – in racing green – and then had the kitchen and conservatory designed around it. Honestly. It's the very centre of our home there. That house is my joy.'

His passion for food has often troubled his long-term stomach problem – he has peptic ulcers. 'I was a curry freak and it would set them off,' he said. 'Some mornings I would wake up and find my voice had gone because the acid would reflux and burn my vocal chords. I had to sleep with my legs lower than my body to ease it. Stress made the ulcers worse, too. I've cut down on the curry.'

But when it comes to washing up, Michael does not excel. 'I make loads of mess and always expect other people to wash and clean up – mainly because I cooked the meal. People know me as a singer and performer but in a truer life I would have been incredibly lazy. I'm lucky to be doing something I love.'

One of the few foods Michael loathes is swede. 'I hate it in any way, shape or form. It should be banned from the face of the Earth for being such a dull, horrible thing,' he said. 'The taste is disgusting and it overpowers everything you eat it with. I have had a lifelong hatred of it and I don't want anything to do with it.'

But he added: 'When you really love food, you know, you really love food. And I do. But you have to be sensible with so much work going on. Naturally your energy burns off the calories and stuff, but I started training and I am sort of much healthier.'

One reason for his good health might be a commitment to complementary medicine. 'The great thing about aromatherapy and massage is that they make you feel so wonderful. I'm convinced that the more relaxed you feel, the less likely you are to become ill.'

Shape and image has always been important to Michael. 'I know that for maximum effect you need to look good while you're doing it. If you are dressed in the right gear and your face looks fine, you have more impact.'

Reaching the age of 30 made him more comfortable when it came to body shape. 'I found it much easier to accept how I looked,' he said. 'I don't starve myself as I used to. I know from experience that going on a crash diet is the quickest way to put on weight. I think happiness is more important than worrying about appearance.'

But when it comes to his outward appearance, he admits to spending 'a fortune' on clothes. Speaking to *OK!* magazine, Michael said: 'I love Gucci, I love Prada, and for knocking about I like Ralph Lauren and Calvin Klein. I used to be nervous about going into "posh" shops because I felt intimidated, but Cathy got me past that because she knows so much about clothes and fashion.'

When it comes to the relationship between Michael and Cathy, this has always been an area of discussion that both have guarded carefully. So what are the facts? He has a soul mate in Cathy McGowan and they live together as partners and undoubtedly love each other.

Michael remains relatively private for the profession he is in. He joked: 'My tip for not being recognised in public is to not wear a big hat and dark sunglasses.'

But more seriously, he told journalist Mark Shenton during an interview with the *Sunday Express* in 2004: 'Cath and I are private. We don't open our home to the press. Something Cath instilled in me early on is that if you let people in, you can't ask them to leave. If I'm doing something like the Eisteddfod and I'm excited and I want people to come, then I'll talk about that and my reasons for doing the gig. But I have always found it very disconcerting when you see people selling their weddings and christenings and private family occasions.'

The very private Michael described it as 'selling themselves to the devil' and he added: 'You won't catch me showing off my home in a celebrity magazine or sharing my life with every Tom, Dick and Harry. I think I must have been approached by every reality television show going – my agent doesn't even bother telling me about them anymore.'

That attitude is a measure of how much Michael wants to be judged purely for his talents as a singer and actor. He said: 'I love my work, I love what I do, and I accept there is a necessary amount you have to do to talk about your work. But I also think that there is a thing that if you reveal too much of yourself then people have less of an imagination and may find it difficult to identify you with the part you are playing or the song you are singing. It is the job of an actor to be kind of enigmatic.'

And enigmatic Michael is. He won't lecture, he won't boast, he is honest to his profession and to those fans who appreciate his work, whether it is acting or singing or his cherished amalgam of them both.

He told his main fan club's website: 'The only advice I can give anybody wanting to pursue a career in this business is first of all develop a very thick skin, second work as hard as you can and do as much as you can in as many different fields as you can. And watch as much as you can, you learn so much from watching other people perform – that is certainly what I did. And get as much experience as possible on stage, even amateur dramatics, putting on stuff with your friends, doing workshops, going to classes, and be prepared to face rejection because it happens to all of us, whatever stage we are at in our careers. But when it works, there is no better job in the world. It isn't a job, it's a joy so go for your dreams always, even if they turn into nightmares.'

And *Music Week* reported that one lesson he is always keen to pass on is this: 'If I was purely a theatre animal, I would be waiting for the next job now and it wouldn't be there. But I have never allowed myself to do that. If I was coming to the end of a stint in *Chitty Chitty Bang Bang*, I would go, "Right, I need to organise a tour and make a new record." I can generate my own work, and on top of that, things will always come along that I wasn't expecting to do, that I hadn't planned on doing. I've never drawn the dole, not yet.'

Michael has always refused to panic about life even with his 50th birthday only a few months off as he entered 2012. He admitted to the *Daily Record* in 2011: 'I'm not as thrilled as I was when approaching my 40th birthday. I'm hating the idea. So much bugs me about it and the worst of it is that I have realised my body doesn't work as well as it did when I was younger.

'If I get ill or hung over, I don't recover as quickly and my eyesight has gone in the past three years. I can no longer read a book without glasses, which is really annoying because I forget to carry them with me and I lose them. I bought really nice ones which I lost in a week. I'm becoming a grumpy old man. How long am I going to be doing this? As long as I'm not dead basically. People in this business don't stop, they slow down – but it is not a job or a career, it is what you do, a way of life, so you can always be tempted back by a good idea or the right role.'

But does he fear that his popularity will wane? 'I have never been in or out of fashion and I have never been that enormous. In terms of record sales, I think you have to be selling as many as, say, Rick Astley did, to then go so monumentally out of fashion. I have never done that, I have always just got on and done my thing. The harder you work, the luckier you seem to get. I work hard, I'm lucky and I have a great time doing what I do,' Michael told *Music Week*.

He draws on memories from his school days to help give an understanding into his thinking on life, saying: 'As a child, I read in a philosophy book that "to dream of the person you'd like to be is to waste the person you are." I play roles but when I am off stage, I always try to be myself.'

Michael, as far back as 1999, said: 'It's all about being happy with the journey you are on. There is no point in going on, otherwise.'

So many have enjoyed his magical musical journey. The passion and expression that this baritone, with the curly mop and soothing personality, puts into his singing brings alive the canter in the melody, the messages behind the lyrics, behind each crafted word, moulding the two into the wonders of each song. And the Michael Ball story is not over. As they say in his beloved theatreland, this one should run and run.

Acknowledgments

The author would like to thank the following sources of information used in part in the compilation of this biography: *BBC Radio 4, Desert Island Discs; Liverpool Echo; Portsmouth News; The Times; Woman's Weekly; Daily Mail; Mail on Sunday; My Weekly; Billy Sloan interview 1994; Radio Gloucestershire; The Guardian; You magazine; Herald Express; Wales Online; The Stage; German Musicals magazine; News of the World; Financial Times; New York Times; New York Post; Rosemary Conley Magazine; Weekly News; JusBall.net; Michael Ball Fan Club; Daily Mirror; The Belfast News Letter; North Wales Daily Post; Daily Express; lastminute.com magazine; Broadwayworld.com; Newsday; Chichester Observer; Independent on Sunday; Dominic McHugh; London Evening Standard; Sunday Times; The Scotsman; The Sun, What's On Stage; Music Week; Bristol*

Evening Post; The Daily Telegraph; The Daily Record; London List; Sunday Express; Yours magazine; California Chronicle; Illawarra Mercury, Westendtheatre.com, The Green, Best magazine, Ents24.com